THINKING AND
WRITING ABOUT
LITERATURE

THINKING AND
WRITING ABOUT
LITERATURE

MICHAEL MEYER
University of Connecticut

BEDFORD BOOKS *of* ST. MARTIN'S PRESS

BOSTON

For Bedford Books
President and Publisher: Charles H. Christensen
General Manager and Associate Publisher: Joan E. Feinberg
Managing Editor: Elizabeth M. Schaaf
Developmental Editor: Karen S. Henry
Production Editor: John Amburg
Production Assistant: Jonathan R. Burns
Copyeditor: Jane Zanichkowsky
Text Design: Sandra Rigney, The Book Department, Inc.
Cover Design: Night & Day Design

For information, write: St. Martin's Press, Inc.
175 Fifth Avenue, New York, NY 10010

Editorial Offices: Bedford Books *of* St. Martin's Press
75 Arlington Street, Boston, MA 02116

ISBN: 0–312–11166–5

Acknowledgments
Diane Ackerman. "A Fine, A Private Place" from *Lady Faustus* by Diane Ackerman. Copyright © 1983 by Diane Ackerman. Reprinted by permission of the author.
Andrew P. Debicki. "New Criticism and Deconstructionism: Two Attitudes in Teaching Poetry" from *Writing and Reading Differently: Deconstruction and the Teaching of Composition and Literature,* edited by G. Douglas Atkins and Michael L. Johnson. Copyright © 1985 by the University Press of Kansas. Reprinted by permission.
Emily Dickinson. "There's a certain Slant of light," " 'Faith' is a fine invention," "I know that He exists," "I never saw a Moor—," "Apparently with no surprise" reprinted by permission of the publishers and the Trustees of Amherst College from *The Poems of Emily Dickinson,* Thomas H. Johnson, ed., Cambridge, Mass.: The Belknap Press of Harvard University Press. Copyright © 1951, 1955, 1979, 1983 by the President and Fellows of Harvard College.
Stanley Fish. "On What Makes an Interpretation Acceptable" from *Is There a Text in This Class?* by Stanley Fish. Reprinted by permission of the publishers from *Is There a Text in This Class?* by Stanley Fish, Cambridge, Mass.: Harvard University Press. Copyright © 1980 by the President and Fellows of Harvard College.
Robert Francis. "Catch" from *The Orb Weaver.* Copyright © 1960 by Robert Francis, Wesleyan University Press. Reprinted by permission of University Press of New England.
Robert Frost. "Mending Wall" from *The Poetry of Robert Frost* edited by Edward Connery Lathem. Copyright 1916, 1930, 1939, © 1967, 1969 by Henry Holt and Company. Copyright 1944, © 1958 by Robert Frost. Copyright © 1967 by Leslie Frost Ballantine. Henry Holt and Company, Publisher.
Henry A. Giroux. "The Canon and Liberal Arts Education," excerpted from "Liberal Arts Education and the Struggle for Public Life: Dreaming about Democracy" *South Atlantic Quarterly* 89:1 (1990), pp. 124–8. Copyright Duke University Press, 1990. Reprinted with permission.

Acknowledgments and copyrights are continued at the back of the book on page 201, which constitutes an extension of the copyright page. It is a violation of the law to reproduce these selections by any means whatsoever without the written permission of the copyright holder.

Preface for Instructors

Thinking and Writing about Literature is a concise guide to reading and writing about fiction, poetry, and drama that treats every stage of the writing process—from generating topics to documenting sources. This book has developed and grown out of the widely adopted *Bedford Introduction to Literature,* Third Edition, particularly its critical reading and writing chapters. Though *Thinking and Writing about Literature* is a new book, major portions of it have been class-tested in hundreds of literature courses and carefully revised and refined over three editions. Common to both books are the assumptions that understanding literature—through reflection, discussion, and writing—enhances its enjoyment and that reading literature offers a valuable and unique means of apprehending life in its richness and diversity. Over the years scores of instructors have offered valuable comments on questionnaires for the *Bedford Introduction to Literature* indicating that any book with such high aspirations had also better provide clear, practical advice about thinking and writing about literature.

This book is designed to do just that. The chapters guide students through the process of generating topics, developing a thesis and building an argument, organizing the paper, writing the first draft, revising, editing for grammar and punctuation, and documenting sources. These essential steps are addressed in the first few chapters and reinforced in subsequent chapters that move progressively from specific types of writing assignments—explication, analysis, comparison and contrast—in Chapter 2 to more particular issues related to reading and writing about fiction, poetry, and drama. A series of detailed questions for writing about each genre highlights topics and concerns readers can use to sharpen their arguments as they think and write about stories, poems, and plays. Along the way brief literary selections are presented so that students can anchor the general critical principles discussed in the text to specific works. In addition, sample papers in these chapters illustrate various types of writing assignments appropriate for each of the three genres.

Chapter 6 builds on the previous chapters by providing an overview of critical strategies for reading and writing. This chapter introduces students to eight contemporary theoretical approaches to literature—formalist, biographical, psychological, historical, sociological (including Marxist and feminist), mythological, reader-response, and deconstructionist. Each approach is applied to Kate Chopin's short story "The Story of an Hour" (as well as other works) to demonstrate what kinds of insights a particular critical strategy offers. Accompanying critical perspectives—essays by contemporary literary critics—reflect many of these schools of criticism.

An opportunity to study a writer in some depth is provided in Chapter 7, which includes four poems by Emily Dickinson along with a sample paper and questions designed to equip students with ways of thinking and writing about multiple works by the same author. This chapter allows students to see how the approaches provided in the preceding chapters can be brought into focus for more of an in-depth (albeit brief) study.

Chapter 8 discusses library research and features a guide to MLA documentation along with a sample documented research paper. Students will find this to be a useful reference source for documentation procedures and models. It also provides an annotated list of helpful sources specifically relevant for developing literary topics. Chapter 9 provides practical information and advice for taking essay examinations in literature courses. Students who sometimes feel bewildered about how to prepare for an essay examination on a semester's worth of reading should find this chapter a welcome supplement to the advice on writing about literature outside of class. Chapter 10 offers a glossary of literary terms consisting of more than 200 items central to the study of literature. Though concise, this glossary provides a clear, thorough resource for students who want to brush up on the elements of literature, a literary concept, or a critical term.

In short, *Thinking and Writing about Literature* serves as an accessible, efficient guide for students who can profit from an overview that focuses on the kind of reading, thinking, and writing necessary for the study of literature.

Acknowledgments

This book has benefited from the ideas, suggestions, and corrections of the many reviewers who provided advice for *The Bedford Introduction to Literature*. I remain grateful to those I have thanked in the prefaces to the editions of that book. I am also indebted to my students for the many papers I have received over the years that I have used in various forms to serve as good and accessible models of student writing. I am particularly grateful to Kathleen Drowne for her solid help on this book and to William E. Sheidley for his astute suggestions. The reviewers who commented specifically on this manuscript also deserve my thanks: David Cowles, Brigham Young University; Terry Everett, Delta State University; Irene Fairley, Northeastern University; Jo Nell Farrar, San Jacinto College; Grace Flisser, Community

College of Philadelphia; Danny Miller, Northern Kentucky University; Charlotte Smith, Virginia Polytechnic Institute and State University; and Gary Tate, Texas Christian University.

At Bedford Books, my debts once again require more time to acknowledge than the deadline allows. Charles H. Christensen and Joan Feinberg initiated this project and launched it with their intelligence, energy, and sound advice. Karen Henry steered the book through rough as well as becalmed moments; her work was as first-rate as it was essential. Verity Winship and Adrian Harris, highly capable assistants, helped with reviewing and research tasks. John Amburg served as a skillful production editor. He was ably assisted by Jonathan Burns. Jane Zanichkowsky provided careful copyediting, and Nancy Bell Scott and Sherri Dietrich did more than meticulous proofreading. All the people at Bedford Books—including Donna Lee Dennison and Ellen Kuhl—helped to make this a pleasant and manageable project, and I thank them.

Contents

THINKING AND WRITING ABOUT LITERATURE

1. Reading and Writing

THE PURPOSE AND VALUE
OF WRITING ABOUT LITERATURE

Introductory literature courses typically include three components: reading, discussion, and writing. Students usually find the readings a pleasure, the class discussions a revelation, and the writing assignments—at least initially—a little intimidating. Writing an analysis of Melville's use of walls in "Bartleby, the Scrivener," for example, may seem considerably more daunting than making a case for animal rights or analyzing a campus newspaper editorial that calls for grade reforms. Like Bartleby, you might want to respond with "I would prefer not to." Literary topics are not, however, all that different from the kinds of papers assigned in English composition courses; many of the same skills are required for both. Regardless of the type of paper, you must develop a thesis and support it with evidence in language that is clear and persuasive.

Whether the subject matter is a marketing survey, a political issue, or a literary work, writing is a method of communicating information and perceptions. Writing teaches. But before writing becomes an instrument for informing the reader, it serves as a means of learning for the writer. An essay is a process of discovery as well as a record of what has been discovered. One of the chief benefits of writing is that we frequently realize what we want to say only after trying out ideas on a page and seeing our thoughts take shape in language.

More specifically, writing about a literary work encourages us to be better readers, because it requires a close examination of the elements of a short story, poem, or play. To determine how plot, character, setting, point of view, style, tone, irony, or any number of other literary elements function in a work, we must study them in relation to one another as well as separately. Speed-reading won't do. To read a text accurately and validly—neither ignoring nor distorting significant details—we must return to the work repeatedly to test our responses and interpretations. By paying attention to details and being sensitive to the author's use of language, we develop a clearer understanding of how the work conveys its effects and meanings—and that's the beginning of literary criticism.

A common misunderstanding about the purpose of literary criticism is that it crankily restricts itself to finding faults in a work. Critical essays are sometimes mistakenly equated with newspaper and magazine reviews of recently published works. Reviews typically include summaries and evaluations to inform readers about a work's nature and quality, but critical essays assume that readers are already familiar with a work. Although a critical essay may point out limitations and flaws, most criticism—and certainly the kind of essay usually written in an introductory literature course—is designed to explain, analyze, and reveal the complexities of a work. Such sensitive consideration increases our appreciation of the writer's achievement and significantly adds to our enjoyment of a short story, poem, or play. In short, the purpose and value of writing about literature are that doing so leads to greater understanding and pleasure.

Nevertheless, students sometimes ask why it is necessary or desirable to write about a literary work. Why not allow stories, poems, and plays to speak for themselves? Isn't it presumptuous to interpret Hemingway, Dickinson, or Shakespeare? These writers do, of course, speak for themselves, but they do so indirectly. Literary criticism does not seek to replace the text by explaining it but to enhance our readings of works by calling attention to significant matters that we might have overlooked or only vaguely sensed.

There are many ways to interpret a literary work and to write about it. Chapter 6, "Critical Strategies for Reading and Writing," offers eight major approaches employed by contemporary literary theorists. An awareness of these approaches—formalist, biographical, psychological, historical, sociological (including Marxist and feminist strategies), mythological, reader-response, and deconstructionist—can help you to determine strategies for your own reading and writing that will open up possibilities in a text that previously might have seemed inaccessible. A familiarity with a variety of critical approaches should demystify literary criticism so that you better understand how thinking and writing about literature can clarify your perceptions of a text.

In this book there is a progression from discussions and examples concerning more general writing assignments to more specialized kinds of writing. Chapter 2 describes basic types of writing assignments—explication, analysis, and comparison and contrast—that can be used not only for writing about literature but for any sort of subject matter. This broad approach is made genre-specific in the subsequent three chapters on writing about fiction, poetry, and drama. The techniques developed in these chapters are complemented by the critical strategies for reading and writing in Chapter 6. These critical strategies, though sophisticated and challenging, offer a means for understanding how your own approach—or a critic's—shapes a discussion of a text. The first and foremost strategy, however, is to read the text carefully.

READING THE WORK CLOSELY

Know the piece of literature you are writing about before you begin your essay. Think about how the work makes you feel and how it is put together. The more familiar you are with how the various elements of the text convey effects and meanings, the more confident you will be explaining whatever perspective on it you ultimately choose. Do not insist that everything make sense on a first reading. Relax and enjoy yourself; you can be attentive and still allow the author's words to work their magic on you. With subsequent readings, however, go more slowly and analytically as you try to establish relations between characters, actions, images, or whatever else seems important. Ask yourself why you respond as you do. Think as you read, and notice how the parts of a work contribute to its overall nature. Whether the work is a short story, poem, or play, you will read relevant portions of it over and over, and you will very likely find more to discuss in each review if the work is rich.

It's best to avoid reading other critical discussions of a work before you are thoroughly familiar with it. There are several good reasons for following this advice. By reading interpretations before you know a work, you deny yourself the pleasure of discovery. That is a bit like starting with the last chapter in a mystery novel. But perhaps even more important than protecting the surprise and delight that a work might offer is that a premature reading of a critical discussion will probably short-circuit your own responses. You will see the work through the critic's eyes and have to struggle with someone else's perceptions and ideas before you can develop your own.

Reading criticism can be useful, but not until you have thought through your own impressions of the text. A guide should not be permitted to become a tyrant. This does not mean, however, that you should avoid background information about a work, for example, that the title of Diane Ackerman's "A Fine, A Private Place" (p. 37) alludes to Andrew Marvell's earlier *carpe diem* poem, "To His Coy Mistress" (p. 36). Knowing something about the author as well as historic and literary contexts can help to create expectations that enhance your reading.

ANNOTATING THE TEXT
AND JOURNAL NOTE TAKING

As you read, get in the habit of making marginal notations in your textbook. If you are working with a library book, use notecards and write down page or line numbers so that you can easily return to annotated passages. Use these cards to record reactions, raise questions, and make comments. They will freshen your memory and allow you to keep track of what goes on in the text.

Whatever method you use to annotate your texts—whether by writing marginal notes, highlighting, underlining, or drawing boxes and circles around important words and phrases—you'll eventually develop a system that allows you to retrieve significant ideas and elements from the text. Another way to record your impressions of a work—like any other experience—is to keep a journal. By writing down your reactions to characters, images, language, actions, and other matters in a reading journal, you can often determine why you like or dislike a work or feel sympathetic or antagonistic to an author or discover paths into a work that might have eluded you if you hadn't preserved your impressions. Your journal notes and annotations may take whatever form you find useful; full sentences and grammatical correctness are not essential (unless they are to be handed in and your instructor requires that), though they might allow you to make better sense of your own reflections days later. The point is simply to put in writing thoughts that you can retrieve when you need them for class discussion or a writing assignment. Consider the following student annotation of the first twenty-four lines of Andrew Marvell's "To His Coy Mistress" and the journal entry that follows it:

Annotated Text

If we had time...

Had we but world enough, and time,
This coyness, lady, were no (crime.) — *Waste life and you steal from yourself*
We would sit down, and think which way
To walk, and pass our long love's day.
Thou by the Indian (Ganges') side   5
Shouldst rubies find; I by the tide
Of (Humber) would complain.° I would   *write love songs*
Love you ten years before the Flood,   *Measurements of time*
And you should, if you please, refuse
Till the conversion of the Jews.   10
My vegetable love should grow° **?**   *Slow, unconscious growth*
Vaster than empires, and more slow;
An hundred years should go to praise
Thine eyes and on thy forehead gaze,
Two hundred to adore each breast,   15
But thirty thousand to the rest:
An age at least to every part,
And the last age should show your heart.
For, lady, you deserve this state,
Nor would I love at lower rate.   20
[But] at my back I always hear   *Lines move faster here—*
Time's wingèd chariot hurrying near;   *tone changes*
And yonder all before us lie
contrast river and desert images (Deserts) of vast (eternity.) — *This eternity rushes in*

4 Reading and Writing

```
      He'd be patient and wait for his "mistress" if they had
   the time--sing songs, praise her, adore her, etc.  But they
   don't have that much time according to him.  He seems to be
   patient but he actually begins by calling patience--her
   coyness--a "crime."  Looks to me like he's got his mind made
   up from the beginning of the poem.  Where's her response?  I'm
   not sure about him.
```

This journal note responds to some of the effects noted in the annotations of the poem; it's an excellent beginning for making sense of the speaker's argument in the poem.

Taking notes will preserve your initial reactions to the work. Many times first impressions are the best. Your response to a peculiar character in a story, a striking phrase in a poem, or a subtle bit of stage business in a play might lead to larger perceptions. The student paper on John Updike's "A & P" (p. 29), for example, began with the student writing "how come?" next to the story's title in her textbook. She thought it strange that the title didn't refer to a character or the story's conflict. That annotated response eventually led her to examine the significance of the setting, which became the central idea of her paper.

You should take detailed notes only after you've read through the work. If you write too many notes during the first reading, you're likely to disrupt your response. Moreover, until you have a sense of the entire work, it will be difficult to determine how connections can be made among its various elements. In addition to recording your first impressions and noting significant passages, characters, actions, and so on, you should consult the Questions for Writing about Fiction (p. 49), Poetry (p. 64), and Drama (p. 86). These questions can assist you in getting inside a work as well as organizing your notes.

Inevitably, you will take more notes than you finally use in the paper. Note taking is a form of thinking aloud, but because your ideas are on paper you don't have to worry about forgetting them. As you develop a better sense of a potential topic, your notes will become more focused and detailed.

CHOOSING A TOPIC

If your instructor assigns a topic or offers a choice from among an approved list of topics, some of your work is already completed. Instead of being asked to come up with a topic about *Antigone,* you may be assigned a three-page essay that specifically discusses "Antigone's Decision to Defy Creon." You also have the assurance that a specified topic will be manageable within the suggested number of pages. Unless you ask your instructor for permission to write on a different or related topic, be certain to address yourself to the assignment. An essay that does not discuss Antigone's decision but instead describes her relationship with her sister would be missing the point. Notice too that there is room even in an assigned topic to develop your own approach. One question that immediately comes to mind is whether Antigone is justified in defying Creon's authority. Assigned topics do not relieve you of thinking about an aspect of a work, but they do focus your thinking.

At some point during the course, you may have to begin an essay from scratch. You might, for example, be asked to write about a short story that somehow impressed you or that seemed particularly well written or filled with insights. Before you start considering a topic, you should have a sense of how long the paper will be, because the assigned length can help to determine the extent to which you should develop your topic. Ideally, the paper's length should be based on how much space you deem necessary to present your discussion clearly and convincingly, but if you have any doubts and no specific guidelines have been indicated, ask. The question is important; a topic that might be appropriate for a three-page paper could be too narrow for ten pages. Three pages would probably be adequate for a discussion of why Sammy quits his job at the A & P in Updike's story. Conversely, it would be futile to try to summarize Updike's use of New England in his fiction in even ten pages; this would have to be narrowed to something like "Images of New England in 'A & P.' " Be sure that the topic you choose can be adequately covered in the assigned number of pages.

Once you have a firm sense of how much you are expected to write, you can begin to decide on your topic. If you are to choose what work to write about, select one that genuinely interests you. Too often students pick a story, poem, or play because it is mercifully short or seems simple. Such works can certainly be the subjects of fine essays, but simplicity should not be the major reason for selecting them. Choose a work that has moved you so that you have something to say about it. The student who wrote about "A & P" was initially attracted to the story's title because she had once worked in a similar store. After reading the story, she became fascinated with its setting because Updike's descriptions seemed so accurate. Her paper then grew out of her curiosity about the setting's purpose. When a writer is engaged in a topic, the paper has a better chance of being interesting to a reader.

After you have settled on a particular work, your notes and annotations of the text should prove useful for generating a topic. The paper on "The A & P as a State of Mind" developed naturally from the notes (p. 29) that the student jotted down about the setting and antagonist. If you think with a pen in your hand, you are likely to find when you review your notes that your thoughts have clustered into one or more topics. Perhaps there are patterns of imagery that seem to make a point about life. There may be scenes that are ironically paired or secondary characters who reveal certain qualities about the protagonist. Your notes and annotations on such aspects can lead you to a particular effect or impression. Having chuckled your way through "A & P," you may discover that your notations about the story's humor point to a serious satire of society's values.

DEVELOPING A THESIS

When you are satisfied that you have something interesting to say about a work and that your notes have led you to a focused topic, you can formulate a thesis, the central idea of the paper. Whereas the topic indicates what the paper focuses on (the setting in "A & P"), the thesis explains what you have to say about the topic (because the intolerant setting of "A & P" is the antagonist in the story, it is crucial to our understanding of Sammy's decision to quit his job). The thesis should be a complete sentence (though sometimes it may require more than one sentence) that establishes your topic in clear, unambiguous language. The thesis may be revised as you get further into the topic and discover what you want to say about it, but once the thesis is firmly established it will serve as a guide for you and your reader, because all the information and observations in your essay should be related to the thesis.

One student, on an initial reading of Andrew Marvell's "To His Coy Mistress" (p. 36), saw that the male speaker of the poem urges a woman to love now before time runs out for them. This reading gave him the impression that the poem is a simple celebration of the pleasures of the flesh, but on subsequent readings he underlined or noted these images: "Time's wingèd chariot hurrying near"; "Deserts of vast eternity"; "marble vault"; "worms"; "dust"; "ashes"; and these two lines: "The grave's a fine and private place, / But none, I think, do there embrace."

By listing these images associated with time and death, he established an inventory that could be separated from the rest of his notes on point of view, character, sounds, and other subjects. Inventorying notes allows patterns to emerge that you might have only vaguely perceived otherwise. Once these images are grouped, they call attention to something darker and more complex in Marvell's poem than a first impression might suggest.

These images may create a different feeling about the poem, but they still don't explain very much. One simple way to generate a thesis about a literary work is to ask the question "why?" Why do these images appear in the poem? Why does Hamlet hesitate to avenge his father's death? Why does Updike choose New England as the setting of "A & P"? Your responses to these kinds of questions can lead to a thesis.

Writers sometimes use free writing to help themselves explore possible answers to such questions. It can be an effective way of generating ideas. Free writing is exactly that: the technique calls for nonstop writing without concern for mechanics or editing of any kind. Free writing for ten minutes or so on a question will result in fragments and repetitions, but it can also produce some ideas. Here's an example of a student's response to the question about the images in "To His Coy Mistress":

```
He wants her to make love.  Love poem.  There's little time.
Her crime.  He exaggerates.  Sincere?  Sly?  What's he want?
She says nothing--he says it all.  What about deserts, ashes,
graves, and worms?  Some love poem.  Sounds like an old Vincent
Price movie.  Full of sweetness but death creeps in.  Death--
hurry hurry!  Tear pleasures.  What passion!  Where's death in
this?  How can a love poem be so ghoulish?  She does nothing.
Maybe frightened?  Convinced?  Why death?  Love and death--
time--death.
```

This free writing contains several ideas; it begins by alluding to the poem's plot and speaker, but the central idea seems to be death. This emphasis led the student to five potential thesis statements for his essay about the poem:

1. "To His Coy Mistress" is a difficult poem.
2. Death in "To His Coy Mistress."
3. There are many images of death in "To His Coy Mistress."
4. "To His Coy Mistress" celebrates the pleasures of the flesh but it also recognizes the power of death to end that pleasure.
5. On the surface, "To His Coy Mistress" is a celebration of the pleasures of the flesh, but this witty seduction is tempered by a chilling recognition of the reality of death.

The first statement is too vague to be useful. In what sense is the poem difficult? A more precise phrasing, indicating the nature of the difficulty, is needed. The second statement is a topic rather than a thesis. Because it is not a sentence, it does not express a complete idea about how the poem treats death. Although this could be an appropriate title, it is inadequate as a thesis statement. The third statement, like the first one, identifies the topic, but even though it is a sentence, it is not a complete idea that tells us anything significant beyond the fact it states. After these preliminary attempts to develop a thesis, the student remembered his first impression of the poem and incorporated it into his thesis statement. The fourth thesis is a useful approach to the poem because it limits the topic and indicates how it will be treated in the paper: the writer will begin with an initial impression of the poem and then go on to qualify it. However, the fifth thesis is better than the fourth because it indicates a shift in tone produced by the ironic relationship between death and flesh. An effective thesis, like this one, makes a clear statement about a manageable topic and provides a firm sense of direction for the paper.

Most writing assignments in a literature course require you to persuade readers that your thesis is reasonable and supported with evidence. Papers that report information without comment or evaluation are simply summaries. A plot summary of Shakespeare's *The Tempest,* for example, would have no thesis, but a paper that discussed how Prospero's oppression of Caliban represents European imperialism and colonialism would argue a thesis. Similarly, a paper that merely pointed out the death images in "To His Coy Mistress" would not contain a thesis, but a paper that attempted to make a case for the death imagery as a grim reminder of how vulnerable flesh is would involve persuasion. In developing a thesis, remember that you are expected not merely to present information but to argue a point.

ARGUING ABOUT LITERATURE

An argumentative essay is designed to make persuasive your interpretation of a work. Arguing about literature doesn't mean that you're engaged in an angry, antagonistic dispute (though controversial topics do sometimes engender heated debates; see for example Harriet Hawkins's reflections in "Should We Study *King Kong* or *King Lear?*" [p. 125]). Instead, argumentation requires that you present your interpretation of a work (or a portion of it) by supporting your thesis with clearly defined terms, ample evidence, and a detailed analysis of relevant portions of the text.

If you have a choice, it's generally best to write about a topic that you feel strongly about. If you're not fascinated by Bartleby the Scrivener's haunting presence in Melville's short story, then perhaps you'll find chilling Emily Greirson's mysterious behavior in Faulkner's "A Rose for Emily," or maybe you can explain why Bartleby's character is so excruciatingly boring to you. If your essay is to be interesting and convincing, what is important is that it be written from a strong point of view that persuasively argues your evaluation, analysis, and interpretation of a work. It is not enough to say that you like or dislike a work; instead you must give your reader some ideas and evidence that can be accepted or rejected based on the quality of the answers to the questions you raise.

One way to come up with persuasive answers is to generate good questions that will lead you further into the text and to critical issues related to it. The critical strategies for reading summarized in Chapter 6 can be a resource for raising questions that can be shaped into an argument. See page 130 for a list of questions for the critical approaches covered in Chapter 6 that should be useful for discovering arguments you might make about a short story, poem, or play. Those questions refer to critical approaches such as Marxist, historical, feminist, reader-response, and deconstructionist strategies. These approaches reflect critics' deep beliefs about the role of literature in our culture, as well as attitudes toward art, politics, and, indeed, people. Depending upon your own values and perceptions (and the nature of the assignment), you may find that arguing a persuasive interpretation from one of these perspectives could be tailored to your own sensibilities. That's no small consideration for writing a convincing and personally satisfying paper.

A deconstructionist's reading of Robert Frost's "Mending Wall" (p. 162), for example, would attempt to destabilize and extend the meanings of the poem (see pages 112–114 for a discussion of deconstructionist strategies), because for the deconstructionist language is slippery and goes beyond what writers may intend it to mean. A question frequently raised in deconstructionist readings is, How are contradictory and opposing meanings expressed in the work? Here's how a deconstructionist might answer that question: "In 'Mending Wall,' the speaker presents himself as being on the side of the imaginative rather than the hidebound, rigid responses to life, seeming to value freedom and openness rather than restrictions and narrowly defined limits."

But a deconstructionist treatment of Frost's speaker might point out that he is condescending and even smug in his superior attitude toward his neighbor's repeating his "father's saying," as if he were "an old-stone savage armed." This condescending attitude hardly suggests a robust sense of community and shared humanity. Moreover, for all the talk about unnecessary conventions and traditions, a deconstructionist would likely be quick to point out that Frost writes the poem in blank verse—unrhymed iambic pentameter—rather than free verse; hence the very regular rhythms of the narrator's speech may be seen to deconstruct its liberationist meaning. Students inclined to explore competing meanings in texts will find a deconstructionist's approach appealing.

ORGANIZING A PAPER

After you have chosen a manageable topic and developed a thesis, a central idea about it, you can begin to organize the argument of your paper. Your thesis, even if it is still somewhat tentative, should help you decide what information will need to be included and provide you with a sense of direction.

Consider again the sample thesis in the section on developing a thesis:

On the surface, "To His Coy Mistress" is a celebration of the pleasures of the flesh, but this witty seduction is tempered by a chilling recognition of the reality of death.

This thesis indicates that the paper can be divided into two parts: the pleasures of the flesh and the reality of death. It also indicates an order: Because the central point is to show that the poem is more than a simple celebration, the pleasures of the flesh should be discussed first so that another, more complex, reading of the poem can follow. If the paper began with the reality of death, its point would be anticlimactic.

Having established such a broad and informal outline, you can draw upon your underlinings, margin notations, and notes for the subheadings and evidence required to explain the major sections of your paper. This next level of detail would look like the following:

1. Pleasures of the flesh
   Part of the traditional tone of love poetry
2. Recognition of death
   Ironic treatment of love
      Diction
      Images
      Figures of speech
      Symbols
      Tone

This list was initially a jumble of terms, but the student arranged the items so that each of the two major sections leads to a discussion of tone. (The student also found it necessary to drop some biographical information from his notes because it was irrelevant to the thesis.) The list indicates that the first part of the paper will establish the traditional tone of love poetry that celebrates the pleasures of the flesh, while the second part will present a more detailed discussion about the ironic recognition of death. The emphasis is on the latter because that is the point to be argued in the paper. Hence, the thesis has helped to organize the parts of the paper, establish an order, and indicate the paper's proper proportions.

The next step is to fill in the subheadings with information from your notes. Many experienced writers find that making lists of information to be included under each subheading is an efficient way to develop paragraphs. For a longer paper (perhaps a research paper), you should be able to develop a paragraph or more on each subheading. On the other hand, a shorter paper may require that you combine several subheadings in a paragraph. You may also discover that while an informal list is adequate for a brief paper, a ten-page assignment could require a more detailed outline. Use the method that is most productive for you. Whatever the length of the essay, your presentation must be in a coherent and logical order that allows your reader to follow the argument and evaluate the evidence. The quality of your reading can be demonstrated only by the quality of your writing.

WRITING A DRAFT

The time for sharpening pencils, arranging your desk, and doing almost anything else instead of writing has ended. The first draft will appear on the page only if you stop avoiding the inevitable and sit, stand up, or lie down to write. It makes no difference how you write, just so you do. Now that you have developed a topic into a tentative thesis, you can assemble your notes and begin to flesh out whatever outline you have made.

Be flexible. Your outline should smoothly conduct you from one point to the next, but do not permit it to railroad you. If a relevant and important idea occurs to you now, work it into the draft. By using the first draft as a means of thinking about what you want to say, you will very likely discover more than your notes originally suggested. Plenty of good writers don't use outlines at all but discover ordering principles as they write. Do not attempt to compose a perfectly correct draft the first time around. Grammar, punctuation, and spelling can wait until you revise. Concentrate on what you are saying. Good writing most often occurs when you are in hot pursuit of an idea rather than in a nervous search for errors.

To make revising easier, leave wide margins and extra space between lines so that you can easily add words, sentences, and corrections. Write on only one side of the paper. Your pages will be easier to keep track of that way, and, if you have to clip a paragraph to place it elsewhere, you will not lose any writing on the other side.

If you are working on a word processor, you can take advantage of its capacity to make additions and deletions as well as move entire paragraphs by making just a few simple keyboard commands. Some software programs can also check spelling and certain grammatical elements in your writing. It's worth remembering, however, that though a clean copy fresh off a printer may look terrific, it will read only as well as the thinking and writing that have gone into it. Many writers prudently store their data on disks and print their pages each time they finish a draft to avoid losing any material because of power failures or other problems. These printouts are also easier to read than the screen when you work on revisions.

Once you have a first draft on paper, you can delete material that is unrelated to your thesis and add material necessary to illustrate your points and make your paper convincing. The student who wrote "The A & P as a State of Mind" wisely dropped a paragraph that questioned whether Sammy displays chauvinistic attitudes toward women. Although this is an interesting issue, it has nothing to do with the thesis, which explains how the setting influences Sammy's decision to quit his job. Instead of including that paragraph, she added one that described Lengel's crabbed response to the girls so that she could lead up to the A & P "policy" he enforces.

Remember that your initial draft is only that. You should go through the paper many times—and then again—working to substantiate and clarify your ideas. You may even end up with several entire versions of the paper.

Rewrite. The sentences within each paragraph should be related to a single topic. Transitions should connect one paragraph to the next so that there are no abrupt or confusing shifts. Awkward or wordy phrasing or unclear sentences and paragraphs should be mercilessly poked and prodded into shape.

Writing the Introduction and Conclusion

After you have clearly and adequately developed the body of your paper, pay particular attention to the introductory and concluding paragraphs. It's probably best to write the introduction—at least the final version of it—last, after you know precisely what you are introducing. Because this paragraph is crucial for generating interest in the topic, it should engage the reader and provide a sense of what the paper is about. There is no formula for writing effective introductory paragraphs, because each writing situation is different—depending on the audience, topic, and approach—but if you pay attention to the introductions of the essays you read, you will notice a variety of possibilities. The introductory paragraph to "The A & P as a State of Mind," for example, is a straightforward explanation of why the story's setting is important for understanding Updike's treatment of the antagonist. The rest of the paper then offers evidence to support this point.

Concluding paragraphs demand equal attention because they leave the reader with a final impression. The conclusion should provide a sense of closure instead of starting a new topic or ending abruptly. In the final paragraph about the significance of the setting in "A & P," the student brings together the reasons Sammy quit his job by referring to his refusal to accept Lengel's store policies. At the same time she makes this point, she also explains the significance of Sammy ringing up the "No Sale" mentioned in her introductory paragraph. Thus, we are brought back to where we began, but we now have a greater understanding of why Sammy quits his job. Of course, the body of your paper is the most important part of your presentation, but do remember that first and last impressions have a powerful impact on readers.

Using Quotations

Quotations can be a valuable means of marshaling evidence to illustrate and support your ideas. A judicious use of quoted material will make your points clearer and more convincing. Here are some guidelines that should help you use quotations effectively.

1. Brief quotations (four lines or fewer of prose or three lines or fewer of poetry) should be carefully introduced and integrated into the text of your paper with quotation marks around them.

> According to the narrator, Bertha "had a reputation for strictness." He tells us that she always "wore dark clothes, dressed her hair simply, and expected contrition and obedience from her pupils."

For brief poetry quotations, use a slash to indicate a division between lines.

> The concluding lines of Blake's "The Tyger" pose a disturbing question: "What immortal hand or eye/Dare frame thy fearful symmetry?"

Lengthy quotations should be separated from the text of your paper. More than three lines of poetry should be double spaced and indented ten spaces from the left margin. More than four lines of prose should also be double spaced and indented ten spaces from the left margin, with the right margin the same as for the text. Do *not* use quotation marks for the passage; the indentation indicates that the passage is a quotation.

> Henry A. Giroux gives an historical view of the function of literary canons:

>> Indeed, the canon was fashioned as a safeguard to insure that the cultural property of such groups was passed on from generation to generation along with the family estates. Thus, in these terms it seems most appropriate that the literary canon should be subject to revision—as it has been before in the course of the expansion of democracy. (2033)

Lengthy quotations should not be used in place of your own writing. Use them only if they are absolutely necessary.

2. If any words are added to a quotation, use brackets to distinguish your addition from the original source.

> "He [Young Goodman Brown] is portrayed as self-righteous and disillusioned."

Any words inside quotation marks and not in brackets must be precisely those of the author. Brackets can also be used to change the grammatical structure of a quotation so that it fits into your sentence.

> Smith argues that Chekhov "present[s] the narrator in an ambivalent light."

If you drop any words from the source, use ellipses (three spaced periods) to indicate the omission.

> "Early to bed . . . makes a man healthy, wealthy, and wise."

Use ellipses following a period to indicate an omission at the end of a sentence.

> "Early to bed and early to rise makes a man healthy. . . ."

Use a single line of spaced periods to indicate the omission of a line or more of poetry or more than one paragraph of prose.

> Nothing would sleep in that cellar, dank as a ditch,
> Bulbs broke out of boxes hunting for chinks in the dark,
>
> . . . .
>
> Nothing would give up life:
> Even the dirt kept breathing a small breath.

3. You will be able to punctuate quoted material accurately and confidently if you observe these conventions.

Place commas and periods inside quotation marks.

"Even the dirt," Roethke insists, "kept breathing a small breath."

Even though a comma does not appear after "dirt" in the original quotation, it is placed inside the quotation mark. The exception to this rule occurs when a parenthetical reference to a source follows the quotation.

"Even the dirt," Roethke insists, "kept breathing a small breath" (11).

Punctuation marks other than commas or periods go outside the quotation marks unless they are part of the material quoted.

What does Roethke mean when he writes that "the dirt kept breathing a small breath"?

Yeats asked, "How can we know the dancer from the dance?"

REVISING AND EDITING

Put some distance—a day or so if you can—between yourself and each draft of your paper. The phrase that seemed just right on Wednesday may be revealed as all wrong on Friday. You'll have a better chance of detecting lumbering sentences and thin paragraphs if you plan ahead and give yourself the time to read your paper from a fresh perspective. Through the process of revision, you can transform a competent paper into an excellent one.

Begin by asking yourself if your approach to the topic requires any rethinking. Is the argument carefully thought out and logically presented? Are there any gaps in the presentation? How well is the paper organized? Do the paragraphs lead into one another? Does the body of the paper deliver what the thesis promises? Is the interpretation sound? Are any relevant and important elements of the work ignored or distorted to advance the thesis? Are the points supported with evidence? These large questions should be addressed before you focus on more detailed matters. If you uncover serious problems as a result of considering these questions, you'll probably have quite a lot of rewriting to do, but at least you will have the opportunity to correct the problems—even if doing so takes several drafts.

A useful technique for spotting awkward or unclear moments in the paper is to read it aloud. You might also try having a friend read it aloud to you. If your handwriting is legible, your friend's reading—perhaps accompanied by hesitations and puzzled expressions—could alert you to passages that need reworking. Having identified problems, you can readily correct them on a word processor or on the draft provided you've skipped lines and used wide margins. The final draft you hand in should be neat and carefully proofread for any inadvertent errors.

The following checklist offers questions to ask about your paper as you revise and edit it. Most of these questions will be familiar to you; however, if you need help with any of them, ask your instructor or review the appropriate section in a composition handbook.

Revision Checklist

1. Is the topic manageable? Is it too narrow or too broad?
2. Is the thesis clear? Is it based on a careful reading of the work?
3. Does the opening paragraph introduce the topic in an interesting manner?
4. Is the paper logically organized? Does it have a firm sense of direction?
5. Is your argument persuasive?
6. Should any material be deleted? Do any important points require further illustration or evidence?
7. Are the paragraphs developed, unified, and coherent? Are any too short or long?
8. Are there transitions linking the paragraphs?
9. Is the tone appropriate? Is it unduly flippant or pretentious?
10. Does the concluding paragraph provide a sense of closure?
11. Is the title engaging and suggestive?
12. Are the sentences clear, concise, and complete?
13. Are simple, complex, and compound sentences used for variety?
14. Have technical terms been used correctly? Are you certain of the meanings of all the words in the paper? Are they spelled correctly?
15. Have you documented any information borrowed from books, articles, or other sources? Have you quoted too much instead of summarizing or paraphrasing secondary material?
16. Have you used a standard format for citing sources (see p. 156)?
17. Have you followed your instructor's guidelines for the manuscript format of the final draft?
18. Have you carefully proofread the final draft?

When you proofread your final draft, you may find a few typographical errors that must be corrected but do not warrant retyping an entire page. Provided there are not more than a handful of such errors throughout the page, they can be corrected as shown in the following passage. This example condenses a short paper's worth of errors; no single passage should be this shabby in your essay.

```
To add a letter or word, use a caret on the line where the
                 is
addition‸needed.  To delete a word draw a single line through
through it.  Run-on words are separated by a vertical|line, and
inadvertent spaces are closed like t͡his.  Transposed letters
are indicated this wa͡y.  New paragraphs are noted with the sign
```

¶in front of where the next paragraph is to begin. ¶Unless you . . .

These sorts of errors can be minimized by using correction fluids or tapes while you type. If you use a word processor, you can eliminate such errors completely by simply entering corrections as you proofread on the screen.

MANUSCRIPT FORM

The novelist and poet Peter De Vries once observed in his characteristically humorous way that he very much enjoyed writing but that he couldn't bear the "paper work." Behind this playful pun is a half-serious impatience with the mechanics of it all. You may feel some of that too, but this is not the time to allow a thoughtful, carefully revised paper to trip over minor details that can be easily accommodated. The final draft you hand in to your instructor should not only read well but look neat. If your instructor does not provide specific instructions concerning the format for the paper, follow these guidelines.

1. Papers (particularly long ones) should be typed on 8½ × 11-inch paper in double space. Avoid transparent paper such as onionskin; it is difficult to read and write comments on. The ribbon should be dark and the letters on the machine clear. If you compose on a word processor with a dot-matrix printer, be certain that the dots are close enough together to be legible. And don't forget to separate your pages and remove the strips of holes on each side of the pages if your printer uses a continuous paper feed. If your instructor accepts handwritten papers, write legibly in ink on only one side of a wide-lined page.

2. Use a one-inch margin at the top, bottom, and sides of each page. Unless you are instructed to include a separate title page, type your name, instructor's name, course number and section, and date on separate lines one inch below the upper-left corner of the first page. Double space between these lines and then center the title two spaces below the date. Do not underline or put quotation marks around your paper's title, but do use quotation marks around the titles of poems, short stories, or other brief works, and underline the titles of books and plays (for instance, Racial Stereotypes in "Battle Royal" and *Fences*). Begin the text of your paper four spaces below the title. If you have used secondary sources, center the heading "Notes" or "Works Cited" one inch from the top of a separate page and then double space between it and the entries.

3. Number each page consecutively, a half inch from the top of the page in the upper-right corner.

4. Gather the pages with a paper clip rather than staples, folders, or some other device. That will make it easier for your instructor to handle the paper.

2. Types of Writing Assignments

The types of papers most frequently assigned in literature classes are explication, analysis, and comparison and contrast. Most writing about literature involves some combination of these skills. This chapter includes a sample explication, an analysis, and a comparison and contrast paper. If you know how to handle these basic kinds of papers, you'll be better prepared to take on more sophisticated assignments as well. (Six additional sample papers are included in this text. For genre-based assignments see the sample papers for writing about fiction [p. 53], poetry [p. 65], and drama [p. 88]. A paper written from the critical perspective of a reader-response approach appears on page 133, and a paper that studies an author in depth through a discussion of four poems by Emily Dickinson is on page 145. For a sample research paper that demonstrates a variety of strategies for documenting outside sources, see page 162.)

EXPLICATION

The purpose of this approach to a literary work is to make the implicit explicit. *Explication* is a detailed explanation of a passage of poetry or prose. Because explication is an intensive examination of a text line by line, it is mostly used to interpret a short poem in its entirety or a brief passage from a long poem, short story, or play. Explication can be used in any kind of paper when you want to be specific about how a writer achieves a certain effect. An explication pays careful attention to language: the connotations of words, allusions, figurative language, irony, symbol, rhythm, sound, and so on. These elements are examined in relation to one another and to the overall effect and meaning of the work.

The simplest way to organize an explication is to move through the passage line by line, explaining whatever seems significant. It is wise to avoid, however, an assembly-line approach that begins each sentence with

"In line one. . . ." Instead, organize your paper in whatever way best serves your thesis. You might find that the right place to start is with the final lines, working your way back to the beginning of the poem or passage. The following sample explication on Dickinson's "There's a certain Slant of light" does just that. The student's opening paragraph refers to the final line of the poem in order to present her thesis. She explains that though the poem begins with an image of light, it is not a bright or cheery poem but one concerned with "the look of Death." Since the last line prompted her thesis, that is where she begins the explication.

You might also find it useful to structure a paper by discussing various elements of literature, so that you have a paragraph on connotative words followed by one on figurative language and so on. However your paper is organized, keep in mind that the aim of an explication is not simply to summarize the passage but to comment on the effects and meanings produced by the author's use of language in it. An effective explication (the Latin word *explicare* means "to unfold") displays a text to reveal how it works and what it signifies. Although writing an explication requires some patience and sensitivity, it is an excellent method for coming to understand and appreciate the elements and qualities that constitute literary art. The sample explication focuses on the following poem.

EMILY DICKINSON (1830–1886)
There's a certain Slant of light   c. 1861

There's a certain Slant of light,
Winter Afternoons —
That oppresses, like the Heft
Of Cathedral Tunes —

Heavenly Hurt, it gives us —   5
We can find no scar,
But internal difference,
Where the Meanings, are —

None may teach it—Any —
'Tis the Seal Despair —   10
An imperial affliction
Sent us of the Air —

When it comes, the Landscape listens —
Shadows—hold their breath —
When it goes, 'tis like the Distance   15
On the look of Death —

A SAMPLE EXPLICATION: A READING OF
DICKINSON'S "THERE'S A CERTAIN SLANT OF LIGHT"

The sample paper by Bonnie Katz is the result of an assignment calling for an explication of about 750 words on any poem by Emily Dickinson. Katz selected "There's a certain Slant of light."

This essay comments on every line of the poem and provides a coherent reading that relates each line to the speaker's intense awareness of death. Although the essay discusses each stanza in the order that it appears, the introductory paragraph provides a brief overview explaining how the poem's images contribute to its total meaning. In addition, the student does not hesitate to discuss a line out of sequence when it can be usefully connected to another phrase. This is especially apparent in the third paragraph, in her discussion of stanzas 2 and 3. The final paragraph describes some of the formal elements of the poem. It might be argued that this discussion could have been integrated into the previous paragraphs rather than placed at the end, but the student does make a connection in her concluding sentence between the pattern of language and its meaning.

Several other matters are worth noticing. The student works quotations into her own sentences to support her points. She quotes exactly as the words appear in the poem, even Dickinson's irregular use of capital letters. When something is added to a quotation to clarify it, it is enclosed in brackets so that the essayist's words will not be mistaken for the poet's: "Seal [of] Despair." A slash is used to separate line divisions as in "imperial affliction/ Sent us of the Air." And, finally, because the essay focuses on a short poem, it is not necessary to include line numbers, though they would be required in a study of a longer work.

Bonnie Katz

Professor Quiello

English 109-2

October 26, 19--

A Reading of Dickinson's

"There's a certain Slant of light"

Because Emily Dickinson did not provide titles for her poetry, editors follow the customary practice of using the first line of a poem as its title. However, a more appropriate title for "There's a certain Slant of light," one that suggests what the speaker in the poem is most concerned about, can be drawn from the poem's last line, which ends with "the look of Death." Although the first line begins with an image of light, nothing bright, carefree, or cheerful appears in the poem. Instead, the predominant mood and images are darkened by a sense of despair resulting from the speaker's awareness of death.

In the first stanza, the "certain Slant of light" is associated with "Winter Afternoons," a phrase that connotes the end of a day, a season, and even life itself. Such light is hardly warm or comforting. Not a ray or beam, this slanting light suggests something unusual or distorted and creates in the speaker a certain slant on life that is consistent with the cold, dark mood that winter afternoons can produce. Like the speaker, most of us have seen and felt this sort of light: it "oppresses" and pervades our sense of things when we encounter it. Dickinson uses the senses of hearing and touch as well as sight to describe the overwhelming oppressiveness that the speaker experiences. The light is transformed into sound by a simile that tells us it is "like the Heft / Of Cathedral

Tunes." Moreover, the "Heft" of that sound--the slow, solemn measures of tolling church bells and organ music--weighs heavily on our spirits. Through the use of shifting imagery, Dickinson evokes a kind of spiritual numbness that we keenly feel and perceive through our senses.

By associating the winter light with "Cathedral Tunes," Dickinson lets us know that the speaker is concerned about more than the weather. Whatever it is that "oppresses" is related by connotation to faith, mortality, and God. The second and third stanzas offer several suggestions about this connection. The pain caused by the light is a "Heavenly Hurt." This "imperial affliction / Sent us of the Air" apparently comes from God above, and yet it seems to be part of the very nature of life. The oppressiveness we feel is in the air, and it can neither be specifically identified at this point in the poem nor be eliminated, for "None may teach it--Any." All we can know is that existence itself seems depressing under the weight of this "Seal [of] Despair." The impression left by this "Seal" is stamped within the mind or soul rather than externally. "We can find no scar," but once experienced, this oppressiveness challenges our faith in life and its "Meanings."

The final stanza does not explain what those "Meanings" are, but it does make clear that the speaker is acutely aware of death. As the winter daylight fades, Dickinson projects the speaker's anxiety onto the surrounding landscape and shadows, which will soon be engulfed by the darkness that follows this light: "[T]he Landscape listens-- / Shadows--hold their breath." This image firmly aligns the winter light in the first stanza with darkness. Paradoxically, the light in this poem illuminates the nature of darkness. Tension is released when the light is completely gone, but what remains is the despair that the "imperial affliction" has imprinted on the speaker's sensibilities, for it is "like the Distance / On the look of Death." There can be no relief from what that "certain Slant of light" has revealed, because what has been experienced is permanent--like the fixed stare in the eyes of someone who is dead.

The speaker's awareness of death is conveyed in a thoughtful, hushed tone. The lines are filled with fluid <u>l</u> and smooth <u>s</u> sounds that are appropriate for the quiet, meditative voice in the poem. The voice sounds tentative and uncertain--perhaps a little frightened. This seems to be re-flected in the slightly irregular meter of the lines. The stanzas are trochaic, with the second and fourth lines of each stanza having five syllables, but no stanza is identical to another because each works a slight variation on the first stanza's seven syllables in the first and third lines. The rhymes also combine exact patterns with variations. The first and third lines of each stanza are not exact rhymes, but the second and fourth lines are exact so that the paired words are more closely related: <u>Afternoons</u>, <u>Tunes</u>; <u>scar</u>, <u>are</u>; <u>Despair</u>, <u>Air</u>; and <u>breath</u>, <u>Death</u>. There is a pattern to the poem, but it is unobtrusively woven into the speaker's voice in much the same way that "the look of Death" is subtly present in the im-ages and language of the poem.

ANALYSIS

The preceding sample essay shows how an explication examines in detail the important elements in a work and relates them to the whole. An analysis, however, usually examines only a single element—such as plot, character, point of view, symbol, tone, or irony—and relates it to the entire work. An analytic topic separates the work into parts and focuses on a specific one; you might consider "Point of View in Updike's 'A & P' " "Patterns of Rhythm in Frost's 'Mending Wall' " or "The Significance of Fortinbras in *Hamlet*." The specific element must be related to the work as a whole or it will appear irrelevant. It is not enough to point out that there are many death images in Marvell's "To His Coy Mistress"; the images must somehow be connected to the poem's overall effect.

Whether an analytic paper is just a few pages or many, it cannot attempt to discuss everything about the work it is considering. Only those elements that are relevant to the topic can be treated. This kind of focusing makes the topic manageable; this is why most papers that you write will probably be some form of analysis. Explications are useful for a short passage, but a line-by-line commentary on a story, play, or long poem simply isn't practical. Because analysis allows you to consider the central effect or meaning of an entire work by studying a single important element, it is a useful and common approach to longer works. The sample analysis paper focuses on the following short story.

JOHN UPDIKE (b. 1932)
A & P   1961

In walks these three girls in nothing but bathing suits. I'm in the third checkout slot, with my back to the door, so I don't see them until they're over by the bread. The one that caught my eye first was the one in the plaid green two-piece. She was a chunky kid, with a good tan and a sweet broad soft-looking can with those two crescents of white just under it, where the sun never seems to hit, at the top of the backs of her legs. I stood there with my hand on a box of HiHo crackers trying to remember if I rang it up or not. I ring it up again and the customer starts giving me hell. She's one of these cash-register-watchers, a witch about fifty with rouge on her cheekbones and no eyebrows, and I know it made her day to trip me up. She'd been watching cash registers for fifty years and probably never seen a mistake before.

By the time I got her feathers smoothed and her goodies into a bag—she gives me a little snort in passing, if she'd been born at the right time they would have burned her over in Salem—by the time I get her on her way the girls had circled around the bread and were coming back, without a pushcart, back my way along the counters, in the aisle between the checkouts and the Special bins. They didn't even have shoes on. There was this chunky one, with the two-piece—it was bright green and the seams on the bra were still sharp and her belly was still pretty pale so I guessed she just got it (the suit)—there was this one, with one of those chubby berry-faces, the lips all bunched together under her nose, this one, and a tall one, with black hair that hadn't quite frizzed right, and one of these sunburns right across under the eyes, and a chin that was too long—you know, the kind of girl other girls think is very "striking" and "attractive" but never quite makes it, as they very well know, which is why they like her so much—and then the third one, that wasn't quite so tall. She was the queen. She kind of led them, the other two peeking around and making their shoulders round. She didn't look around, not this queen, she just walked straight on slowly, on these long white prima-donna legs. She came down a little hard on her heels, as if she didn't walk in her bare feet that much, putting down her heels and then letting the weight move along to her toes as if she was testing the floor with every step, putting a little deliberate extra action into it. You never know for sure how girls' minds work (do you really think it's a mind in there or just a little buzz like a bee in a glass jar?) but you got the idea she had talked the other two into coming in here with her, and now she was showing them how to do it, walk slow and hold yourself straight.

She had on a kind of dirty-pink—beige maybe, I don't know—bathing suit with a little nubble all over it and, what got me, the straps were down. They were off her shoulders looped loose around the cool tops of her arms, and I guess as a result the suit had slipped a little on her, so all around the top of the cloth there was this shining rim. If it hadn't been there you wouldn't have known there could have been anything whiter than those shoulders. With the straps pushed off, there was nothing between the top of the suit and the top of her head except just *her*, this clean bare plane of the top of her chest down from the shoulder bones like a dented sheet of metal tilted in the light. I mean, it was more than pretty.

She had sort of oaky hair that the sun and salt had bleached, done up in a bun that was unraveling, and a kind of prim face. Walking into the A & P with your straps down, I suppose it's the only kind of face you *can* have. She held her head so high her neck, coming up out of those white shoulders, looked kind of stretched, but I didn't mind. The longer her neck was, the more of her there was.

She must have felt in the corner of her eye me and over my shoulder 5 Stokesie in the second slot watching, but she didn't tip. Not this queen. She kept her eyes moving across the racks, and stopped, and turned so slow it made my stomach rub the inside of my apron, and buzzed to the other two, who kind of huddled against her for relief, and then they all three of them went up the cat-and-dog-food-breakfast-cereal-macaroni-rice-raisins-seasonings-spreads-spaghetti-soft-drinks-crackers-and-cookies aisle. From the third slot I look straight up this aisle to the meat counter, and I watched them all the way. The fat one with the tan sort of fumbled with the cookies, but on second thought she put the package back. The sheep pushing their carts down the aisle—the girls were walking against the usual traffic (not that we have one-way signs or anything)—were pretty hilarious. You could see them, when Queenie's white shoulders dawned on them, kind of jerk, or hop, or hiccup, but their eyes snapped back to their own baskets and on they pushed. I bet you could set off dynamite in an A & P and the people would by and large keep reaching and checking oatmeal off their lists and muttering "Let me see, there was a third thing, began with A, asparagus, no, ah, yes, applesauce!" or whatever it is they do mutter. But there was no doubt, this jiggled them. A few houseslaves in pin curlers even looked around after pushing their carts past to make sure what they had seen was correct.

You know, it's one thing to have a girl in a bathing suit down on the beach, where what with the glare nobody can look at each other much anyway, and another thing in the cool of the A & P, under the fluorescent lights, against all those stacked packages, with her feet paddling along naked over our checker-board green-and-cream rubber-tile floor.

"Oh Daddy," Stokesie said beside me. "I feel so faint."

"Darling," I said. "Hold me tight." Stokesie's married, with two babies chalked up on his fuselage already, but as far as I can tell that's the only difference. He's twenty-two, and I was nineteen this April.

"Is it done?" he asks, the responsible married man finding his voice. I forgot to say he thinks he's going to be manager some sunny day, maybe in 1990 when it's called the Great Alexandrov and Petrooshki Tea Company or something.

What he meant was, our town is five miles from a beach, with a big 10 summer colony out on the Point, but we're right in the middle of town, and the women generally put on a shirt or shorts or something before they get out of the car into the street. And anyway these are usually women with six children and varicose veins mapping their legs and nobody, including them, could care less. As I say, we're right in the middle of town, and if you stand at our front doors you can see two banks and the Congregational church and the newspaper store and three real-estate offices and about twenty-seven old freeloaders tearing up Central Street because the sewer broke again. It's not as if we're on the Cape, we're north of Boston and there's people in this town haven't seen the ocean for twenty years.

The girls had reached the meat counter and were asking McMahon something. He pointed, they pointed, and they shuffled out of sight behind a pyramid of Diet Delight peaches. All that was left for us to see was old McMahon patting his mouth and looking after them sizing up their joints. Poor kids, I began to feel sorry for them, they couldn't help it.

Now here comes the sad part of the story, at least my family says it's sad, but I don't think it's so sad myself. The store's pretty empty, it being Thursday afternoon, so there was nothing much to do except lean on the register and wait for the girls to show up again. The whole store was like a pinball machine and I didn't know which tunnel they'd come out of. After a while they come around out of the far aisle, around the light bulbs, records at discount of the Caribbean Six or Tony Martin Sings or some such gunk you wonder they waste the wax on, sixpacks of candy bars, and plastic toys done up in cellophane that fall apart when a kid looks at them anyway. Around they come, Queenie still leading the way, and holding a little gray jar in her hands. Slots Three through Seven are unmanned and I could see her wondering between Stokes and me, but Stokesie with his usual luck draws an old party in baggy gray pants who stumbles up with four giant cans of pineapple juice (what do these bums *do* with all that pineapple juice? I've often asked myself). So the girls come to me. Queenie puts down the jar and I take it into my fingers icy cold. Kingfish Fancy Herring Snacks in Pure Sour Cream: 49¢. Now her hands are empty, not a ring or a bracelet, bare as God made them, and I wonder where the money's coming from. Still with that prim look she lifts a folded dollar bill out of the hollow at the center of her nubbled pink top. The jar went heavy in my hand. Really, I thought that was so cute.

Then everybody's luck begins to run out. Lengel comes in from haggling with a truck full of cabbages on the lot and is about to scuttle into that door marked MANAGER behind which he hides all day when the girls touch his eye. Lengel's pretty dreary, teaches Sunday school and the rest, but he doesn't miss that much. He comes over and says, "Girls, this isn't the beach."

Queenie blushes, though maybe it's just a brush of sunburn I was noticing for the first time, now that she was so close. "My mother asked me to pick up a jar of herring snacks." Her voice kind of startled me, the way voices do when you see the people first, coming out so flat and dumb yet kind of tony, too, the way it ticked over "pick up" and "snacks." All of a sudden I slid right down her voice into the living room. Her father and the other men were standing around in ice-cream coats and bow ties and the women were in sandals picking up herring snacks on toothpicks off a big glass plate and they were all holding drinks the color of water with olives and sprigs of mint in them. When my parents have somebody over they get lemonade and if it's a real racy affair Schlitz in tall glasses with "They'll Do It Every Time" cartoons stenciled on.

"That's all right," Lengel said. "But this isn't the beach." His repeating this struck me as funny, as if it had just occurred to him, and he had been thinking all these years the A & P was a great big dune and he was the head lifeguard. He didn't like my smiling—as I say he doesn't miss much—but he concentrates on giving the girls that sad Sunday-school-superintendent stare.

Queenie's blush is no sunburn now, and the plump one in plaid, that I liked better from the back—a really sweet can—pipes up, "We weren't doing any shopping. We just came in for the one thing."

"That makes no difference," Lengel tells her, and I could see from the way his eyes went that he hadn't noticed she was wearing a two-piece before. "We want you decently dressed when you come in here."

"We *are* decent," Queenie says suddenly, her lower lip pushing, getting sore now that she remembers her place, a place from which the crowd that runs the A & P must look pretty crummy. Fancy Herring Snacks flashed in her very blue eyes.

"Girls, I don't want to argue with you. After this come in here with your shoulders covered. It's our policy." He turns his back. That's policy for you. Policy is what the kingpins want. What the others want is juvenile delinquency.

All this while, the customers had been showing up with their carts but, 20
you know, sheep, seeing a scene, they had all bunched up on Stokesie, who
shook open a paper bag as gently as peeling a peach, not wanting to miss
a word. I could feel in the silence everybody getting nervous, most of all
Lengel, who asks me, "Sammy, have you rung up their purchase?"

I thought and said "No" but it wasn't about that I was thinking. I go
through the punches, 4, 9, GROC. TOT—it's more complicated than you think,
and after you do it often enough, it begins to make a little song, that you
hear words to, in my case "Hello *(bing)* there, you *(gung)* hap-py *pee*-pul
(splat)!"—the *splat* being the drawer flying out. I uncrease the bill, tenderly
as you may imagine, it just having come from between the two smoothest
scoops of vanilla I had ever known were there, and pass a half and a penny
into her narrow pink palm, and nestle the herrings in a bag and twist its
neck and hand it over, all the time thinking.

The girls, and who'd blame them, are in a hurry to get out, so I say "I
quit" to Lengel quick enough for them to hear, hoping they'll stop and watch
me, their unsuspected hero. They keep right on going, into the electric eye;
the door flies open and they flicker across the lot to their car, Queenie and
Plaid and Big Tall Goony-Goony (not that as raw material she was so bad),
leaving me with Lengel and a kink in his eyebrow.

"Did you say something, Sammy?"

"I said I quit."

"I thought you did." 25

"You didn't have to embarrass them."

"It was they who were embarrassing us."

I started to say something that came out "Fiddle-de-doo." It's a saying
of my grandmother's, and I know she would have been pleased.

"I don't think you know what you're saying," Lengel said.

"I know you don't," I said. "But I do." I pull the bow at the back of my 30
apron and start shrugging it off my shoulders. A couple customers that had
been heading for my slot begin to knock against each other, like scared pigs
in a chute.

Lengel sighs and begins to look very patient and old and gray. He's
been a friend of my parents for years. "Sammy, you don't want to do this
to your Mom and Dad," he tells me. It's true, I don't. But it seems to me that
once you begin a gesture it's fatal not to go through with it. I fold the apron,
"Sammy" stitched in red on the pocket, and put it on the counter, and drop
the bow tie on top of it. The bow tie is theirs, if you've ever wondered.
"You'll feel this for the rest of your life," Lengel says, and I know that's true,
too, but remembering how he made the pretty girl blush makes me so
scrunchy inside I punch the No Sale tab and the machine whirs "pee-pul"
and the drawer splats out. One advantage to this scene taking place in
summer, I can follow this up with a clean exit, there's no fumbling around
getting your coat and galoshes, I just saunter into the electric eye in my
white shirt that my mother ironed the night before, and the door heaves
itself open, and outside the sunshine is skating around on the asphalt.

I look around for my girls, but they're gone, of course. There wasn't anybody but some young married screaming with her children about some candy they didn't get by the door of a powder-blue Falcon station wagon. Looking back in the big windows, over the bags of peat moss and aluminum lawn furniture stacked on the pavement, I could see Lengel in my place in the slot, checking the sheep through. His face was dark gray and his back stiff, as if he'd just had an injection of iron, and my stomach kind of fell as I felt how hard the world was going to be to me hereafter.

A SAMPLE ANALYSIS: THE A & P
AS A STATE OF MIND

Nancy Lager's paper analyzes the setting in John Updike's "A & P." The assignment simply asked for an essay of approximately 750 words on a short story written in the twentieth century. The approach was left to the student.

The idea for this essay began with Lager asking herself why Updike used "A & P" as the title. The initial answer to the question was that "the setting is important in this story." This answer was the rough beginning of a tentative thesis. What still had to be explained, though, was how the setting is important. To determine the significance of the setting, Lager jotted down some notes based on her underlinings and marginal notations.

```
A & P
"usual traffic"
lights and tile
"electric eye"
shoppers like "sheep," "houseslaves," "pigs"
"Alexandrov and Petrooshki"--Russia

New England Town
typical: bank, church, etc.
traditional
conservative
proper
near Salem--witch trials
puritanical
intolerant

Lengel
"manager"
"doesn't miss that much" (like lady shopper)
Sunday school
"It's our policy"
spokesman for A & P values
```

From these notes Lager saw that Lengel serves as the voice of the A & P. He is, in a sense, a personification of the intolerant atmosphere of the setting. This insight led to another version of her thesis statement: "The setting of 'A & P' is the antagonist of the story." That explained at least some of the

(Text continued on page 32)

Nancy Lager

Professor Taylor

English 102-12

April 1, 19--

The A & P as a State of Mind

The setting of John Updike's "A & P" is crucial to our understanding of Sammy's decision to quit his job. Although Sammy is the central character in the story and we learn that he is a principled, good-natured nineteen-year-old with a sense of humor, Updike seems to invest as much effort in describing the setting as he does in Sammy. The setting is the antagonist and plays a role that is as important as Sammy's. The title, after all, is not "Youthful Rebellion" or "Sammy Quits" but "A & P." Even though Sammy knows that his quitting will make life more difficult for him, he instinctively insists upon rejecting what the A & P comes to represent in the story. When he rings up a "No Sale" and "saunter[s]" out of the store, he leaves behind not only a job but the rigid state of mind associated with the A & P.

Sammy's descriptions of the A & P present a setting that is ugly, monotonous, and rigidly regulated. The fluorescent light is as blandly cool as the "checker-board green-and-cream rubber-tile floor." We can see the uniformity Sammy describes because we have all been in chain stores. The "usual traffic" moves in one direction (except for the swimsuited girls, who move against it), and everything is neatly ordered and categorized in tidy aisles. The dehumanizing routine of this environment is suggested by Sammy's offhanded references to the typical shoppers as "sheep," "houseslaves," and "pigs." They

seem to pace through the store in a stupor; as Sammy tells us,
not even dynamite could move them.

The A & P is appropriately located "right in the middle"
of a proper, conservative, traditional New England town north
of Boston. This location, coupled with the fact that the
town is only five miles from Salem, the site of the famous
seventeenth-century witch trials, suggests a narrow, intolerant social atmosphere in which there is no room for stepping
beyond the boundaries of what is regarded as normal and
proper. The importance of this setting can be appreciated
even more if we imagine the action taking place in, say, a
mellow suburb of southern California. In this prim New England setting, the girls in their bathing suits are bound to
offend somebody's sense of propriety.

As soon as Lengel sees the girls, the inevitable conflict
begins. He embodies the dull conformity represented by the
A & P. As "manager," he is both the guardian and enforcer of
"policy." When he gives the girls "that sad Sunday-school-
superintendent stare," we know we are in the presence of the
A & P's version of a dreary bureaucrat who "doesn't miss that
much." He is as unsympathetic and unpleasant as the woman
"with rouge on her cheekbones and no eyebrows" who pounces on
Sammy for ringing up her "HiHo crackers" twice. Like the
"electric eye" in the doorway, her vigilant eyes allow nothing
to escape their notice. For Sammy the logical extension of
Lengel's "policy" is the half-serious notion that one day the
A & P might be known as the "Great Alexandrov and Petrooshki
Tea Company." Sammy's connection between what he regards as
mindless "policy" and Soviet oppression is obviously an exag-

geration, but the reader is invited to entertain the similarities anyway.

The reason Sammy quits his job has less to do with defending the girls than with his own sense of what it means to be a decent human being. His decision is not an easy one. He doesn't want to make trouble or disappoint his parents, and he knows his independence and self-reliance (the other side of New England tradition) will make life more complex for him. In spite of his own hesitations, he finds himself blurting out "Fiddle-de-doo" to Lengel's policies and in doing so knows that his grandmother "would have been pleased." Sammy's "No Sale" rejects the crabbed perspective on life that Lengel represents as manager of the A & P. This gesture is more than just negative, however, for as he punches in that last entry on the cash register, "the machine whirs 'pee-pul.' " His decision to quit his job at the A & P is an expression of his refusal to regard policies as more important than people.

---

setting's importance. By seeing Lengel as a spokesman for "A & P" policies, she could view him as a voice that articulates the morally smug atmosphere created by the setting. Finally, she considered why it is significant that the setting is the antagonist, and this generated her last thesis: "Because the intolerant setting of 'A & P' is the antagonist in the story, it is crucial to our understanding of Sammy's decision to quit his job." This thesis sentence does not appear precisely in these words in the essay, but it is the backbone of the introductory paragraph.

The remaining paragraphs consist of details that describe the A & P in the second paragraph, the New England town in the third, Lengel in the fourth, and Sammy's reasons for quitting in the concluding paragraph. Paragraphs 2, 3, and 4 are largely based on Lager's notes, which she used as an outline once her thesis was established. The essay is sharply focused, well organized, and generally well written. In addition, it suggests a number of useful guidelines for analytic papers.

1. Only those points related to the thesis are included. In another type of paper the role of the girls in the bathing suits, for example, might have been considerably more prominent.
2. The analysis keeps the setting in focus while at the same time indicating how it is significant in the major incident in the story— Sammy's quitting.
3. The title is a useful lead into the paper; it provides a sense of what the topic is. In addition, the title is drawn from a sentence (the final one of the first paragraph) that clearly explains its meaning.
4. The introductory paragraph is direct and clearly indicates the paper will argue that the setting serves as the antagonist of the story.
5. Brief quotations are deftly incorporated into the text of the paper to illustrate points. We are told what we need to know about the story as evidence is provided to support ideas. There is no unnecessary plot summary. Because "A & P" is only a few pages in length and is an assigned topic, page numbers are not included after quoted phrases. If the story were longer, page numbers would be helpful for the reader.
6. The paragraphs are well developed, unified, and coherent. They flow naturally from one to another. Notice, for example, the smooth transition worked into the final sentence of the third paragraph and the first sentence of the fourth paragraph.
7. Lager makes excellent use of her careful reading and notes by finding revealing connections among the details she has observed. The store's "electric eye," for instance, is related to the woman's and Lengel's watchfulness.
8. As events are described, the present tense is used. This avoids awkward tense shifts and lends an immediacy to the discussion.
9. The concluding paragraph establishes the significance of why the setting should be seen as the antagonist and provides a sense of closure by referring again to Sammy's "No Sale," which has been mentioned at the end of the first paragraph.
10. In short, Lager has demonstrated that she has read the work closely, has understood the relation of the setting to the major action, and has argued her thesis convincingly by using evidence from the story.

COMPARISON AND CONTRAST

Another essay assignment in literature courses often combined with analytic topics is the type that requires you to write about similarities and differences between or within works. You might be asked to discuss "How Sounds Express Meanings in William Hathaway's 'Oh, Oh' and Robert Francis's 'Catch,' " or "Sammy's and Stokesie's Attitudes about Conformity in

Updike's 'A & P.' " A *comparison* of either topic would emphasize their similarities, while a *contrast* would stress their differences. It is possible, of course, to include both perspectives in a paper if you find significant likenesses and differences. A comparison of Andrew Marvell's "To His Coy Mistress" and Richard Wilbur's "A Late Aubade" would, for example, yield similarities, because each poem describes a man urging his lover to make the most of their precious time together; however, important differences also exist in the tone and theme of each poem that would constitute a contrast. (You should, incidentally, be aware that the term *comparison* is sometimes used inclusively to refer to both similarities and differences. If you are assigned a comparison of two works, be sure that you understand what your instructor's expectations are; you may be required to include both approaches in the essay.)

When you choose your own topic, the paper will be more successful—more manageable—if you write on works that can be meaningfully related to each other. Although Robert Herrick's "To the Virgins, to Make Much of Time" and Shakespeare's *Hamlet* both have something to do with hesitation, the likelihood of anyone making a connection between the two that reveals something interesting and important is remote—though perhaps not impossible if the topic were conceived imaginatively and tactfully. That is not to say that comparisons of works from different genres should be avoided, but the relation between them should be strong, as would a treatment of female identity in Kate Chopin's "The Story of an Hour" (p. 46) and Susan Glaspell's *Trifles* (p. 73). Choose a topic that encourages you to ask significant questions about each work; the purpose of a comparison or contrast is to understand the works more clearly for having examined them together.

Choose works to compare or contrast that intersect with each other in some significant way. They may, for example, be written by the same author, in the same genre, or about the same subject. Perhaps you can compare their use of some technique, such as irony or point of view. Regardless of the specific topic, be sure to have a thesis that allows you to organize your paper around a central idea that argues a point about the two works. If you merely draw up a list of similarities or differences without a thesis in mind, your paper will be little more than a series of observations with no apparent purpose. Keep in the foreground of your thinking what the comparison or contrast reveals about the works.

There is no single way to organize comparative papers since each topic is likely to have its own particular issues to resolve, but it is useful to be aware of two basic patterns that can be helpful with a comparison, a contrast, or a combination of both. One method that can be effective for relatively short papers consists of dividing the paper in half, first discussing one work and then the other. Here, for example, is a partial informal outline for a discussion of Sophocles' *Oedipus the King* and

Shakespeare's *Hamlet;* the topic is a comparison and contrast: "Oedipus and Hamlet as Tragic Figures."

1. Oedipus
    a. The nature of the conflict
    b. Strengths and stature
    c. Weaknesses and mistakes
    d. What is learned
2. Hamlet
    a. The nature of the conflict
    b. Strengths and stature
    c. Weaknesses and mistakes
    d. What is learned

This organizational strategy can be effective provided that the second part of the paper combines the discussion of Hamlet with references to Oedipus so that the thesis is made clear and the paper unified without being repetitive. If the two characters were treated entirely separately, then the discussion would be merely parallel rather than integrated. In a lengthy paper, this organization probably would not work well because a reader would have difficulty remembering the points made in the first half as he or she reads on.

Thus for a longer paper it is usually better to create a more integrated structure that discusses both works as you take up each item in your outline. Here is the second basic pattern using the elements in partial outline just cited.

1. The nature of the conflict
    a. Oedipus
    b. Hamlet
2. Strengths and stature
    a. Oedipus
    b. Hamlet
3. Weaknesses and mistakes
    a. Oedipus
    b. Hamlet
4. What is learned
    a. Oedipus
    b. Hamlet

This pattern allows you to discuss any number of topics without requiring that your reader recall what you first said about the conflict Oedipus confronts before you discuss Hamlet's conflicts fifteen pages later. However you structure your comparison or contrast paper, make certain that a reader can follow its elements and keep track of its thesis. The sample comparison paper focuses on the following two poems.

ANDREW MARVELL (1621–1678)

To His Coy Mistress   1681

Had we but world enough, and time,
This coyness, lady, were no crime.
We would sit down, and think which way
To walk, and pass our long love's day.
Thou by the Indian Ganges'° side   5
Shouldst rubies find; I by the tide
Of Humber° would complain.° I would   *write love songs*
Love you ten years before the Flood,
And you should, if you please, refuse
Till the conversion of the Jews.   10
My vegetable love should grow°
Vaster than empires, and more slow;
An hundred years should go to praise
Thine eyes and on thy forehead gaze,
Two hundred to adore each breast,   15
But thirty thousand to the rest:
An age at least to every part,
And the last age should show your heart.
For, lady, you deserve this state,
Nor would I love at lower rate.   20
    But at my back I always hear
Time's wingèd chariot hurrying near;
And yonder all before us lie
Deserts of vast eternity.
Thy beauty shall no more be found,   25
Nor in thy marble vault shall sound
My echoing song; then worms shall try
That long preserved virginity,
And your quaint honor turn to dust,
And into ashes all my lust.   30
The grave's a fine and private place,
But none, I think, do there embrace.
    Now, therefore, while the youthful hue
Sits on thy skin like morning dew,
And while thy willing soul transpires°   *breathes forth* 35
At every pore with instant fires,
Now let us sport us while we may,
And now, like amorous birds of prey,
Rather at once our time devour
Than languish in his slow-chapped° power.   *slow-jawed*   40
Let us roll all our strength and all
Our sweetness up into one ball,

---

5 *Ganges:* A river in India sacred to the Hindus.   7 *Humber:* A river that flows through Marvell's native town, Hull.   11 *My vegetable love . . . grow:* A slow, unconscious growth.

And tear our pleasures with rough strife
Thorough° the iron gates of life.   *through*
Thus, though we cannot make our sun   45
Stand still, yet we will make him run.

DIANE ACKERMAN (b. 1948)
A Fine, a Private Place   1983

He took her one day
under the blue horizon
where long sea fingers
parted like beads
hitched in the doorway   5
of an opium den,
and canyons mazed the deep
reef with hollows,
cul-de-sacs, and narrow boudoirs,
and had to ask twice   10
before she understood
his stroking her arm
with a marine feather
slobbery as aloe pulp
was wooing, or saw the octopus   15
in his swimsuit
stretch one tentacle
and ripple its silky bag.

While bubbles rose
like globs of mercury,   20
they made love
mask to mask, floating
with oceans of air between them,
she his sea-geisha
in an orange kimono   25
of belts and vests,
her lacquered hair waving,
as Indigo Hamlets
tattooed the vista,
and sunlight   30
cut through the water,
twisting its knives
into corridors of light.

His sandy hair
and sea-blue eyes,   35
his kelp-thin waist
and chest ribbed wider

than a sandbar
where muscles domed
clear and taut as shells   40
(freckled cowries,
flat, brawny scallops
the color of dawn),
his sea-battered hands
gripping her thighs   45
like tawny starfish
and drawing her close
as a pirate vessel
to let her board:
who was this she loved?   50

Overhead, sponges
sweating raw color
jutted from a coral arch,
Clown Wrasses°   *brightly colored tropical fish*
hovered like fireworks,   55
and somewhere an abalone opened
its silver wings.
Part of a lusty dream
under aspic, her hips rolled
like a Spanish galleon,   60
her eyes swam
and chest began to heave.
Gasps melted on the tide.
Knowing she would soon be
breathless as her tank,   65
he pumped his brine
deep within her,
letting sea water drive it
through petals
delicate as anemone veils   70
to the dark purpose
of a conch-shaped womb.
An ear to her loins
would have heard the sea roar.

When panting ebbed,   75
and he signaled *Okay?*
as lovers have asked,
land or waterbound
since time heaved ho,
he led her to safety: 80
shallower realms,
heading back toward
the boat's even keel,
though ocean still petted her
cell by cell, murmuring   85

along her legs and neck,
caressing her
with pale, endless arms.

Later, she thought often
of that blue boudoir,   90
pillow-soft and filled
with cascading light,
where together
they'd made a bell
that dumbly clanged   95
beneath the waves
and minutes lurched
like mountain goats.
She could still see
the quilted mosaics   100
that were fish
twitching spangles overhead,
still feel the ocean
inside and out, turning her
evolution around.   105

She thought of it miles
and fathoms away, often,
at odd moments: watching
the minnow snowflakes
dip against the windowframe,   110
holding a sponge
idly under tap-gush,
sinking her teeth
into the cleft
of a voluptuous peach.   115

A SAMPLE COMPARISON:
MARVELL AND ACKERMAN SEIZE THE DAY

The following paper is in response to an assignment that required a
comparison and contrast—about 1,000 words—of two assigned poems. The
student chose to write an analysis of two "seize the day" poems written
three hundred years apart.

Although these two poems are fairly lengthy, Stephanie Smith's brief
analysis of them is satisfying because she specifically focuses on the male
and female *carpe diem* voices of Andrew Marvell's "To His Coy Mistress"
(p. 36) and Diane Ackerman's "A Fine, A Private Place" (p. 37). After introducing the topic in the first paragraph, she takes up the two poems in a pattern
similar to the first outline suggested for "Oedipus and Hamlet as

(Text continued on page 44)

Stephanie Smith

English 210-10

Professor Monroe

April 2, 19--

Marvell and Ackerman Seize the Day

In her 1983 poem "A Fine, A Private Place," Diane Ackerman never mentions Andrew Marvell's 1681 poem "To His Coy Mistress." However, her one-line allusion to Marvell's famous
argument to his lover is all the reference she needs. Through
a contemporary lens, she firmly qualifies Marvell's
seventeenth-century masculine perspective. Marvell's speaker
attempts to woo a young woman and convince her to have sexual
relations with him. His seize-the-day rhetoric argues that
"his mistress" should let down her conventional purity and
enjoy the moment, his logic being that we are grave-bound anyway, so why not? Although his poetic pleading is effective,
both stylistically and argumentatively, Marvell's speaker obviously assumes that the coy mistress will succumb to his
grasps at her sexuality. Further, and most important for Ackerman, the speaker takes for granted that the female must be
persuaded to love. His smooth talk leaves no room for a feminine perspective, be it a slap in the face or a sharing of his
carpe diem attitudes. Ackerman accommodates Marvell's masculine speaker but also deftly takes poetic license in the cause
of female freedom and sensuously lays out her own fine and
private place. Through describing a personal sexual encounter
both sensually and erotically, Ackerman's female speaker demonstrates that women have just as many lustful urges as the
men who would seduce them; she presents sex as neither solely
a male quest nor a female sacrifice. "A Fine, A Private

Place" takes a female perspective on sex, and enthusiastically enjoys the pleasure of it.

"To His Coy Mistress" is in a regular rhyme scheme, as each line rhymes with the next--almost like a compilation of couplets. And this, accompanied by traditional iambic tetrameter, lays the foundation for a forcefully flowing speech, a command for the couple to just do it. By the end of the poem the speaker seems to expect his mistress to capitulate. Marvell's speaker declares at the start that if eternity were upon them, he would not mind putting sex aside and paying her unending homage.

> Had we but world enough, and time,
>
> This coyness, lady, were no crime.
>
> We would sit down, and think which way
>
> To walk, and pass our long love's day (lines 1-4).

He proclaims he would love her "ten years before the Flood" (8) and concedes that she "should, if you please, refuse / Till the conversion of the Jews" (9-10). This eternal love-land expands as Marvell asserts that his "vegetable love should grow / Vaster than empires, and more slow" (11-12). Every part of her body would be admired for an entire "age" because "lady, you deserve this state, / Nor would I love at lower rate" (19-20). He would willingly wait but, alas, circumstances won't let him. She'll have to settle for the here and now, and he must show her that life is not an eternity but rather an alarm clock.

The speaker laments that "at my back I always hear / Time's wingèd chariot hurrying near" (21-22). He then cleverly draws a picture of what exactly eternity does have in store for them, namely barren "Deserts" where her "beauty

shall no more be found" (25) while "worms shall try / That
long preserved virginity" (27-28) and her "quaint honor turn
to dust" (29). This death imagery is meant to frighten her
for not having lived enough. He astutely concedes that "The
grave's a fine and private place, / But none, I think, do
there embrace" (31-32), thereby making even more vivid the
nightmare he has just laid before her. Although he must make
his grim argument, he does not want to dampen the mood, so he
quickly returns to her fair features.

"Now," the speaker proclaims, "while the youthful hue /
Sits on thy skin like morning dew, / . . . Now let us sport us
while we may" (33-34, 37). The speaker has already made the
decision for her. Through sex, their energies will become
one--they will "roll" their "strength" and "sweetness up into
one ball" (41) as they "tear" their "pleasures with rough
strife" (43). If the two of them cannot have eternity and
make the "sun / Stand still" (45-46), then they will seize the
day, combine and celebrate their humanity, and "make [the sun]
run" (46). The speaker makes a vivid case in favor of living
for the moment. His elaborate images of the devotion his mistress deserves, the inevitability of death, and the viva-
ciousness of human life are compelling. Three hundred years
later, however, Diane Ackerman demonstrates that women no
longer need this lesson, because they share the same desires.

Ackerman's title is taken directly from "To His Coy Mistress." This poet's fine and private place is not the grave,
as it was in Marvell's poetic persuasion, but rather her
underwater sexual encounter. Ackerman's familiarity with
Marvell informs us that she knows about death and its implica-

tions. More importantly, her speaker needs no rationale to
live fully, she just does. She has sex on her own, willingly,
knowingly, and thoroughly.

Unlike "To His Coy Mistress," the poem has no rhyme
scheme and has little meter or conventional form. The free
verse tells the sexual story in an unconfined, open way. The
poem flows together with sensual, sexual images drawn from the
mystical, vibrant, undersea world. The speaker and her lover
float

> under the blue horizon
> where long sea fingers
> parted like beads
> hitched in the doorway
> of an opium den (2-6).

Whereas Marvell's lovers race against time, Ackerman's seem to
bathe in it. Within this sultry setting the "canyons mazed
the deep / reef with hollows, / cul-de-sacs, and narrow boudoirs" (7-9) that evoke erotic images. Her lover's "stroking
her arm / with a marine feather / slobbery as aloe pulp"
(12-14) constitutes foreplay, and when "the octopus / in his
swimsuit / stretch[es] one tentacle / ripple[s] its silky bag"
(15-18), she becomes a willing partner. In this "lusty dream"
(58), "her hips rolled" (59), "her eyes swam / and chest began
to heave" (61-62), and the sea also becomes a willing partner
in their love-making as the underwater waves help drive his
brine "through petals / . . . to the dark purpose / of a
conch-shaped womb" (69-72).

After "panting ebbed" (75), they return to "shallower
realms, / heading back toward / the boat's even keel" (81-83),

away from the sensual, wild, sea-world in which they reveled.
However, the speaker has not literally or figuratively exhausted the waters yet. The "ocean still petted her / cell by
cell, murmuring" (84-85). Though she emerges from the water
and the encounter, the experience stays with her as a satisfying memory.

   Her sensual memories of the encounter allow her to savor
the moment, in contrast to Marvell's speaker, whose desperate,
urgent tone is filled with tension rather than the relief of
consummation. In the final section of the poem (106-15), we
see that the speaker's sexual encounter is an experience that
stays with her "miles / and fathoms away." The erotic language of the sea is in her own voice as she looks out at "minnow snowflakes" while "holding a sponge / idly under [a] tap-
gush." As water seems to cascade all around her, the memory
of her underwater experience surfaces in the sensuous image of
"sinking her teeth / into the cleft / of a voluptuous peach."
Ackerman's subject does not have to be persuaded by an excited
man to be a sexual being; her sexuality seeps into every day
of her life, and we marvel at the depth of her sensuality.
Unlike Marvell's speaker, who remains eternally poised to
"tear our pleasures," Ackerman's speaker is steeped in those
pleasures.

Tragic Figures." Notice how Smith works in subsequent references to Marvell's poem as she discusses Ackerman's so that her treatment is integrated
and we are reminded why she is comparing and contrasting the two works.
Her final paragraph sums up her points without being repetitive and reiterates
the thesis with which she began.

3. Reading and Writing about Fiction

RESPONDING TO FICTION

Reading a literary work responsively can be an intensely demanding activity. Henry David Thoreau—about as intense and demanding a reader and writer as they come—insists that "books must be read as deliberately and reservedly as they were written." Thoreau is right about the necessity for a conscious, sustained involvement with a literary work. Imaginative literature does demand more from us than, say, browsing through *People* magazine in a dentist's waiting room, but Thoreau makes the process sound a little more daunting than it really is. For when we respond to the demands of responsive reading, our efforts are usually rewarded with pleasure as well as understanding. Careful, deliberate reading—the kind that engages a reader's imagination as it calls forth the writer's—is a means of exploration that can take a reader outside whatever circumstance or experience previously defined his or her world. Just as we respond moment by moment to people and situations in our lives, we also respond to literary works as we read them, though we may not be fully aware of how we are affected at each point along the way. The more conscious we are of how and why we respond to works in particular ways, the more likely we are to be imaginatively engaged in our reading.

In a very real sense both the reader and the author create the literary work. How a reader responds to a story, poem, or play will help to determine its meaning. The author arranges the various elements that constitute his or her craft—elements such as plot, character, setting, point of view, and symbolism, which are defined in the Glossary of Literary Terms (p. 175)—but the author cannot completely control the reader's response any more than a person can absolutely predict how a remark or action will be received by a stranger, friend, or even family member. Few authors *tell* readers how to respond. Our sympathy, anger, confusion, laughter, sadness, or whatever the feeling might be is left up to us to experience. Writers may have the talent to evoke such feelings, but they don't have the power and authority to enforce them. Because of the range of possible responses produced by imaginative literature, there is no single, correct, definitive response or interpretation. There can be readings that are wrongheaded or foolish, and some readings are better than others—that is, more responsive to a work's details and more persuasive—but that doesn't mean there is only one possible reading of a work. (See the Questions for Writing about Fiction on p. 49 for a sense of the range of possible approaches to fiction.)

Experience tells us that different people respond differently to the same work. Recall, for example, how often you've heard Melville's *Moby-Dick* described as one of the greatest American novels. This, however, is how a reviewer in *New Monthly Magazine* described the book when it was published in 1851: it is "a huge dose of hyperbolical slang, maudlin sentimentalism and tragic-comic bubble and squeak." Melville surely did not intend or desire this response; but there it is, and neither was it a singular, isolated reaction. This reading—like any reading—was influenced by the values, assumptions, and expectations that the readers brought to the novel from both previous readings and life experiences. The reviewer's refusal to take the book seriously may have missed the boat from the perspective of many other readers of *Moby-Dick,* but it indicates that even "classics" (perhaps especially those kinds of works) can generate disparate readings.

Consider the following brief story by Kate Chopin, a writer whose fiction (like Melville's) sometimes met with indifference or hostility in her own time. As you read, keep track of your responses to the central character, Mrs. Mallard. Write down your feelings about her in a substantial paragraph when you finish the story. Think, for example, about how you respond to the emotions she expresses concerning news of her husband's death. What do you think of her feelings about marriage? Do you think you would react the way she does under similar circumstances?

KATE CHOPIN (1851–1904)
The Story of an Hour   1894

Knowing that Mrs. Mallard was afflicted with a heart trouble, great care was taken to break to her as gently as possible the news of her husband's death.

It was her sister Josephine who told her, in broken sentences; veiled hints that revealed in half concealing. Her husband's friend Richards was there, too, near her. It was he who had been in the newspaper office when intelligence of the railroad disaster was received, with Brently Mallard's name leading the list of "killed." He had only taken the time to assure himself of its truth by a second telegram, and had hastened to forestall any less careful, less tender friend in bearing the sad message.

She did not hear the story as many women have heard the same, with a paralyzed inability to accept its significance. She wept at once, with sudden, wild abandonment, in her sister's arms. When the storm of grief had spent itself she went away to her room alone. She would have no one follow her.

There stood, facing the open window, a comfortable, roomy armchair. Into this she sank, pressed down by a physical exhaustion that haunted her body and seemed to reach into her soul.

She could see in the open square before her house the tops of trees that were all aquiver with the new spring life. The delicious breath of rain was in the air. In the street below a peddler was crying his wares. The notes of a distant song which some one was singing reached her faintly, and countless sparrows were twittering in the eaves.

There were patches of blue sky showing here and there through the clouds that had met and piled one above the other in the west facing her window.

She sat with her head thrown back upon the cushion of the chair, quite motionless, except when a sob came up into her throat and shook her, as a child who has cried itself to sleep continues to sob in its dreams.

She was young, with a fair, calm face, whose lines bespoke repression and even a certain strength. But now there was a dull stare in her eyes, whose gaze was fixed away off yonder on one of those patches of blue sky. It was not a glance of reflection, but rather indicated a suspension of intelligent thought.

There was something coming to her and she was waiting for it, fearfully. What was it? She did not know; it was too subtle and elusive to name. But she felt it, creeping out of the sky, reaching toward her through the sounds, the scents, the color that filled the air.

Now her bosom rose and fell tumultuously. She was beginning to recognize this thing that was approaching to possess her, and she was striving to beat it back with her will—as powerless as her two white slender hands would have been.

When she abandoned herself a little whispered word escaped her slightly parted lips. She said it over and over under her breath: "free, free, free!" The vacant stare and the look of terror that had followed it went from her eyes. They stayed keen and bright. Her pulses beat fast, and the coursing blood warmed and relaxed every inch of her body.

She did not stop to ask if it were or were not a monstrous joy that held her. A clear and exalted perception enabled her to dismiss the suggestion as trivial.

She knew that she would weep again when she saw the kind, tender hands folded in death; the face that had never looked save with love upon her, fixed and gray and dead. But she saw beyond that bitter moment a long procession of years to come that would belong to her absolutely. And she opened and spread her arms out to them in welcome.

There would be no one to live for her during those coming years; she would live for herself. There would be no powerful will bending hers in that blind persistence with which men and women believe they have a right to impose a private will upon a fellow-creature. A kind intention or a cruel intention made the act seem no less a crime as she looked upon it in that brief moment of illumination.

And yet she had loved him—sometimes. Often she had not. What did it matter! What could love, the unsolved mystery, count for in face of this possession of self-assertion which she suddenly recognized as the strongest impulse of her being! 15

"Free! Body and soul free!" she kept whispering.

Josephine was kneeling before the closed door with her lips to the keyhole, imploring for admission. "Louise, open the door! I beg; open the door—you will make yourself ill. What are you doing, Louise? For heaven's sake open the door."

"Go away. I am not making myself ill." No; she was drinking in a very elixir of life through that open window.

Her fancy was running riot along those days ahead of her. Spring days, and summer days, and all sorts of days that would be her own. She breathed a quick prayer that life might be long. It was only yesterday she had thought with a shudder that life might be long.

She arose at length and opened the door to her sister's importunities. There was a feverish triumph in her eyes, and she carried herself unwittingly like a goddess of Victory. She clasped her sister's waist, and together they descended the stairs. Richards stood waiting for them at the bottom. 20

Some one was opening the front door with a latchkey. It was Brently Mallard who entered, a little travel-stained, composedly carrying his gripsack and umbrella. He had been far from the scene of accident, and did not even know there had been one. He stood amazed at Josephine's piercing cry; at Richards' quick motion to screen him from the view of his wife.

But Richards was too late.

When the doctors came they said she had died of heart disease—of joy that kills.

Did you find Mrs. Mallard a sympathetic character? Some readers think that she is callous, selfish, and unnatural—even "monstrous"—because she ecstatically revels in her newly discovered sense of freedom so soon after learning of her husband's presumed death. Others read her as a victim of her inability to control her own life in a repressive, male-dominated society. Is it possible to hold both views simultaneously, or are they mutually exclusive? Are your views in any way influenced by your being male or female? Does your age affect your perception? What about your social and economic background? Does your nationality, race, or religion in any way shape your attitudes? Do you have particular views about the institution of marriage that inform your assessment of Mrs. Mallard's character? Have other reading experiences—perhaps a familiarity with some of Chopin's other stories—predisposed you one way or another to Mrs. Mallard?

Understanding potential influences might be useful in determining whether a particular response to Mrs. Mallard is based primarily on the story's details and their arrangement or on an overt or subtle bias that is brought to the story. If you unconsciously project your beliefs and assumptions onto a literary work, you run the risk of distorting it to accommodate your prejudice. Your feelings can be a reliable guide to interpretation, but you should be aware of what those feelings are based on.

Often specific questions about literary works cannot be answered definitively. For example, Chopin does not explain why Mrs. Mallard suffers a heart attack at the end of this story. Is the shock of seeing her "dead" husband simply too much for this woman "afflicted with a heart trouble"? Does she die of what the doctors call a "joy that kills" because she was so glad to see her husband? Is she so profoundly guilty about feeling "free" at her husband's expense that she has a heart attack? Is her death a kind of willed suicide in reaction to her loss of freedom? Your answers to these questions will depend on which details you emphasize in your interpretation of the story and the kinds of perspectives and values you bring to it. If, for example, you read the story from a feminist perspective, you would be likely to pay close attention to Chopin's comments about marriage in paragraph 14. Or if you read the story as an oblique attack on the insensitivity of physicians of the period, you might want to find out if Chopin wrote elsewhere about doctors (she did) and compare her comments with historic sources. (A number of critical strategies for reading, including feminist and historical approaches, appear in Chapter 6.)

Reading responsively makes you an active participant in the process of creating meaning in a literary work. The experience that you and the author create will most likely not be identical to another reader's encounter with the same work, but then that's true of nearly any experience you'll have, and it is part of the pleasure of reading. Indeed, talking and writing about literature is a way of sharing responses so that they can be enriched and deepened.

QUESTIONS FOR WRITING ABOUT FICTION

The following questions can help you consider important elements of fiction that reveal your responses to a story's effects and meanings. The questions are general, so they will not always be relevant to a particular story. Many of them, however, should prove useful for thinking, talking, and writing about a work of fiction. If you are uncertain about the meaning of a term used in a question, consult the Glossary of Literary Terms beginning on page 175 of this book. You should also find useful the discussion of various critical approaches to literature in Chapter 6, "Critical Strategies for Reading and Writing."

Plot

1. Does the plot conform to a formula? Is it like those of any other stories you have read? Did you find it predictable?
2. What is the source and nature of the conflict for the protagonist? Was your major interest in the story based on what happens next or on some other concern? What does the title reveal now that you've finished the story?
3. Is the story told chronologically? If not, in what order is it told, and what is the effect of that order on your response to the action?
4. What does the exposition reveal? Are flashbacks used? Did you see any foreshadowings? Where is the climax?
5. Is the conflict resolved at the end? Would you characterize the ending as happy, unhappy, or somewhere in between?
6. Is the plot unified? Is each incident somehow related to some other element in the story?

Character

7. Do you identify with the protagonist? Who (or what) is the antagonist?
8. Does your response to any characters change as you read? What do you think caused the change? Do any characters change and develop in the course of the story? How?
9. Are round, flat, or stock characters used? Is their behavior motivated and plausible?
10. How does the author reveal characters? Are they directly described or indirectly presented? Are the characters' names used to convey something about them?
11. What is the purpose of the minor characters? Are they individualized, or do they primarily represent ideas or attitudes?

Setting

12. Is the setting important in shaping your response? If it were changed, would your response to the story's action and meaning be significantly different?
13. Is the setting used symbolically? Are the time, place, and atmosphere related to the theme?
14. Is the setting used as an antagonist?

Point of View

15. Who tells the story? Is it a first-person or third-person narrator? Is it a major or minor character or one who does not participate in the action at all? How much does the narrator know? Does the point of view change at all in the course of the story?
16. Is the narrator reliable and objective? Does the narrator appear too innocent, emotional, or self-deluded to be trusted?

17. Does the author directly comment on the action?
18. If told from a different point of view, how would your response to the story change? Would anything be lost?

Symbolism

19. Did you notice any symbols in the story? Are they actions, characters, settings, objects, or words?
20. How do the symbols contribute to your understanding of the story?

Theme

21. Did you find a theme? If so, what is it?
22. Is the theme stated directly, or is it developed implicitly through the plot, characters, or some other element?
23. Is the theme a confirmation of your values, or does it challenge them?

Style, Tone, and Irony

24. Do you think the style is consistent and appropriate throughout the story? Do all the characters use the same kind of language, or did you hear different voices?
25. Would you describe the level of diction as formal or informal? Are the sentences short and simple, long and complex, or some combination?
26. How does the author's use of language contribute to the tone of the story? Did it seem, for example, intense, relaxed, sentimental, nostalgic, humorous, angry, sad, or remote?
27. Do you think the story is worth reading more than once? Does the author's use of language bear close scrutiny so that you feel and experience more with each reading?

Critical Strategies

28. Is there a particular critical approach that seems especially appropriate for this story? (See the discussion of "Critical Strategies for Reading and Writing" beginning on p. 94.)
29. How might biographical information about the author help to determine the central concerns of the story?
30. How might historical information about the story provide a useful context for interpretation?
31. What kinds of evidence from the story are you focusing on to support your interpretation? Does your interpretation leave out any important elements that might undercut or qualify your interpretation?
32. To what extent do your own experiences, values, beliefs, and assumptions inform your interpretation?
33. Given that there are a variety of ways to interpret the story, which one seems the most useful to you?

Charles Dickens is well known for creating characters who have stepped off the pages of his fictions into the imaginations and memories of his readers. His characters are successful not because readers might have encountered such people in their own lives, but because his characterizations are vivid and convincing. He manages to make strange and eccentric people appear familiar. The following excerpt from *Hard Times* is the novel's entire first chapter. In it Dickens introduces and characterizes a school principal addressing a classroom full of children. The sample paper on page 53 provides a character analysis based on this chapter and on the questions listed under character in the Questions for Writing about Fiction offered above. The assignment called for a character analysis of no more than 300 words.

CHARLES DICKENS (1812–1870)
From *Hard Times*   1854

"Now, what I want is, Facts. Teach these boys and girls nothing but Facts. Facts alone are wanted in life. Plant nothing else, and root out everything else. You can only form the minds of reasoning animals upon Facts: nothing else will ever be of any service to them. This is the principle on which I bring up my own children, and this is the principle on which I bring up these children. Stick to Facts, sir!"

The scene was a plain, bare, monotonous vault of a schoolroom, and the speaker's square forefinger emphasized his observations by underscoring every sentence with a line on the schoolmaster's sleeve. The emphasis was helped by the speaker's square wall of a forehead, which had his eyebrows for its base, while his eyes found commodious cellarage in two dark caves, overshadowed by the wall. The emphasis was helped by the speaker's mouth, which was wide, thin, and hard set. The emphasis was helped by the speaker's voice, which was inflexible, dry, and dictatorial. The emphasis was helped by the speaker's hair, which bristled on the skirts of his bald head, a plantation of firs to keep the wind from its shining surface, all covered with knobs, like the crust of a plum pie, as if the head had scarcely warehouse-room for the hard facts stored inside. The speaker's obstinate carriage, square coat, square legs, square shoulders—nay, his very neckcloth, trained to take him by the throat with an unaccommodating grasp, like a stubborn fact, as it was—all helped the emphasis.

"In this life, we want nothing but Facts, sir; nothing but Facts!"

The speaker, and the schoolmaster, and the third grown person present, all backed a little, and swept with their eyes the inclined plane of little vessels then and there arranged in order, ready to have imperial gallons of facts poured into them until they were full to the brim.

A SAMPLE CHARACTER ANALYSIS: CHARACTER REVEALED IN FOUR PARAGRAPHS

Kim Schleicher

English 109

Professor White

September 29, 19--

Character Revealed in Four Paragraphs

Charles Dickens's one-page description of a school principal in <u>Hard Times</u> is an extremely brief chapter, but it
seems complete as a characterization nonetheless. We are
given enough information, or "Facts," as the principal would
put it, to recognize in him a destructively practical personality that is antagonistic to any human impulse that is in-
stinctive, creative, and spontaneous in the "little vessels"
who are "arranged in order" (not just seated) before him.

The principal is a flat one-dimensional character rather
than a psychologically complex round character, and he is
clearly a stock figure who is immediately recognizable, but he
is made fascinating owing to the vivid description of him that
Dickens provides. The principal's utilitarian educational
values are announced in the first paragraph, where he reveals
that he regards his students as nothing more than "reasoning
animals" who must be shaped, controlled, and filled with
"Facts." If this crabbed approach to education isn't enough
to alert the reader to Dickens's negative assessment of the
principal, then the physical descriptions in the second paragraph of both the schoolroom and its principal teacher make
clear his cold, hard, obstinate character.

The schoolroom--like the principal's mind, it seems--is a

"plain, bare, monotonous vault" that, ironically, contains
nothing of any value. The adjectives used to describe the
principal reveal his rigid personality. Everything about him
emphasizes this square stiffness, from his forefinger and
forehead to his "square coat, square legs, [and] square shoulders." His mouth is "thin, and hard set"; his voice is "inflexible, dry, and dictatorial"; and his head is wildly bald.
All he can say and think is that "In this life, we want nothing but Facts, sir; nothing but Facts!"

The principal is every student's nightmare. He teaches
by rote and he insists that his students learn by rote. There
is no room for anything but stark, rigid facts that must be
memorized and regurgitated on command. The principal demands
that he and his ideas be taken seriously, but Dickens's description of his principal's character makes that impossible.
Interestingly enough, we do not learn this character's name
until the beginning of the next chapter, when Dickens informs
us that this starchy educator is called Mr. Gradgrind, the
perfect name for a principal who embodies such deadening principles.

4. Reading and Writing about Poetry

RESPONDING TO POETRY

Perhaps the best way to begin reading poetry responsively is not to allow yourself to be intimidated by it. Come to it, initially at least, the way you might listen to a song on the radio. You probably listen to a song several times before you hear it all, before you have a sense of how it works, where it's going, and how it gets there. You don't worry about analyzing a song when you listen to it, even though after repeated experiences with it you know and anticipate a favorite part and know, on some level, why it works for you. Give yourself a chance to respond to poetry. The hardest work has already been done by the poet, so all you need to do at the start is listen for the pleasure produced by the poet's arrangement of words.

Try reading the following poem aloud. Read it aloud before you read it silently. You may stumble once or twice, but you'll make sense of it if you pay attention to its punctuation and don't stop at the end of every line where there is no punctuation. The title gives you an initial sense of what the poem is about.

MARGE PIERCY (b. 1936)
The Secretary Chant 1973

My hips are a desk.
From my ears hang
chains of paper clips.
Rubber bands form my hair.
My breasts are wells of mimeograph ink.   5
My feet bear casters.
Buzz. Click.
My head is a badly organized file.

My head is a switchboard
where crossed lines crackle.   10
Press my fingers
and in my eyes appear
credit and debit.
Zing. Tinkle.
My navel is a reject button.   15
From my mouth issue canceled reams.
Swollen, heavy, rectangular
I am about to be delivered
of a baby
Xerox machine.   20
File me under W
because I wonce
was
a woman.

What is your response to this secretary's chant? The point is simple
enough—she feels dehumanized by her office functions—but the pleasures
are manifold. Piercy makes the speaker's voice sound mechanical by using
short bursts of sound and by having her make repetitive, flat, matter-of-fact
statements ("My breasts . . . My feet . . . My head . . . My navel"). "The
Secretary Chant" makes a serious statement about how such women are
reduced to functionaries. The point is made, however, with humor since we
are asked to visualize the misappropriation of the secretary's body—her
identity—as it is transformed into little more than a piece of office equipment,
which seems to be breaking down in the final lines, when we learn that she
"wonce / was / a woman." Is there the slightest hint of something subversive
in this misspelling of "wonce"? Maybe so, but the humor is clear enough,
particularly if you try to make a drawing of what this dehumanized secretary
has become.

The next poem creates a different kind of mood. Think about the title,
"Those Winter Sundays," before you begin reading the poem. What associations do you have with winter Sundays? What emotions does the phrase
evoke in you?

ROBERT HAYDEN (1913–1980)
Those Winter Sundays   1962

Sundays too my father got up early
and put his clothes on in the blueblack cold,
then with cracked hands that ached
from labor in the weekday weather made
banked fires blaze. No one ever thanked him.   5
I'd wake and hear the cold splintering, breaking,

When the rooms were warm, he'd call,
and slowly I would rise and dress,
fearing the chronic angers of that house,

Speaking indifferently to him,   10
who had driven out the cold
and polished my good shoes as well.
What did I know, what did I know
of love's austere and lonely offices?

Did the poem match the feelings you have about winter Sundays? Either
way your response can be useful in reading the poem. For most of us Sundays
are days at home; they might be cozy and pleasant experiences or they might
be dull and depressing. Whatever they are, Sundays are more evocative than,
say, Tuesdays. Hayden uses that response to call forth a sense of missed
opportunity in the poem. The person who reflects on those winter Sundays
didn't know until much later how much he had to thank his father for "love's
austere and lonely offices." This is a poem about a cold past and a present
reverence for his father—elements brought together by the phrase "Winter
Sundays." *His* father? You may have noticed that the poem doesn't use a
masculine pronoun; hence the voice could be a woman's. Does the sex of
the voice make any difference to your reading? Would it make any difference
about which details are included or what language is used?

What is most important about your initial readings of a poem is that
you ask questions. If you read responsively, you'll find yourself asking all
kinds of questions about the words, descriptions, sounds, and structures of
a poem. The specifics of those questions will be generated by the particular
poem. We don't, for example, ask how humor is achieved in "Those Winter
Sundays" because there is none, but it is worth asking what kind of tone is
established by the description of "the chronic angers of that house." The
Questions for Writing about Poetry (p. 64) will help you to formulate questions about a variety of specific elements in poetry, such as speaker, image,
metaphor, symbol, rhyme, and rhythm. (These and many other elements are
defined in the Glossary of Literary Terms [p. 175].) For the moment, however,
read the following poem several times and note your response at different
points in the poem. Then write down a half dozen questions or so about
what produces your response to the poem.

JOHN UPDIKE (b. 1932)
Dog's Death   1969

She must have been kicked unseen or brushed by a car.
Too young to know much, she was beginning to learn
To use the newspapers spread on the kitchen floor
And to win, wetting there, the words, "Good dog! Good dog!"

We thought her shy malaise was a shot reaction.   5
The autopsy disclosed a rupture in her liver.
As we teased her with play, blood was filling her skin
And her heart was learning to lie down forever.

Monday morning, as the children were noisily fed
And sent to school, she crawled beneath the youngest's bed.   10
We found her twisted and limp but still alive.
In the car to the vet's, on my lap, she tried

To bite my hand and died. I stroked her warm fur
And my wife called in a voice imperious with tears.
Though surrounded by love that would have upheld her,   15
Nevertheless she sank and, stiffening, disappeared.

Back home, we found that in the night her frame,
Drawing near to dissolution, had endured the shame
Of diarrhoea and had dragged across the floor
To a newspaper carelessly left there. *Good dog.*   20

Here's a simple question to get started with your own questions: what would its effect have been if Updike had titled the poem "Good Dog" instead of "Dog's Death"?

UNDERSTANDING THE PLEASURE OF WORDS

The impulse to create and appreciate poetry is as basic to human experience as language itself. Although no one can point to the precise origins of poetry, it is one of the most ancient of the arts, because it has existed ever since human beings discovered pleasure in language. The tribal ceremonies of peoples without written language suggest evidence that the earliest primitive cultures incorporated rhythmic patterns of words into their rituals. These chants, very likely accompanied by the music of a simple beat and the dance of a measured step, expressed what people regarded as significant and memorable in their lives. They echoed the concerns of the chanters and the listeners by chronicling acts of bravery, fearsome foes, natural disasters, mysterious events, births, deaths, and whatever else brought people pain or pleasure, bewilderment or revelation. Later cultures, such as the ancient Greeks, made poetry an integral part of religion.

Thus, from its very beginnings, poetry has been associated with what has mattered most to people. These concerns—whether natural or supernatural—can, of course, be expressed without vivid images, rhythmic patterns, and pleasing sounds, but human beings have always sensed a magic in words that goes beyond rational, logical understanding. Poetry is not simply a method of communication; it is a unique kind of experience in itself.

What is special about poetry? What makes it valuable? Why should we read it? How is reading it different from reading prose? To begin with, poetry pervades our world in a variety of forms, ranging from advertising jingles to song lyrics. These may seem to be a long way from the chants heard around a primitive camp fire, but they serve some of the same purposes. Like poems printed in a magazine or book, primitive chants, catchy jingles, and popular songs attempt to stir the imagination through the carefully measured use of words.

Although reading poetry usually makes more demands than does the kind of reading used to skim a magazine or newspaper, the appreciation of poetry comes naturally enough to anyone who enjoys playing with words. Play is an important element of poetry. Consider, for example, how the following words appeal to the children who gleefully chant them in playgrounds.

> I scream, you scream
> We all scream
> For ice cream.

These lines are an exuberant evocation of the joy of ice cream. Indeed, chanting the words turns out to be as pleasurable as eating ice cream. In poetry, the expression of the idea is as important as the idea expressed.

But is "I scream . . ." poetry? Some poets and literary critics would say that it certainly is one kind of poem, because the children who chant it experience some of the pleasures of poetry in its measured beat and repeated sounds. However, other poets and critics would define poetry more narrowly and insist, for a variety of reasons, that this isn't true poetry but merely doggerel, a term used for lines whose subject matter is trite and whose rhythm and sounds are monotonously heavy-handed.

Although probably no one would argue that "I scream . . ." is a great poem, it does contain some poetic elements that appeal, at the very least, to children. Does that make it poetry? The answer depends on one's definition, but poetry has a way of breaking loose from definitions. Because there are nearly as many definitions of poetry as there are poets, Edwin Arlington Robinson's succinct observations are useful: "Poetry has two outstanding characteristics. One is that it is undefinable. The other is that it is eventually unmistakable."

This comment places more emphasis on how a poem affects a reader than on how a poem is defined. By characterizing poetry as "undefinable," Robinson acknowledges that it can include many different purposes, subjects, emotions, styles, and forms. What effect does the following poem have on you?

WILLIAM HATHAWAY (b. 1944)
Oh, Oh   1982

My girl and I amble a country lane,
moo cows chomping daisies, our own

sweet saliva green with grass stems.
"Look, look," she says at the crossing,
"the choo-choo's light is on." And sure   5
enough, right smack dab in the middle
of maple dappled summer sunlight
is the lit headlight—so funny.
An arm waves to us from the black window.
We wave gaily to the arm. "When I hear   10
trains at night I dream of being president,"
I say dreamily. "And me first lady," she
says loyally. So when the last boxcars,
named after wonderful, faraway places,
and the caboose chuckle by we look   15
eagerly to the road ahead. And there,
poised and growling, are fifty Hell's Angels.

    Hathaway's poem serves as a convenient reminder that poetry can be full of surprises. Even on a first reading there is no mistaking the emotional reversal created by the last few words of this poem. With the exception of the final line, the poem's language conjures up an idyllic picture of a young couple taking a pleasant walk down a country lane. Contented as "moo cows," they taste the sweetness of the grass, hear peaceful country sounds, and are dazzled by "dappled summer sunlight." Their future together seems to be all optimism as they anticipate "wonderful, faraway places" and the "road ahead." Full of confidence, this couple, like the reader, is unprepared for the shock to come. When we see those "fifty Hell's Angels," we are confronted with something like a bucket of cold water in the face.

    But even though our expectations are abruptly and powerfully reversed, we are finally invited to view the entire episode from a safe distance—the distance provided by the delightful humor in this poem. After all, how seriously can we take a poem that is titled "Oh, Oh"? The poet has his way with us, but we are brought in on the joke too. The terror takes on comic proportions as the innocent couple is confronted by no fewer than *fifty* Hell's Angels. This is the kind of raucous overkill that informs a short animated film produced some years ago titled *Bambi Meets Godzilla:* you might not have seen it, but you know how it ends. The poem's good humor comes through when we realize how pathetically inadequate the response of "Oh, Oh" is to the circumstances.

    As you can see, reading a description of what happens in a poem is not the same as experiencing a poem. The exuberance of "I scream . . . " and the surprise of Hathaway's "Oh, Oh" are in the hearing or reading rather than in the retelling. A paraphrase is a prose restatement of the central ideas of a poem in your own language. Consider the difference between the following poem and the paraphrase that follows it. What is missing from the paraphrase?

ROBERT FRANCIS (1901–1987)
Catch   1950

Two boys uncoached are tossing a poem together,
Overhand, underhand, backhand, sleight of hand, every hand,
Teasing with attitudes, latitudes, interludes, altitudes,
High, make him fly off the ground for it, low, make him stoop,
Make him scoop it up, make him as-almost-as-possible miss it,   5
Fast, let him sting from it, now, now fool him slowly,
Anything, everything tricky, risky, nonchalant,
Anything under the sun to outwit the prosy,
Over the tree and the long sweet cadence down,
Over his head, make him scramble to pick up the meaning,   10
And now, like a posy, a pretty one plump in his hands.

Paraphrase: A poet's relationship to a reader is similar to a game of catch. The poem, like a ball, should be pitched in a variety of ways to challenge and create interest. Boredom and predictability must be avoided if the game is to be engaging and satisfying.

A paraphrase can help us achieve a clearer understanding of a poem, but, unlike a poem, it misses all the sport and fun. It is the poem that "outwit[s] the prosy," because the poem serves as an example of what it suggests poetry should be. Moreover, the two players—the poet and the reader—are "uncoached." They know how the game is played, but their expectations do not preclude spontaneity and creativity or their ability to surprise and be surprised. The solid pleasure of the workout—of reading poetry—is the satisfaction derived from exercising your imagination and intellect.

That pleasure is worth emphasizing. Poetry uses language to move and delight even when it includes a cast of fifty Hell's Angels. The pleasure is in having the poem work its spell on us. For that to happen, it is best to relax and enjoy poetry rather than worrying about definitions of it. Pay attention to what the poet throws you. We read poems for emotional and intellectual discovery—to feel and experience something about the world and ourselves. The ideas in poetry—what can be paraphrased in prose—are important, but the real value of a poem consists in the words that work their magic by allowing us to feel, see, and be more than we were before. Perhaps the best way to approach a poem is similar to what Francis's "Catch" implies: expect to be surprised; stay on your toes; and concentrate on the delivery. The strategies for reading poetry are somewhat different from those for reading prose. Try these suggestions for approaching poetry.

SUGGESTIONS FOR APPROACHING POETRY

1. Assume that it will be necessary to read a poem more than once. Give yourself a chance to become familiar with what the poem has

to offer. Like a piece of music, a poem becomes more pleasurable with each encounter.

2. Do pay attention to the title; it will often provide a helpful context for the poem and serve as an introduction to it. Updike's "Dog's Death" is precisely what its title describes.

3. As you read the poem for the first time, avoid becoming entangled in words or lines that you don't understand. Instead, give yourself a chance to take in the entire poem before attempting to resolve problems encountered along the way.

4. On a second reading, identify any words or passages that you don't understand. Look up words you don't know; these might include names, places, historical and mythical references, or anything else that is unfamiliar to you.

5. Read the poem aloud (or perhaps have a friend read it to you). You'll probably discover that some puzzling passages suddenly fall into place when you hear them. You'll find that nothing helps, though, if the poem is read in an artificial, exaggerated manner. Read in as natural a voice as possible, with slight pauses at line breaks. Silent reading is preferable to imposing a te-tumpty-te-tum reading on a good poem.

6. Read the punctuation. Poems use punctuation marks—in addition to the space on the page—as signals for readers. Be especially careful not to assume that the end of a line marks the end of a sentence, unless it is concluded by punctuation. Consider, for example, the opening lines of Hathaway's "Oh, Oh."

My girl and I amble a country lane,
moo cows chomping daisies, our own
sweet saliva green with grass stems.

Line 2 makes little or no sense if a reader stops after "own." Keeping track of the subjects and verbs will help you find your way among the sentences.

7. Annotate the text by writing notes in the margin, highlighting, underlining, and drawing boxes and circles around important words and phrases. A reading journal can also help you to preserve initial ideas and responses that might be useful for generating a paper topic or help you to respond to an assigned topic (see p. 4 for an example of annotations on Marvell's "To His Coy Mistress").

8. Paraphrase the poem to determine whether you understand what happens in it. As you work through each line of the poem, a paraphrase will help you to see which words or passages need further attention.

9. Try to get a sense of who is speaking and what the setting or situation is. Don't assume that the speaker is the author; often it is a created character.

10. Assume that each element in the poem has a purpose. Try to explain how the elements of the poem work together.

11. Be generous. Be willing to entertain perspectives, values, experiences, and subjects that you might not agree with or approve. Even if you loathe baseball, you should be able to comprehend its imaginative use in Francis's "Catch."

12. Try developing a coherent approach to the poem that helps you to shape a discussion of the text. See Chapter 6, "Critical Strategies for Reading and Writing" (p. 94), to consider formalist, biographical, historical, psychological, feminist, and other possible critical approaches.

13. Don't expect to produce a definitive reading. Many poems do not resolve all the ideas, issues, or tensions in them, and so it is not always possible to drive their meaning into an absolute corner. Your reading will explore rather than define the poem. Poems are not trophies to be stuffed and mounted. They're usually more elusive. And don't be afraid that a close reading will damage the poem. Poems aren't hurt when we analyze them; instead, they come alive as we experience them and put into words what we discover through them.

A list of more specific questions for writing about poetry employing the literary terms defined in the Glossary (p. 175) begins on page 64. That list, like the suggestions just made, raises issues and questions that can help you to read just about any poem closely and write about it with confidence. These strategies should be a useful means for getting inside poems to understand how they work. Furthermore, because reading poetry inevitably increases sensitivity to language, you're likely to find yourself a better reader of words in any form—whether in a novel, a newspaper editorial, an advertisement, a political speech, or a conversation—after having studied poetry. In short, many of the reading skills that make poetry accessible also open up the world you inhabit.

You'll probably find some poems amusing or sad, some fierce or tender, and some fascinating or dull. You may find, too, some poems that will get inside you. Their kinds of insights—the poet's and yours—are what Emily Dickinson had in mind when she defined poetry this way: "If I read a book and it makes my whole body so cold no fire can ever warm me, I know that it is poetry. If I feel physically as if the top of my head were taken off, I know that it is poetry." Dickinson's response may be more intense than most—poetry was, after all, at the center of her life—but you too might find yourself moved by poems in unexpected ways. In any case, as Edwin Arlington Robinson knew, poetry is, to an alert and sensitive reader, "eventually unmistakable."

QUESTIONS FOR WRITING ABOUT POETRY

The following questions can help you respond to important elements that reveal a poem's effects and meanings. The questions are general, so not all of them will necessarily be relevant to a particular poem. Many, however, should prove useful for thinking, talking, and writing about poetry. If you are uncertain about the meaning of a term used in a question, consult the Glossary of Literary Terms beginning on page 175.

Before addressing these questions, read the poem you are studying in its entirety. Don't worry about interpretation on a first reading; allow yourself the pleasure of enjoying whatever makes itself apparent to you. Then on subsequent readings, use the questions to understand and appreciate how the poem works.

1. Who is the speaker? Is it possible to determine the speaker's age, sex, sensibilities, level of awareness, and values?
2. Is the speaker addressing anyone in particular?
3. How do you respond to the speaker? favorably? negatively? What is the situation? Are there any special circumstances that inform what the speaker says?
4. Is there a specific setting of time and place?
5. Does reading the poem aloud help you to understand it?
6. Does a paraphrase reveal the basic purpose of the poem?
7. What does the title emphasize?
8. Is the theme presented directly or indirectly?
9. Do any allusions enrich the poem's meaning?
10. How does the diction reveal meaning? Are any words repeated? Do any carry evocative connotative meanings? Are there any puns or other forms of verbal wit?
11. Are figures of speech used? How does the figurative language contribute to the poem's vividness and meaning?
12. Do any objects, persons, places, events, or actions have allegorical or symbolic meanings? What other details in the poem support your interpretation?
13. Is irony used? Are there any examples of situational irony, verbal irony, or dramatic irony? Is understatement or paradox used?
14. What is the tone of the poem? Is the tone consistent?
15. Does the poem use onomatopoeia, assonance, consonance, or alliteration? How do these sounds affect you?
16. What sounds are repeated? If there are rhymes, what is their effect? Do they seem forced or natural? Is there a rhyme scheme? Do the rhymes contribute to the poem's meaning?
17. Do the lines have a regular meter? What is the predominant meter? Are there significant variations? Does the rhythm seem appropriate for the tone of the poem?

18. Does the poem's form—its overall structure—follow an established pattern? Do you think the form is a suitable vehicle for the poem's meaning and effects?

19. Is the language of the poem intense and concentrated? Do you think it warrants more than one or two close readings?

20. Did you enjoy the poem? What, specifically, pleased or displeased you about what was expressed and how it was expressed?

21. Is there a particular critical approach that seems especially appropriate for this poem? (See the discussion of "Critical Strategies for Reading and Writing" beginning on p. 94.)

22. How might biographical information about the author help to determine the central concerns of the poem?

23. How might historical information about the poem provide a useful context for interpretation?

24. To what extent do your own experiences, values, beliefs, and assumptions inform your interpretation?

25. What kinds of evidence from the poem are you focusing on to support your interpretation? Does your interpretation leave out any important elements that might undercut or qualify your interpretation?

26. Given that there are a variety of ways to interpret the poem, which one seems the most useful to you?

A SAMPLE ANALYSIS: "CATCH": ON "TOSSING A POEM TOGETHER"

The following sample paper on Robert Francis's "Catch" (p. 61) was written in response to a 750-word assignment that asked the student to discuss the use of metaphor in the poem. Notice that Chris Leggett's paper is clearly focused and well organized. His discussion of the use of metaphor in the poem keeps on track from beginning to end without any detours concerning unrelated topics. His own title draws upon the central metaphor of the poem, and he organizes the paper around four key words used in the poem: "attitudes, latitudes, interludes [and] altitudes." These four words constitute the heart of the paper's four paragraphs, and they are effectively framed by introductory and concluding paragraphs. Moreover, the paper's transitions between paragraphs clearly indicate that its author was not merely tossing a paper together.

Chris Leggett

Professor Lyles

English 203-1

November 9, 19--

"Catch:" On "Tossing a Poem Together"

The word "catch" is an attention getter. It usually means that something is about to be hurled at someone, and that he or she is expected to catch it. "Catch" can also signal a challenge to another player if the toss is purposefully difficult. Robert Francis, in his poem "Catch," uses the extended metaphor of two boys playing catch to explore the considerations a poet makes when "tossing a poem together." Line 3 of "Catch" enumerates these considerations metaphorically as "attitudes, latitudes, interludes, [and] altitudes." While regular prose is typically straightforward and easily understood, poetry usually takes great effort to understand and appreciate. To exemplify this, Francis presents the reader not with a normal game of catch with the ball flying back and forth in a repetitive and predictable fashion, but a physically challenging game in which one must concentrate, scramble, and exert oneself to catch the ball, as one must stretch the intellect to truly grasp a poem.

The first consideration mentioned by Francis is attitude. Attitude, when applied to the game of catch, indicates the ball's pitch in flight, upward, downward, or straight. It could also describe the players' attitudes toward each other, or the game in general. Below this literal level lies attitude's meaning in relation to poetry. Attitude in this case represents a poem's tone. A poet may "tease with attitude" by

experimenting with different tones to achieve the desired mood
to be conveyed. The underlying tone of "Catch" is a playful
one, set and reinforced by the use of a game. This playful-
ness is further reinforced by words and phrases such as "teasing," "outwit," and "fool him."

Considered also in the metaphorical game of catch is latitude, which, when applied to the game, suggests the range the
object may be thrown, how high, how low, or how far. Poetic
latitude, along similar lines, considers a poem's breadth, or
the scope of topic. Taken one level further, latitude suggests freedom from normal restraints or limitations, indicating the ability to go outside the norm to find originality of
expression. The entire game of catch described in Francis's
poem reaches outside the normal expectations of something
being merely tossed back and forth in a predictable manner.
The ball is thrown in almost every conceivable fashion, "overhand, underhand . . . every hand." Other words describing
the throws, such as "tricky," "risky," "fast," "slowly," and
"Anything under the sun," express endless latitude for
avoiding predictability in Francis's game of catch and metaphorically in writing poetry.

During a game of catch the ball could be thrown at different intervals, establishing the game's rhythm or disrupting
it altogether. Other intervening features such as the field
being played on or the weather could also affect the game.
These features of the game are considered in the game with the
use of the word "interludes." "Interlude" in the poetic sense
represents the poem's form, which can similarly establish or
diminish rhythm or enhance meaning. Lines 6 and 9 respec-

tively show a broken and a flowing rhythm. Line 6 begins rapidly as a hard toss is described that stings the catcher's
hand. The rhythm of the line is immediately slowed, however,
by the word "now" followed by a comma, followed by the rest of
the line. In contrast, line 9 flows smoothly as the reader
visualizes the ball flying over the tree and sailing downward.
The words chosen for this line function perfectly. The phrase
"the long sweet cadence down" establishes a sweet cadence that
reads smoothly and rolls off the tongue easily. Choice of
diction not only affects the poem's rhythmic flow but also establishes through connotative language the various levels at
which the poem can be understood, represented in "Catch" as
altitude.

While "altitude" when referring to the game of catch
means how high an object is thrown, in poetry it could refer
to the level of diction, lofty or down to earth, formal or informal. It suggests also the levels at which a poem can be
comprehended, the literal as well as the interpretive. In
Francis's game of catch the ball is thrown high to make the
player reach, or low to make him stoop, or over his head to
make him scramble, implying that the player should have to
exert himself to catch it. So too, then, should the reader of
poetry put forth great effort to understand the full meaning
of a poem. Francis exemplifies this consideration in writing
poetry not only by giving "Catch" an enjoyable literal meaning
concerning the game of catch, but also a rich metaphorical
meaning--reflecting the process of writing poetry. Francis
uses several phrases and words with multiple meanings. The
phrase "tossing a poem together" can be understood as tossing

something back and forth, or the process of constructing a
poem. While "prosy" suggests prose itself, it also means the
mundane or the ordinary. In the poem's final line the word
"posy" of course represents a flower, while it is also a vari-
ant of the word "poesy," meaning poetry, or the practice of
composing poetry.

Francis effectively describes several considerations to
be taken in writing poetry in order to "outwit the prosy."
His use of the extended metaphor in "Catch" shows that a poem
must be unique, able to be comprehended on multiple levels,
and a challenge to the reader. The various rhythms in the
lines of "Catch" each exemplify the ideas expressed within
them. While achieving an enjoyable poem on the literal level,
Francis has also achieved a rich metaphorical meaning. The
poem offers a good workout both physically and intellectually.

5. Reading and Writing about Drama

RESPONDING TO DRAMA

The publication of a short story, novel, or poem represents for most writers the final step in a long creative process that might have begun with an idea, issue, emotion, or question that demanded expression. Playwrights—writers who make plays—may begin a work in the same way as other writers, but rarely are they satisfied with only its publication, because most dramatic literature—what we call plays—is written to be performed by actors on a stage before an audience. Playwrights typically create a play keeping in mind not only readers but also actors, producers, directors, costumers, designers, technicians, and a theater full of other support staff who have a hand in presenting the play to a live audience.

Drama is literature equipped with arms, legs, tears, laughs, whispers, shouts, and gestures that are alive and immediate. Indeed, the word drama derives from the Greek word *dran,* meaning "to do" or "to perform." The text of many plays—the script—may come to life fully only when the written words are transformed into a performance. Although there are plays that do not invite production, they are relatively few. Such plays, written to be read rather than performed, are called closet dramas. In this kind of work (primarily associated with nineteenth-century English literature), literary art outweighs all other considerations. The majority of playwrights, however, view the written word as the beginning of a larger creation and hope that a producer will deem their scripts worthy of production.

Given that most playwrights intend their works to be performed, it might be argued that reading a play is a poor substitute for seeing it acted on a stage—perhaps something like reading a recipe without having access to the ingredients and a kitchen. This analogy is tempting, but it overlooks the literary dimensions of a script; the words we hear on a stage were written first. Read from a page, these words can feed an imagination in ways that a recipe cannot satisfy a hungry cook. We can fill in a play's missing faces, voices, actions, and settings in much the same way that we imagine these elements in a short story or novel. Like any play director, we are free to include as many ingredients as we have an appetite for.

This imaginative collaboration with the playwright creates a mental world that can be nearly as real and vivid as a live performance. Sometimes readers find that they prefer their own reading of a play to a director's interpretation. Shakespeare's Hamlet, for instance, has been presented as a whining son, but you may read him as a strong prince. Rich plays often accommodate a wide range of imaginative responses to their texts. Reading, then, is an excellent way to appreciate and evaluate a production of a play. Moreover, reading is valuable in its own right, because it allows us to enter the playwright's created world even when a theatrical production is unavailable.

Reading a play, however, requires more creative imagining than sitting in an audience watching actors on a stage presenting lines and actions before you. As a reader you become the play's director; you construct an interpretation based on the playwright's use of language, development of character, arrangement of incidents, description of settings, and directions for staging. Keeping track of the playwright's handling of these elements will help you to organize your response to the play. You may experience suspense, fear, horror, sympathy, or humor, but whatever experience a play evokes, ask yourself why you respond to it as you do. You may discover that your assessment of Hamlet's character is different from someone else's, but whether you find him heroic, indecisive, neurotic, or a complex of competing qualities, you'll be better equipped to articulate your interpretation of him if you pay attention to your responses and ask yourself questions as you read. Consider, for example, how his reactions might be similar to or different from your own. How does his language reveal his character? Does his behavior seem justified? How would you play the role yourself? What actor do you think might best play the Hamlet that you have created in your imagination? Why would he or she (women have also played Hamlet onstage) fill the role best?

These kinds of questions (see Questions for Writing about Drama, p. 86) can help you to think and talk about your responses to a play. Happily, such questions needn't—and often can't—be fully answered as you read the play. Frequently you must experience the entire play before you can determine how its elements work together. That's why reading a play can be such a satisfying experience. You wouldn't think of asking a live actor onstage to repeat her lines because you didn't quite comprehend their significance, but you can certainly reread a page in a book. Rereading allows you to replay language, characters, and incidents carefully and thoroughly to your own satisfaction.

TRIFLES

In the following play, Susan Glaspell skillfully draws on many dramatic elements and creates an intense story that is as effective on the page as it is in the theater. A reading of this play and the discussion that follows it will help you to understand how a play conveys its effects and meanings so that you are better equipped to write about drama. The sample student paper on page 88 compares the themes of *Trifles* with Henrik Ibsen's *A Doll House*.

Glaspell wrote *Trifles* in 1916 for the Provincetown Players on Cape Cod, in Massachusetts. Their performance of the work helped her develop a reputation as a writer sensitive to feminist issues. The year after *Trifles* was produced, Glaspell transformed the play into a short story titled "A Jury of Her Peers."

Glaspell's life in the Midwest provided her with the setting for *Trifles*. Born and raised in Davenport, Iowa, she graduated from Drake University in 1899 and then worked for a short time as a reporter on the *Des Moines News,* until her short stories were accepted in magazines such as *Harper's* and *Ladies' Home Journal.* Glaspell moved to the Northeast when she was in her early thirties to continue writing fiction and drama. She published some twenty plays, novels, and more than forty short stories. *Alison's House,* based on Emily Dickinson's life, earned her a Pulitzer Prize for drama in 1931. *Trifles* and "A Jury of Her Peers" remain, however, Glaspell's best-known works.

Glaspell wrote *Trifles* to complete a bill that was to feature several one-act plays by Eugene O'Neill. In *The Road to the Temple* (1926) she recalls how the play came to her as she sat in the theater looking at a bare stage. First, "the stage became a kitchen. . . . Then the door at the back opened, and people all bundled up came in—two or three men. I wasn't sure which, but sure enough about the two women, who hung back, reluctant to enter that kitchen. When I was a newspaper reporter out in Iowa, I was sent downstate to do a murder trial, and I never forgot going to the kitchen of a woman who had been locked up in town."

Trifles is about a murder committed in a midwestern farmhouse, but the play goes beyond the kinds of questions raised by most whodunit stories. The murder is the occasion instead of the focus. The play's major concerns are the moral, social, and psychological aspects of the assumptions and perceptions of the men and women who search for the murderer's motive. Glaspell is finally more interested in the meaning of Mrs. Wright's life than in the details of Mr. Wright's death.

As you read the play keep track of your responses to the characters and note in the margin the moments when Glaspell reveals how men and women respond differently to the evidence before them. What do those moments suggest about the kinds of assumptions these men and women make about themselves and each other? How do their assumptions compare with your own?

SUSAN GLASPELL (1882-1948)
Trifles

1916

Characters

George Henderson, county attorney
Henry Peters, sheriff
Lewis Hale, a neighboring farmer
Mrs. Peters
Mrs. Hale

SCENE: *The kitchen in the now abandoned farmhouse of John Wright, a gloomy kitchen, and left without having been put in order—the walls covered with a faded wall paper. Down right is a door leading to the parlor. On the right wall above this door is a built-in kitchen cupboard with shelves in the upper portion and drawers below. In the rear wall at right, up two steps is a door opening onto stairs leading to the second floor. In the rear wall at left is a door to the shed and from there to the outside. Between these two doors is an old-fashioned black iron stove. Running along the left wall from the shed door is an old iron sink and sink shelf, in which is set a hand pump. Downstage of the sink is an uncurtained window. Near the window is an old wooden rocker. Center stage is an unpainted wooden kitchen table with straight chairs on either side. There is a small chair down right. Unwashed pans under the sink, a loaf of bread outside the breadbox, a dish towel on the table—other signs of incompleted work. At the rear the shed door opens and the Sheriff comes in followed by the County Attorney and Hale. The Sheriff and Hale are men in middle life, the County Attorney is a young man; all are much bundled up and go at once to the stove. They are followed by the two women—the Sheriff's wife, Mrs. Peters, first; she is a slight wiry woman, a thin nervous face. Mrs. Hale is larger and would ordinarily be called more comfortable looking, but she is disturbed now and looks fearfully about as she enters. The women have come in slowly, and stand close together near the door.*

County Attorney (at stove rubbing his hands): This feels good. Come up to the fire, ladies.
Mrs. Peters (after taking a step forward): I'm not—cold.
Sheriff (unbuttoning his overcoat and stepping away from the stove to right of table as if to mark the beginning of official business): Now, Mr. Hale, before we move things about, you explain to Mr. Henderson just what you saw when you came here yesterday morning.
County Attorney (crossing down to left of the table): By the way, has anything been moved? Are things just as you left them yesterday?
Sheriff (looking about): It's just about the same. When it dropped below zero last night I thought I'd better send Frank out this morning to make a fire for us—*(sits right of center table)* no use getting pneumonia with a big case on, but I told him not to touch anything except the stove—and you know Frank.
County Attorney: Somebody should have been left here yesterday.
Sheriff: Oh—yesterday. When I had to send Frank to Morris Center for that man who went crazy—I want you to know I had my hands full yesterday. I knew

you could get back from Omaha by today and as long as I went over everything here myself——

County Attorney: Well, Mr. Hale, tell just what happened when you came here yesterday morning.

Hale (crossing down to above table): Harry and I had started to town with a load of potatoes. We came along the road from my place and as I got here I said, "I'm going to see if I can't get John Wright to go in with me on a party telephone." I spoke to Wright about it once before and he put me off, saying folks talked too much anyway, and all he asked was peace and quiet—I guess you know about how much he talked himself; but I thought maybe if I went to the house and talked about it before his wife, though I said to Harry that I didn't know as what his wife wanted made much difference to John——

County Attorney: Let's talk about that later, Mr. Hale. I do want to talk about that, but tell now just what happened when you got to the house.

Hale: I didn't hear or see anything; I knocked at the door, and still it was all quiet inside. I knew they must be up, it was past eight o'clock. So I knocked again, and I thought I heard somebody say, "Come in." I wasn't sure, I'm not sure yet, but I opened the door—this door *(indicating the door by which the two women are still standing)* and there in that rocker—*(pointing to it)* sat Mrs. Wright. *(They all look at the rocker down left.)*

County Attorney: What—was she doing?

Hale: She was rockin' back and forth. She had her apron in her hand and was kind of—pleating it.

County Attorney: And how did she—look?

Hale: Well, she looked queer.

County Attorney: How do you mean—queer?

Hale: Well, as if she didn't know what she was going to do next. And kind of done up.

County Attorney (takes out notebook and pencil and sits left of center table): How did she seem to feel about your coming?

Hale: Why, I don't think she minded—one way or other. She didn't pay much attention. I said, "How do, Mrs. Wright, it's cold, ain't it?" And she said, "Is it?"—and went on kind of pleating at her apron. Well, I was surprised; she didn't ask me to come up to the stove, or to set down, but just sat there, not even looking at me, so I said, "I want to see John." And then she—laughed. I guess you would call it a laugh. I thought of Harry and the team outside, so I said a little sharp: "Can't I see John?" "No," she says, kind o' dull like. "Ain't he home?" says I. "Yes," says she, "he's home." "Then why can't I see him?" I asked her, out of patience. " 'Cause he's dead," says she. *"Dead?"* says I. She just nodded her head, not getting a bit excited, but rockin' back and forth. "Why—where is he?" says I, not knowing what to say. She just pointed upstairs—like that. *(Himself pointing to the room above.)* I started for the stairs, with the idea of going up there. I walked from there to here—then I says, "Why, what did he die of?" "He died of a rope round his neck," says she, and just went on pleatin' at her apron. Well, I went out and called Harry. I thought I might—need help. We went upstairs and there he was lyin'——

County Attorney: I think I'd rather have you go into that upstairs, where you can point it all out. Just go on now with the rest of the story.

Hale: Well, my first thought was to get that rope off. It looked . . . *(stops; his face twitches)* . . . but Harry, he went up to him, and he said, "No, he's dead all right, and we'd better not touch anything." So we went back downstairs. She was still sitting that same way. "Has anybody been notified?" I asked. "No," says she, unconcerned. "Who did this, Mrs. Wright?" said Harry. He said it businesslike—and she stopped pleatin' of her apron. "I don't know," she says. "You don't *know?*" says Harry. "No," says she. "Weren't you sleepin' in the bed with him?" says Harry. "Yes," says she, "but I was on the inside." "Somebody slipped a rope round his neck and strangled him and you didn't wake up?" says Harry. "I didn't wake up," she said after him. We must 'a' looked as if we didn't see how that could be, for after a minute she said, "I sleep sound." Harry was going to ask her more questions but I said maybe we ought to let her tell her story first to the coroner, or the sheriff, so Harry went fast as he could to Rivers' place, where there's a telephone.

County Attorney: And what did Mrs. Wright do when she knew that you had gone for the coroner?

Hale: She moved from the rocker to that chair over there *(pointing to a small chair in the down right corner)* and just sat there with her hands held together and looking down. I got a feeling that I ought to make some conversation, so I said I had come in to see if John wanted to put in a telephone, and at that she started to laugh, and then she stopped and looked at me—scared. *(The County Attorney, who has had his notebook out, makes a note.)* I dunno, maybe it wasn't scared. I wouldn't like to say it was. Soon Harry got back, and then Dr. Lloyd came and you, Mr. Peters, and so I guess that's all I know that you don't.

County Attorney (rising and looking around): I guess we'll go upstairs first— and then out to the barn and around there. *(To the Sheriff.)* You're convinced that there was nothing important here—nothing that would point to any motive?

Sheriff: Nothing here but kitchen things. *(The County Attorney, after again looking around the kitchen, opens the door of a cupboard closet in right wall. He brings a small chair from right—gets on it and looks on a shelf. Pulls his hand away, sticky.)*

County Attorney: Here's a nice mess. *(The women draw nearer up center.)*

Mrs. Peters (to the other woman): Oh, her fruit; it did freeze. *(To the Lawyer.)* She worried about that when it turned so cold. She said the fire'd go out and her jars would break.

Sheriff (rises): Well, can you beat the women! Held for murder and worryin' about her preserves.

County Attorney (getting down from chair): I guess before we're through she may have something more serious than preserves to worry about. *(Crosses down right center.)*

Hale: Well, women are used to worrying over trifles. *(The two women move a little closer together.)*

County Attorney (with the gallantry of a young politician): And yet, for all their worries, what would we do without the ladies? *(The women do not unbend. He goes below the center table to the sink, takes a dipperful of water from the pail, and pouring it into a basin, washes his hands. While he is doing this the Sheriff and Hale cross to cupboard, which they inspect. The County Attorney starts to wipe his hands on the roller towel, turns it for a cleaner place.)* Dirty towels! *(Kicks his foot against the pans under the sink.)* Not much of a housekeeper, would you say, ladies?

Mrs. Hale (stiffly): There's a great deal of work to be done on a farm.

County Attorney: To be sure. And yet *(with a little bow to her)* I know there are some Dickson County farmhouses which do not have such roller towels. *(He gives it a pull to expose its full length again.)*

Mrs. Hale: Those towels get dirty awful quick. Men's hands aren't always as clean as they might be.

County Attorney: Ah, loyal to your sex, I see. But you and Mrs. Wright were neighbors. I suppose you were friends, too.

Mrs. Hale (shaking her head): I've not seen much of her of late years. I've not been in this house—it's more than a year.

County Attorney (crossing to women up center): And why was that? You didn't like her?

Mrs. Hale: I liked her all well enough. Farmers' wives have their hands full, Mr. Henderson. And then———

County Attorney: Yes———?

Mrs. Hale (looking about): It never seemed a very cheerful place.

County Attorney: No—it's not cheerful. I shouldn't say she had the homemaking instinct.

Mrs. Hale: Well, I don't know as Wright had, either.

County Attorney: You mean that they didn't get on very well?

Mrs. Hale: No, I don't mean anything. But I don't think a place'd be any cheerfuller for John Wright's being in it.

County Attorney: I'd like to talk more of that a little later. I want to get the lay of things upstairs now. *(He goes past the women to up right where steps lead to a stair door.)*

Sheriff: I suppose anything Mrs. Peters does'll be all right. She was to take in some clothes for her, you know, and a few little things. We left in such a hurry yesterday.

County Attorney: Yes, but I would like to see what you take, Mrs. Peters, and keep an eye out for anything that might be of use to us.

Mrs. Peters: Yes, Mr. Henderson. *(The men leave by up right door to stairs. The women listen to the men's steps on the stairs, then look about the kitchen.)*

Mrs. Hale (crossing left to sink): I'd hate to have men coming into my kitchen, snooping around and criticizing. *(She arranges the pans under sink which the Lawyer had shoved out of place.)*

Mrs. Peters: Of course it's no more than their duty. *(Crosses to cupboard up right.)*

Mrs. Hale: Duty's all right, but I guess that deputy sheriff that came out to make the fire might have got a little of this on. *(Gives the roller towel a pull.)* Wish I'd thought of that sooner. Seems mean to talk about her for not having things slicked up when she had to come away in such a hurry. *(Crosses right to Mrs. Peters at cupboard.)*

Mrs. Peters (who has been looking through cupboard, lifts one end of towel that covers a pan): She had bread set. *(Stands still.)*

Mrs. Hale (eyes fixed on a loaf of bread beside the breadbox, which is on a low shelf of the cupboard): She was going to put this in there. *(Picks up loaf, abruptly drops it. In a manner of returning to familiar things.)* It's a shame about her fruit. I wonder if it's all gone. *(Gets up on the chair and looks.)* I think there's some here that's all right, Mrs. Peters. Yes—here; *(holding it toward the window)* this is cherries, too. *(Looking again.)* I declare I believe that's the only one. *(Gets down, jar in her hand. Goes to the sink and wipes it off on the outside.)* She'll feel awful bad after all her hard work in the hot weather. I remember the afternoon I put up my cherries last summer. *(She puts the jar on the big kitchen table, center of the room. With a sigh, is about to sit down in the rocking chair. Before she is seated realizes what chair it is; with a slow look at it, steps back. The chair which she has touched rocks back and forth. Mrs. Peters moves to center table and they both watch the chair rock for a moment or two.)*

Mrs. Peters (shaking off the mood which the empty rocking chair has evoked. Now in a businesslike manner she speaks): Well I must get those things from the front room closet. *(She goes to the door at the right but, after looking into the other room, steps back.)* You coming with me, Mrs. Hale? You could help me carry them. *(They go in the other room; reappear, Mrs. Peters carrying a dress, petticoat, and skirt, Mrs. Hale following with a pair of shoes.)* My, it's cold in there. *(She puts the clothes on the big table and hurries to the stove.)*

Mrs. Hale (right of center table examining the skirt): Wright was close. I think maybe that's why she kept so much to herself. She didn't even belong to the Ladies' Aid. I suppose she felt she couldn't do her part, and then you don't enjoy things when you feel shabby. I heard she used to wear pretty clothes and be lively, when she was Minnie Foster, one of the town girls singing in the choir. But that—oh, that was thirty years ago. This all you want to take in?

Mrs. Peters: She said she wanted an apron. Funny thing to want, for there isn't much to get you dirty in jail, goodness knows. But I suppose just to make her feel more natural. *(Crosses to cupboard.)* She said they was in the top drawer in this cupboard. Yes, here. And then her little shawl that always hung behind the door. *(Opens stair door and looks.)* Yes, here it is. *(Quickly shuts door leading upstairs.)*

Mrs. Hale (abruptly moving toward her): Mrs. Peters?

Mrs. Peters: Yes, Mrs. Hale? *(At up right door.)*

Mrs. Hale: Do you think she did it?

Mrs. Peters (in a frightened voice): Oh, I don't know.

Mrs. Hale: Well, I don't think she did. Asking for an apron and her little shawl. Worrying about her fruit.

Mrs. Peters (starts to speak, glances up, where footsteps are heard in the room above. In a low voice): Mr. Peters says it looks bad for her. Mr. Henderson is awful sarcastic in a speech and he'll make fun of her sayin' she didn't wake up.

Mrs. Hale: Well, I guess John Wright didn't wake when they was slipping that rope under his neck.

Mrs. Peters (crossing slowly to table and placing shawl and apron on table with other clothing): No, it's strange. It must have been done awful crafty and still. They say it was such a—funny way to kill a man, rigging it all up like that.

Mrs. Hale (crossing to left of Mrs. Peters at table): That's just what Mr. Hale said. There was a gun in the house. He says that's what he can't understand.

Mrs. Peters: Mr. Henderson said coming out that what was needed for the case was a motive; something to show anger, or—sudden feeling.

Mrs. Hale (who is standing by the table): Well, I don't see any signs of anger around here. *(She puts her hand on the dish towel, which lies on the table, stands looking down at table, one-half of which is clean, the other half messy.)* It's wiped to here. *(Makes a move as if to finish work, then turns and looks at loaf of bread outside the breadbox. Drops towel. In that voice of coming back to familiar things.)* Wonder how they are finding things upstairs. *(Crossing below table to down right.)* I hope she had it a little more red-up up there. You know, it seems kind of *sneaking.* Locking her up in town and then coming out here and trying to get her own house to turn against her!

Mrs. Peters: But, Mrs. Hale, the law is the law.

Mrs. Hale: I s'pose 'tis. *(Unbuttoning her coat.)* Better loosen up your things, Mrs. Peters. You won't feel them when you go out. *(Mrs. Peters takes off her fur tippet, goes to hang it on chair back left of table, stands looking at the work basket on floor near down left window.)*

Mrs. Peters: She was piecing a quilt. *(She brings the large sewing basket to the center table and they look at the bright pieces, Mrs. Hale above the table and Mrs. Peters left of it.)*

Mrs. Hale: It's a log cabin pattern. Pretty, isn't it? I wonder if she was goin' to quilt it or just knot it? *(Footsteps have been heard coming down the stairs. The Sheriff enters followed by Hale and the County Attorney.)*

Sheriff: They wonder if she was going to quilt it or just knot it! *(The men laugh, the women look abashed.)*

County Attorney (rubbing his hands over the stove): Frank's fire didn't do much up there, did it? Well, let's go out to the barn and get that cleared up. *(The men go outside by up left door.)*

Mrs. Hale (resentfully): I don't know as there's anything so strange, our takin' up our time with little things while we're waiting for them to get the evidence. *(She sits in chair right of table smoothing out a block with decision.)* I don't see as it's anything to laugh about.

Mrs. Peters (apologetically): Of course they've got awful important things on their minds. *(Pulls up a chair and joins Mrs. Hale at the left of the table.)*

Mrs. Hale (examining another block): Mrs. Peters, look at this one. Here, this is the one she was working on, and look at the sewing! All the rest of it has been so nice and even. And look at this! It's all over the place! Why, it looks as if she didn't know what she was about! *(After she has said this they look at each other, then start to glance back at the door. After an instant Mrs. Hale has pulled at a knot and ripped the sewing.)*

Mrs. Peters: Oh, what are you doing, Mrs. Hale?

Mrs. Hale (mildly): Just pulling out a stitch or two that's not sewed very good. *(Threading a needle.)* Bad sewing always made me fidgety.

Mrs. Peters (with a glance at door, nervously): I don't think we ought to touch things.

Mrs. Hale: I'll just finish up this end. *(Suddenly stopping and leaning forward.)* Mrs. Peters?

Mrs. Peters: Yes, Mrs. Hale?

Mrs. Hale: What do you suppose she was so nervous about?

Mrs. Peters: Oh—I don't know. I don't know as she was nervous. I sometimes sew awful queer when I'm just tired. *(Mrs. Hale starts to say something, looks at Mrs. Peters, then goes on sewing.)* Well, I must get these things wrapped up. They may be through sooner than we think. *(Putting apron and other things together.)* I wonder where I can find a piece of paper, and string. *(Rises.)*

Mrs. Hale: In that cupboard, maybe.

Mrs. Peters (crosses right looking in cupboard): Why, here's a bird-cage. *(Holds it up)*. Did she have a bird, Mrs. Hale?

Mrs. Hale: Why, I don't know whether she did or not—I've not been here for so long. There was a man around last year selling canaries cheap, but I don't know as she took one; maybe she did. She used to sing real pretty herself.

Mrs. Peters (glancing around): Seems funny to think of a bird here. But she must have had one, or why would she have a cage? I wonder what happened to it?

Mrs. Hale: I s'pose maybe the cat got it.

Mrs. Peters: No, she didn't have a cat. She's got that feeling some people have about cats—being afraid of them. My cat got in her room and she was real upset and asked me to take it out.

Mrs. Hale: My sister Bessie was like that. Queer, ain't it?

Mrs. Peters (examining the cage): Why, look at this door. It's broke. One hinge is pulled apart. *(Takes a step down to Mrs. Hale's right.)*

Mrs. Hale (looking too): Looks as if someone must have been rough with it.

Mrs. Peters: Why, yes. *(She brings the cage forward and puts it on the table.)*

Mrs. Hale (glancing toward up left door): I wish if they're going to find any evidence they'd be about it. I don't like this place.

Mrs. Peters: But I'm awful glad you came with me, Mrs. Hale. It would be lonesome for me sitting here alone.

Mrs. Hale: It would, wouldn't it? *(Dropping her sewing.)* But I tell you what I do wish, Mrs. Peters. I wish I had come over sometimes when *she* was here. I—*(looking around the room)*—wish I had.

Mrs. Peters: But of course you were awful busy, Mrs. Hale—your house and your children.

Mrs. Hale (rises and crosses left): I could've come. I stayed away because it weren't cheerful—and that's why I ought to have come. I—*(looking out left window)*—I've never liked this place. Maybe because it's down in a hollow and you don't see the road. I dunno what it is, but it's a lonesome place and always was. I wish I had come over to see Minnie Foster sometimes. I can see now—*(Shakes her head.)*

Mrs. Peters (left of table and above it): Well, you mustn't reproach yourself, Mrs. Hale. Somehow we just don't see how it is with other folks until—something turns up.

Mrs. Hale: Not having children makes less work—but it makes a quiet house, and Wright out to work all day, and no company when he did come in. *(Turning from window.)* Did you know John Wright, Mrs. Peters?

Mrs. Peters: Not to know him; I've seen him in town. They say he was a good man.

Mrs. Hale: Yes—good; he didn't drink, and kept his word as well as most, I guess, and paid his debts. But he was a hard man, Mrs. Peters. Just to pass the time of day with him— *(Shivers.)* Like a raw wind that gets to the bone. *(Pauses, her eye falling on the cage.)* I should think she would 'a' wanted a bird. But what do you suppose went with it?

Mrs. Peters: I don't know, unless it got sick and died. *(She reaches over and swings the broken door, swings it again, both women watch it.)*

Mrs. Hale: You weren't raised round here, were you? *(Mrs. Peters shakes her head.)* You didn't know—her?

Mrs. Peters: Not till they brought her yesterday.

Mrs. Hale: She—come to think of it, she was kind of like a bird herself—real sweet and pretty, but kind of timid and—fluttery. How—she—did—change. *(Silence: then as if struck by a happy thought and relieved to get back to every-day things. Crosses right above Mrs. Peters to cupboard, replaces small chair used to stand on to its original place down right.)* Tell you what, Mrs. Peters, why don't you take the quilt in with you? It might take up her mind.

Mrs. Peters: Why, I think that's a real nice idea, Mrs. Hale. There couldn't possibly be any objection to it could there? Now, just what would I take? I wonder if her patches are in here—and her things. *(They look in the sewing basket.)*

Mrs. Hale (crosses to right of table): Here's some red. I expect this has got sewing things in it. *(Brings out a fancy box.)* What a pretty box. Looks like something somebody would give you. Maybe her scissors are in here. *(Opens box. Suddenly puts her hand to her nose.)* Why——— *(Mrs. Peters bends nearer, then turns her face away.)* There's something wrapped up in this piece of silk.

Mrs. Peters: Why, this isn't her scissors.

Mrs. Hale (lifting the silk): Oh, Mrs. Peters——— *(Mrs. Peters bends closer.)*

Mrs. Peters: It's the bird.

Mrs. Hale: But, Mrs. Peters—look at it! Its neck! Look at its neck! It's all—other side *to.*

Mrs. Peters: Somebody—wrung—its—neck. *(Their eyes meet. A look of growing comprehension, of horror. Steps are heard outside. Mrs. Hale slips box under quilt pieces, and sinks into her chair. Enter Sheriff and County Attorney. Mrs. Peters steps down left and stands looking out of window.)*

County Attorney (as one turning from serious things to little pleasantries): Well, ladies, have you decided whether she was going to quilt it or knot it? *(Crosses to center above table.)*

Mrs. Peters: We think she was going to—knot it. *(Sheriff crosses to right of stove, lifts stove lid, and glances at fire, then stands warming hands at stove.)*

County Attorney: Well, that's interesting, I'm sure. *(Seeing the bird-cage.)* Has the bird flown?

Mrs. Hale (putting more quilt pieces over the box): We think the—cat got it.

County Attorney (preoccupied): Is there a cat? *(Mrs. Hale glances in a quick covert way at Mrs. Peters.)*

Mrs. Peters (turning from window takes a step in): Well, not *now.* They're superstitious, you know. They leave.

County Attorney (to Sheriff Peters, continuing an interrupted conversation): No sign at all of anyone having come from the outside. Their own rope. Now let's go up again and go over it piece by piece. *(They start upstairs.)* It would have to have been someone who knew just the———— *(Mrs. Peters sits down left of table. The two women sit there not looking at one another, but as if peering into something and at the same time holding back. When they talk now it is in the manner of feeling their way over strange ground, as if afraid of what they are saying, but as if they cannot help saying it.)*

Mrs. Hale (hesitatively and in hushed voice): She liked the bird. She was going to bury it in that pretty box.

Mrs. Peters (in a whisper): When I was a girl—my kitten—there was a boy took a hatchet, and before my eyes—and before I could get there———— *(Covers her face an instant.)* If they hadn't held me back I would have— *(catches herself, looks upstairs where steps are heard, falters weakly)*—hurt him.

Mrs. Hale (with a slow look around her): I wonder how it would seem never to have had any children around. *(Pause.)* No, Wright wouldn't like the bird—a thing that sang. She used to sing. He killed that, too.

Mrs. Peters (moving uneasily): We don't know who killed the bird.

Mrs. Hale: I knew John Wright.

Mrs. Peters: It was an awful thing was done in this house that night, Mrs. Hale. Killing a man while he slept, slipping a rope around his neck that choked the life out of him.

Mrs. Hale: His neck. Choked the life out of him. *(Her hand goes out and rests on the bird-cage.)*

Mrs. Peters (with rising voice): We don't know who killed him. We don't *know.*

Mrs. Hale (her own feeling not interrupted): If there'd been years and years of nothing, then a bird to sing to you, it would be awful—still, after the bird was still.

Mrs. Peters (something within her speaking): I know what stillness is. When we homesteaded in Dakota, and my first baby died—after he was two years old, and me with no other then————

Mrs. Hale (moving): How soon do you suppose they'll be through looking for the evidence?

Mrs. Peters: I know what stillness is. *(Pulling herself back.)* The law has got to punish crime, Mrs. Hale.

Mrs. Hale (not as if answering that): I wish you'd seen Minnie Foster when she wore a white dress with blue ribbons and stood up there in the choir and sang. *(A look around the room.)* Oh, I *wish* I'd come over here once in a while! That was a crime! That was a crime! Who's going to punish that?

Mrs. Peters (looking upstairs): We mustn't—take on.

Mrs. Hale: I might have known she needed help! I know how things can be—for women. I tell you, it's queer, Mrs. Peters. We live close together and we live far apart. We all go through the same things—it's all just a different kind of the same thing. *(Brushes her eyes, noticing the jar of fruit, reaches out for it.)* If I was you I wouldn't tell her her fruit was gone. Tell her it *ain't.* Tell her it's all right. Take this in to prove it to her. She—she may never know whether it was broke or not.

Mrs. Peters (takes the jar, looks about for something to wrap it in; takes petticoat from the clothes brought from the other room, very nervously begins winding this around the jar. In a false voice): My, it's a good thing the men couldn't hear us. Wouldn't they just laugh! Getting all stirred up over a little thing like a—dead canary. As if that could have anything to do with—with—wouldn't they *laugh! (The men are heard coming downstairs.)*

Mrs. Hale (under her breath): Maybe they would—maybe they wouldn't.

County Attorney: No, Peters, it's all perfectly clear except a reason for doing it. But you know juries when it comes to women. If there was some definite thing. *(Crosses slowly to above table. Sheriff crosses down right. Mrs. Hale and Mrs. Peters remain seated at either side of table.)* Something to show—something to make a story about—a thing that would connect up with this strange way of doing it——— *(The women's eyes meet for an instant. Enter Hale from outer door.)*

Hale (remaining by door): Well, I've got the team around. Pretty cold out there.

County Attorney: I'm going to stay awhile by myself. *(To the Sheriff.)* You can send Frank out for me, can't you? I want to go over everything. I'm not satisfied that we can't do better.

Sheriff: Do you want to see what Mrs. Peters is going to take in? *(The Lawyer picks up the apron, laughs.)*

County Attorney: Oh, I guess they're not very dangerous things the ladies have picked out. *(Moves a few things about, disturbing the quilt pieces which cover the box. Steps back.)* No, Mrs. Peters doesn't need supervising. For that matter a sheriff's wife is married to the law. Ever think of it that way, Mrs. Peters?

Mrs. Peters: Not—just that way.

Sheriff (chuckling): Married to the law. *(Moves to down right door to the other room.)* I just want you to come in here a minute, George. We ought to take a look at these windows.

County Attorney (scoffingly): Oh, windows!

Sheriff: We'll be right out, Mr. Hale. *(Hale goes outside. The Sheriff follows the County Attorney into the room. Then Mrs. Hale rises, hands tight together, looking intensely at Mrs. Peters, whose eyes make a slow turn, finally meeting Mrs. Hale's. A moment Mrs. Hale holds her, then her own eyes point the way to where the box is concealed. Suddenly Mrs. Peters throws back quilt pieces and tries to put the box in the bag she is carrying. It is too big. She opens box, starts to take bird out, cannot touch it, goes to pieces, stands there helpless. Sound of a knob turning in the other room. Mrs. Hale snatches the box and puts it in the pocket of her big coat. Enter County Attorney and Sheriff, who remains down right.)*

County Attorney (crosses to up left door facetiously): Well, Henry, at least we found out that she was not going to quilt it. She was going to—what is it you call it, ladies?

Mrs. Hale (standing center below table facing front, her hand against her pocket): We call it—knot it, Mr. Henderson.

Curtain.

UNDERSTANDING THE ELEMENTS OF DRAMA

Trifles is a one-act play; in other words, the entire play takes place in a single location and unfolds as one continuous action. As in a short story, the characters in a one-act play are presented economically, and the action is sharply focused. In contrast, full-length plays can include many characters as well as different settings in place and time. The main divisions of a full-length play are typically acts; their ends are indicated by lowering a curtain or turning up the houselights. Playwrights frequently employ acts to accommodate changes in time, setting, characters on stage, or mood. In many full-length plays, such as Shakespeare's *Hamlet,* acts are further divided into scenes; according to tradition a scene changes when the location of the action changes or when a new character enters. Acts and scenes are conventions that are understood and accepted by audiences because they have come, through usage and time, to be recognized as familiar techniques. The major convention of a one-act play is that it typically consists of only a single scene; nevertheless, one-act plays contain many of the elements of drama that characterize their full-length counterparts.

One-act plays create their effects through compression. They especially lend themselves to modestly budgeted productions with limited stage facilities, such as those put on by little theater groups. However, the potential of a one-act play to move audiences and readers is not related to its length. As *Trifles* shows, one-acts represent a powerful form of dramatic literature.

The single location that comprises the setting for *Trifles* is described at the very beginning of the play; it establishes an atmosphere that will later influence our judgment of Mrs. Wright. The kitchen, "gloomy" and with walls "covered with a faded wall paper," is disordered, bare, and sparsely equipped with a stove, sink, and rocker—each of them "old"—an unpainted table, some chairs, three doors, and an uncurtained window. The only color mentioned is, appropriately, black. These details are just enough to allow us to imagine the stark, uninviting place where Mrs. Wright spent most of her time. Moreover, "signs of incompleted work," coupled with the presence of the sheriff and county attorney, create an immediate tension by suggesting that something is terribly wrong. Before a single word is spoken, suspense is created as the characters enter. This suspenseful situation causes an anxious uncertainty about what will happen next.

The setting is further developed through the use of exposition, a device that provides the necessary background information about the characters and their circumstances. For example, we immediately learn through dialogue—the verbal exchanges between characters—that Mr. Henderson, the county attorney, is just back from Omaha. This establishes the setting as somewhere in the Midwest, where winters can be brutally cold and barren. We also find out that John Wright has been murdered and that his wife has been arrested for the crime.

Even more important, Glaspell deftly characterizes the Wrights through exposition alone. Mr. Hale's conversation with Mr. Henderson explains how Mr. Wright's body was discovered, but it also reveals that Wright was a noncommunicative man, who refused to share a "party telephone" and who did not consider "what his wife wanted." Later Mrs. Hale adds to this characterization when she tells Mrs. Peters that though Mr. Wright was an honest, good man who paid his bills and did not drink, he was a "hard man" and "Like a raw wind that gets to the bone." Mr. Hale's description of Mrs. Wright sitting in the kitchen dazed and disoriented gives us a picture of a shattered, exhausted woman. But it is Mrs. Hale who again offers further insights when she describes how Minnie Foster, a sweet, pretty, timid young woman who sang in the choir, was changed by her marriage to Mr. Wright and by her childless, isolated life on the farm.

This information about Mr. and Mrs. Wright is worked into the dialogue throughout the play in order to suggest the nature of the conflict or struggle between them, a motive, and, ultimately, a justification for the murder. In the hands of a skillful playwright, exposition is not merely a mechanical device, it can provide important information while simultaneously developing characterizations and moving the action forward.

The action is shaped by the plot, the author's arrangement of incidents in the play that gives the story a particular focus and emphasis. Plot involves more than simply what happens; it involves how and why things happen. Glaspell begins with a discussion of the murder. Why? She could have begun with the murder itself: the distraught Mrs. Wright looping the rope around her husband's neck. The moment would be dramatic and horribly vivid. We neither see the body nor hear very much about it. When Mr. Hale describes finding Mr. Wright's body, Glaspell has the county attorney cut him off by saying, "I think I'd rather have you go into that upstairs, where you can point it all out. Just go on now with the rest of the story." It is precisely the "rest of the story" that interests Glaspell. Her arrangement of incidents prevents us from sympathizing with Mr. Wright. We are, finally, invited to see Mrs. Wright instead of her husband as the victim.

Mr. Henderson's efforts to discover a motive for the murder appear initially to be the play's focus, but the real conflicts are explored in what seems to be a subplot, a secondary action that reinforces or contrasts with the main plot. The discussions between Mrs. Hale and Mrs. Peters and the tensions between the men and the women turn out to be the main plot because they address the issues that Glaspell chooses to explore. Those issues are not about murder but about marriage and how men and women relate to each other.

The protagonist of *Trifles,* the central character with whom we tend to identify, is Mrs. Hale. The antagonist, the character who is in some kind of opposition to the central character, is the county attorney, Mr. Henderson. These two characters embody the major conflicts presented in the play because each speaks for a different set of characters who represent disparate values. Mrs. Hale and Mr. Henderson are developed less individually than as representative types.

Mrs. Hale articulates a sensitivity to Mrs. Wright's miserable life as well as an awareness of how women are repressed in general by men; she also helps Mrs. Peters to arrive at a similar understanding. When Mrs. Hale defends Mrs. Wright's soiled towels from Mr. Henderson's criticism, Glaspell has her say more than the county attorney is capable of hearing. The stage directions, the playwright's instructions about how the actors are to move and behave, indicate that Mrs. Hale responds "stiffly" to Mr. Henderson's disparagements: "Men's hands aren't always as clean as they might be." Mrs. Hale eventually comes to see that the men are, in a sense, complicit because it was insensitivity like theirs that drove Mrs. Wright to murder.

Mr. Henderson, on the other hand, represents the law in a patriarchal, conventional society that blithely places a minimal value on the concerns of women. In his attempt to gather evidence against Mrs. Wright, he implicitly defends men's severe dominance over women. He also patronizes Mrs. Hale and Mrs. Peters. Like Sheriff Peters and Mr. Hale, he regards the women's world as nothing more than "kitchen things" and "trifles." Glaspell, however, patterns the plot so that the women see more about Mrs. Wright's motives than the men do and shows that the women have a deeper understanding of justice.

Many plays are plotted in what has come to be called a pyramidal pattern, because the plot is divided into three essential parts. Such plays begin with a rising action, in which complication creates conflict for the protagonist. The resulting tension builds to the second major division, known as the climax, when the action reaches a final crisis, a turning point that has a powerful effect on the protagonist. The third part consists of falling action; here the tensions are diminished in the resolution of the plot's conflicts and complications (the resolution is also referred to as the conclusion or dénouement, a French word meaning "unknotting"). These divisions may occur at different times. There are many variations to this pattern. The terms are helpful for identifying various moments and movements within a given plot, but they are less useful if seen as a means of reducing dramatic art to a formula.

Because *Trifles* is a one-act play, this pyramidal pattern is less elaborately worked out than it might be in a full-length play, but the basic elements of the pattern can still be discerned. The complication consists mostly of Mrs. Hale's refusal to assign moral or legal guilt to Mrs. Wright's murder of her husband. Mrs. Hale is able to discover the motive in the domestic details that are beneath the men's consideration. The men fail to see the significance of the fruit jars, messy kitchen, and badly sewn quilt.

At first Mrs. Peters seems to voice the attitudes associated with the men. Unlike Mrs. Hale, who is "more comfortable looking," Mrs. Peters is "a slight wiry woman" with "a thin nervous face" who sounds like her husband, the sheriff, when she insists, "the law is the law." She also defends the men's patronizing attitudes, because "they've got awful important things on their minds." But Mrs. Peters is a foil—a character whose behavior and values contrast with the protagonist's—only up to a point. When the most telling clue is discovered, Mrs. Peters suddenly understands, along with Mrs. Hale, the motive for the killing. Mrs. Wright's caged life was no longer tolerable to her after her husband had killed the bird (which was the one bright spot in her life and which represents her early life as the young Minnie Foster). This revelation brings about the climax, when the two women must decide whether to tell the men what they have discovered. Both women empathize with Mrs. Wright as they confront this crisis, and their sense of common experience leads them to withhold the evidence.

This resolution ends the play's immediate conflicts and complications. Presumably, without a motive the county attorney will have difficulty prosecuting Mrs. Wright—at least to the fullest extent of the law. However, the larger issues related to the theme, the central idea or meaning of the play, are left unresolved. The men have both missed the clues and failed to perceive the suffering that acquits Mrs. Wright in the minds of the two women. The play ends with Mrs. Hale's ironic answer to Mr. Henderson's question about quilting. When she says "knot it," she gives him part of the evidence he needs to connect Mrs. Wright's quilting with the knot used to strangle her husband. Mrs. Hale knows—and we know—that Mr. Henderson will miss the clue she offers because he is blinded by his own self-importance and assumptions.

Though brief, *Trifles* is a masterful representation of dramatic elements working together to keep both audiences and readers absorbed in its characters and situations.

QUESTIONS FOR WRITING ABOUT DRAMA

The questions in this section can help you consider important elements that reveal a play's effects and meanings. These questions are general and will not, therefore, always be relevant to a particular play. Many of them, however, should prove useful for thinking, talking, and writing about drama. If you are uncertain about the meaning of a term used in a question, consult the Glossary of Literary Terms beginning on page 175.

1. Did you enjoy the play? What, specifically, pleased or displeased you about what was expressed and how it was expressed?
2. What is the significance of the play's title? How does it suggest the author's overall emphasis?
3. What information do the stage directions provide about the characters, action, and setting? Are these directions primarily descriptive, or are they also interpretive?
4. How is the exposition presented? What does it reveal? How does

the playwright's choice *not* to dramatize certain events on stage help to determine what the focus of the play is?

5. In what ways is the setting important? Would the play be altered significantly if the setting were changed?

6. Are foreshadowings used to suggest what is to come? Are flashbacks used to dramatize what has already happened?

7. What is the major conflict the protagonist faces? What complications constitute the rising action? Where is the climax? Is the conflict resolved?

8. Are one or more subplots used to qualify or complicate the main plot? Is the plot unified so that each incident somehow has a function that relates it to some other element in the play?

9. Does the author purposely avoid a pyramidal plot structure of rising action, climax, and falling action? Is the plot experimental? Is the plot logically and chronologically organized, or is it fantastical or absurd? What effects are produced by the plot? How does it reflect the author's view of life?

10. Who is the protagonist? Who (or what) is the antagonist?

11. By what means does the playwright reveal character? What do the characters' names, physical qualities, actions, and words convey about them? What do the characters reveal about each other?

12. What is the purpose of the minor characters? Are they individualized, or do they primarily represent ideas or attitudes? Are any character foils used?

13. Do the characters all use the same kind of language, or is their speech differentiated? Is it formal or informal? How do the characters' diction and manner of speaking serve to characterize them?

14. Does your response to the characters change in the course of the play? What causes the change?

15. Are words and images repeated in the play so that they take on special meanings? Which speeches seem particularly important? Why?

16. How does the playwright's use of language contribute to the tone of the play? Is the dialogue, for example, predominantly light, humorous, relaxed, sentimental, sad, angry, intense, or violent?

17. Are any symbols used in the play? Which actions, characters, settings, objects, or words convey more than their literal meanings?

18. Are any unfamiliar theatrical conventions used that present problems in understanding the play? How does knowing more about the nature of the theater from which the play originated help to resolve these problems?

19. Is the theme stated directly, or is it developed implicitly through the plot, characters, or some other element? Does the theme confirm or challenge most people's values?

20. How does the play reflect the values of the society in which it is set and in which it was written?

21. How does the play reflect or challenge your own values?
22. Is there a recording, film, or videocassette of the play available in your library or media center? How does this version compare with your own reading?
23. How would you produce the play on a stage? Consider scenery, costumes, casting, and characterizations. What would you emphasize most in your production?
24. Is there a particular critical approach that seems especially appropriate for this play (see the discussion "Critical Strategies for Reading and Writing" beginning on p. 94)?
25. How might biographical information about the author help the reader to grasp the central concerns of the play?
26. How might historical information about the play provide a useful context for interpretation?
27. To what extent do your own experiences, values, beliefs, and assumptions inform your interpretation?
28. What kinds of evidence from the play are you focusing on to support your interpretation? Does your interpretation leave out any important elements that might undercut or qualify your interpretation?
29. Given that there are a variety of ways to interpret the play, which one seems the most useful to you?

A SAMPLE COMPARISON: RECLAIMING THE SELF IN "TRIFLES" AND "A DOLL HOUSE"

The following paper was written in response to an assignment that required a comparison and contrast—about 750 words—of two assigned plays. *A Doll House* dramatizes the tensions of a nineteenth-century middle-class marriage in which the wife, Nora Helmer, struggles to step beyond the limited identity imposed on her by society and her husband, Torvald. Although the Helmers' pleasant apartment seems an unlikely setting for the fierce conflicts that develop, the issues raised in the play are unmistakably real. *A Doll House* affirms the necessity to reject hypocrisy, complacency, cowardice, and stifling conventions if life is to have dignity and meaning. The sample paper focuses upon the protagonist's struggle for self-definition in each play.

Stephanie Smith

Professor Barrina-Barrou

English 109-2

October 6, 19--

     Reclaiming the Self in <u>Trifles</u> and <u>A Doll House</u>

    Despite their early publication dates both Susan Glas-
pell's <u>Trifles</u> (1916) and Henrik Ibsen's <u>A Doll House</u> (1879)
can be regarded as works of feminist literature. Each play
depicts the life of a woman who has been suppressed, oppressed, and subjugated by a patronizing, patriarchal husband.
Glaspell's Mrs. Wright is eventually driven to kill the husband who robbed her of every last twitch of her identity,
whereas Ibsen's Nora, instead of physically removing her self-
righteous, identity-depriving husband, leaves the scene herself. She walks out on him for good, her own good. These
plays dramatize the hypocrisy and ingrained discrimination of
male-dominated society while simultaneously speaking to the
dangers for women who succumb to such hierarchies. Both Mrs.
Wright and Nora follow the roles mapped out for them by their
husbands. Their lives are directed by society's patriarchal
expectations, but their selves are lost somewhere along the
way.

    In <u>Trifles</u>, Mrs. Wright is described as someone who used
to have a flair for life. Her neighbor, Mrs. Hale, comments
that the last time Mrs. Wright appeared happy and vivacious
was before she was married, or more importantly, when she was
Minnie Foster and not Mrs. Wright. Mrs. Hale laments, "I
heard she used to wear pretty clothes and be lively, when she
was Minnie Foster, one of the town girls singing in the choir"

(Glaspell 769). But after thirty years of marriage, Mrs. Wright is now worried about her canned preserves and being without an apron during her stay in jail. This subservient image was so accepted in society that Mrs. Peters, the sheriff's wife, speculates that Mrs. Wright must want her apron to "feel more natural." Any other roles would be considered uncharacteristic.

These wifely roles are predicated on the supposition that women have no ability to make complicated decisions, to think critically, or to rely on themselves. As the title suggests, the men in this story think of homemaking as much less important than a husband's bread-winning role. Mr. Hale remarks, "Well, women are used to worrying over trifles" (Glaspell 762). Hence, women are forced into a domestic, secondary role, like it or not, and are not even respected for that. Mr. Hale, Mr. Peters, and the court attorney all dismiss the dialogue between Mrs. Peters and Mrs. Hale as feminine chitchat. Further, the court attorney allows the women to leave the Wrights' house unsupervised and even adds that "a sheriff's wife is married to the law." In other words, the wife is merely an extension of the husband. Even so, the system the men have set up for their wives and their disregard for it after the rules and boundaries have been laid down prove to be the men's downfall. The evidence that Mrs. Wright killed her husband is interwoven in Mrs. Hale's and Mrs. Peter's conversations about Mrs. Wright's sewing and her pet bird. The knots in her quilt match those in the rope used to strangle Mr. Wright, and the bird is found dead, the last symbol of Mrs. Wright's vitality taken by her husband.

Unable to play the role anymore, Mrs. Wright is foreign to herself and therefore lives a lie. As Mrs. Hale proclaims, "It looks as if she didn't know what she was about!" (Glaspell 765). Minnie Foster was spiritually dead.

Nora also lives a lie because she becomes little more than a toy for her husband. She was her husband's "little lark," chided and patronized with descriptions ranging from "featherhead" to "blind, incompetent child." Nora hears these labels for so long that she even uses her husband's words to describe herself. Mrs. Wright's bird symbolizes her lost ability to sing and soar freely, while Nora's feathered images keep her grounded and confined to her husband's expectations. She is literally dehumanized.

To be this good little wife, Nora forges a signature on a loan application so she will have money to take her sick husband to Italy. Since forgery is a form of falsifying an identity, the crime seems more than fitting. It is her area of expertise. Her husband, Helmer, is more fastidious. As president of the bank, Helmer fears for his reputation when a disgruntled worker threatens to create a scandal. He shuns his wife but soon learns that this worker will not release the information and so he forgives Nora; however, the damage is done. Nora has seen the light and heads out into it.

Nora shows evidence of rejecting her role earlier on. Just as Mrs. Wright's sewing became irregular and harried-- like the knots that matched those in the murder rope--Nora says of her masquerade clothes, "I'd love to rip them into a million pieces!" (Ibsen 1046). Again she uses a form of disguise, but this time she wants to rip it to shreds. She

fights to preserve her forgery secret, but also begins to realize the necessity of preserving her sense of herself. By
the end of the play, Nora understands the destructiveness of
having little or no self-identity. Helmer tells her that
"there's no one who gives up honor for love," but Nora blankly
responds, "Millions of women have done just that" (Ibsen
1074). Nora leaves the scene bereft of self-definition, but at
least she no longer labors under her husband's imposed limitations. Both Nora and Mrs. Wright must still find their place
in the feminine, but more importantly they must find peace in
themselves. Nevertheless, each character has found a place in
the sensibilities of contemporary feminists who see in Nora
and Mrs. Wright the necessity for women to define themselves.

Works Cited

Glaspell, Susan. <u>Trifles</u>. Meyer 760-70.

Ibsen, Henrik. <u>A Doll House</u>. Meyer 1026-75.

Meyer, Michael, ed. <u>The Compact Bedford Introduction to</u>
<u>Literature: Reading, Thinking, and Writing</u>. 3rd. ed.
Boston: Bedford-St. Martin's P, 1994.

6. Critical Strategies for Reading and Writing

CRITICAL THINKING

Maybe this has happened to you: the assignment is to write an analysis of some aspect of a work, let's say Nathaniel Hawthorne's *The Scarlet Letter*, that interests you and takes into account critical sources that comment on and interpret the work. You cheerfully begin research in the library but quickly find yourself bewildered by several seemingly unrelated articles. The first traces the thematic significance of images of light and darkness in the novel; the second makes a case for Hester Prynne as a liberated woman; the third argues that Arthur Dimmesdale's guilt is a projection of Hawthorne's own emotions; and the fourth analyzes the introduction, "The Custom House," as an attack on bourgeois values. These disparate treatments may seem random and capricious—a confirmation of your worst suspicions that interpretations of literature are hit-or-miss excursions into areas that you know little about or didn't know even existed. But if you understand that the articles are written from different perspectives—formalist, feminist, psychological, and Marxist—and that the purpose of each is to enhance your understanding of the novel by discussing a particular element of it, then you can see that their varying strategies represent potentially interesting ways of opening up the text that might otherwise never have occurred to you. There are many ways to approach a text, and a useful first step is to develop a sense of direction, an understanding of how a perspective—your own or a critic's—shapes a discussion of a text.

This chapter offers an introduction to critical approaches to literature by outlining a variety of strategies for reading and writing about fiction, poetry, or drama. These strategies include approaches that have long been practiced by readers who have used, for example, the insights gleaned from biography and history to illuminate literary works as well as more recent approaches, such as those used by feminist, reader-response, and deconstructionist critics. Each of these perspectives is sensitive to point of view, symbol, tone, irony, and other elements defined in the Glossary of Literary Terms

(p. 175), but each also casts those elements in a special light. The formalist approach emphasizes how the elements within a work achieve their effects, whereas biographical and psychological approaches lead outward from the work to consider the author's life and other writings. Even broader approaches, such as historical and sociological perspectives, connect the work to historic, social, and economic forces. Mythological readings represent the broadest approach, because they discuss the cultural and universal responses readers have to a work.

Any given strategy raises its own types of questions and issues while seeking particular kinds of evidence to support itself. An awareness of the assumptions and methods that inform an approach can help you to understand better the validity and value of a given critic's strategy for making sense of a work. More important, such an understanding can widen and deepen the responses of your own reading.

The critical thinking that goes into understanding a professional critic's approach to a work is not foreign to you because you have already used essentially the same kind of thinking to understand the work itself. The skills you have developed to produce a literary *analysis* that, for example, describes how a character, symbol, or rhyme scheme supports a theme are also useful for reading literary criticism, because such skills allow you to keep track of how the parts of a critical approach create a particular reading of a literary work. When you analyze a story, poem, or play by closely examining how its various elements relate to the whole, your *interpretation*—your articulation of what the work means to you as supported by an analysis of its elements—necessarily involves choosing what you focus upon in the work. The same is true of professional critics.

Critical readings presuppose choices in the kinds of material that are discussed. An analysis of the setting of John Updike's "A & P" (p. 24) would probably bring into focus the oppressive environment the protagonist associates with the store, rather than, say, the economic history of that supermarket chain. (For a student's analysis of the setting in "A & P," see p. 29.) The economic history of a supermarket chain might be useful to a Marxist critic concerned with how class relations are revealed in "A & P," but for a formalist critic interested in identifying the unifying structures of the story such information would be irrelevant. Each of these approaches raises different questions, examines different evidence, and employs different assumptions to interpret "A & P." Being aware of those differences—teasing them out so that you can see how they lead to competing conclusions—is a useful way to analyze the analysis itself. What is left out of an interpretation is sometimes as significant as what is included. As you read the critics, it's worth reminding yourself that your own critical thinking skills can help you to determine the usefulness of a particular approach.

The following overview is neither exhaustive in the types of critical approaches covered nor complete in its presentation of the complexities inherent in them, but it should help you to develop an appreciation of the intriguing possibilities that attend literary interpretation. The emphasis in this chapter is on ways of thinking and writing about literature rather than on daunting lists of terms, names, and movements. Although a working knowledge of critical schools may be valuable and necessary for a fully informed use of a given critical approach, the aim here is more modest and practical. This chapter is no substitute for the shelves of literary criticism that can be found in your library, but it does suggest how readers using different perspectives organize their responses to texts.

The summaries of critical approaches that follow are descriptive, not evaluative. Each approach has its advantages and limitations, but those matters are best left to further study. Like literary artists, critics have their personal values, tastes, and styles. The appropriateness of a specific critical approach will depend, at least in part, on the nature of the literary work under discussion as well as on your own sensibilities and experience. However, any approach, if it is to enhance understanding, requires sensitivity, tact, and an awareness of the various literary elements of the text, including, of course, its use of language. Successful critical approaches avoid eccentric decodings that reveal so-called hidden meanings which are not only hidden but totally absent from the text. Literary criticism attempts, like any valid hypothesis, to account for phenomena—the text—without distorting or misrepresenting what it describes.

THE LITERARY CANON: DIVERSITY AND CONTROVERSY

Before looking at the various critical approaches discussed in this chapter, it makes sense to consider first which literature has been traditionally considered worthy of such analysis. In recent years many more works by women, minorities, and writers from around the world have been considered by scholars, critics, and teachers to merit serious study and inclusion in what is known as the literary canon. This increasing diversity has been celebrated by those who believe that multiculturalism taps new sources for the discovery of great literature while raising significant questions about language, culture, and society. At the same time, others have perceived this diversity as a threat to the established, traditional canon of Western culture.

The debates concerning who should be read, taught, and written about have sometimes been acrimonious as well as lively and challenging. Bitter arguments have been waged recently on campuses and in the press over what has come to be called "political correctness." Two camps—roughly—have formed around these debates: liberals and conservatives (the appropriateness of these terms is debatable but the oppositional positioning is unmistakable). The liberals are said to insist upon politically correct views from colleagues and students opening up the curriculum to multicultural texts from Asia, Africa, Latin America, and elsewhere, and to encourage more informed attitudes about race, class, gender, and sexual orientation. These revisionists, seeking a change in traditional attitudes, are sometimes accused of intimidating the opposition into silence and substituting ideological dogma for reason and truth. The conservatives are also portrayed as ideologues; in their efforts to preserve what they regard as the best from the past, they refuse to admit that Western classics, mostly written by white male Europeans, represent only a portion of human experience. These traditionalists are seen as advocating values that are neither universal nor eternal but merely privileged and entrenched. Conservatives are charged with refusing to acknowledge that their values also represent a political agenda, which is implicit in their preference for the works of canonical authors such as Homer, Virgil, Shakespeare, Milton, Tolstoy, and Faulkner. The reductive and contradictory nature of this national debate between liberals and conservatives has been neatly summed up by Katha Pollitt: "Read the conservatives' list [of canonical works] and produce a nation of sexists and racists—or a nation of philosopher kings. Read the liberals' list and produce a nation of spiritual relativists—or a nation of open-minded world citizens" ("Canon to the Right of Me . . . ," *The Nation,* Sept. 23, 1991, p. 330).

These troubling and extreme alternatives can be avoided, of course, if the issues are not approached from such absolutist positions. Solutions to these issues cannot be suggested in this limited space, and, no doubt, solutions will evolve over time, but we can at least provide a perspective. Books— regardless of what list they are on—are not likely to unite a fragmented nation or to disunite a unified one. It is perhaps more useful and accurate to see issues of canonicity as reflecting political changes rather than being the primary causes of them. This is not to say that books don't have an impact on readers—*Uncle Tom's Cabin,* for instance, certainly galvanized antislavery sentiments in nineteenth-century America—but that book lists do not by themselves preserve or destroy the status quo.

It's worth noting that the curricula of American universities have always undergone significant and, some would say, wrenching changes. Only a little more than one hundred years ago there was strong opposition to teaching English, as well as other modern languages, alongside programs dominated by Greek and Latin. Only since the 1920s has American literature been made a part of the curriculum, and just five decades ago writers such as James Joyce, Virginia Woolf, Franz Kafka, and Ernest Hemingway were regarded with the same raised eyebrows that today might be raised about contemporary writers such as Gish Jen, Tim O'Brien, Rita Dove, or Fay Weldon. New voices do not drown out the past; they build on it, and eventually become part of the past as newer writers take their place alongside them. Neither resistance to change nor a denial of the past will have its way with the canon. Though both impulses are widespread, neither is likely to dominate the other, because there are too many reasonable, practical readers and teachers who instead of replacing Shakespeare, Melville, and other canonical writers have supplemented them with neglected writers from Western and other cultures. These readers experience the current debates about the canon not as a binary opposition but as an opportunity to explore important questions about continuity and change in our literature, culture, and society.

FORMALIST STRATEGIES

Formalist critics focus on the formal elements of a work—its language, structure, and tone. A formalist reads literature as an independent work of art rather than as a reflection of the author's state of mind or as a representation of a moment in history. Historic influences on a work, an author's intentions, or anything else outside the work are generally not treated by formalists (this is particularly true of the most famous modern formalists, known as the New Critics, who dominated American criticism from the 1940s through the 1960s). Instead, formalists offer intense examinations of the relationship between form and meaning within a work, emphasizing the subtle complexity of how a work is arranged. This kind of close reading pays special attention to what are often described as *intrinsic* matters in a literary work, such as diction, irony, paradox, metaphor, and symbol, as well as larger elements, such as plot, characterization, and narrative technique. Formalists examine how these elements work together to give a coherent shape to a work while contributing to its meaning. The answers to the questions formalists raise about how the shape and effect of a work are related come from the work itself. Other kinds of information that go beyond the text—biography, history, politics, economics, and so on—are typically regarded by formalists as *extrinsic* matters, which are considerably less important than what goes on within the autonomous text.

Poetry especially lends itself to close readings, because a poem's relative brevity allows for detailed analyses of nearly all its words and how they achieve their effects. For a student's formalist reading of how a pervasive sense of death is worked into a poem, see "A Reading of Dickinson's 'There's a certain Slant of light' " (p. 20).

Formalist strategies are also useful for analyzing drama and fiction. In his well-known essay "The World of *Hamlet*," Maynard Mack explores Hamlet's character and predicament by paying close attention to the words and images that Shakespeare uses to build a world in which appearances mask reality and mystery is embedded in scene after scene. Mack points to recurring terms, such as *apparition, seems, assume,* and *put on,* as well as repeated images of acting, clothing, disease, and painting, to indicate the treacherous surface world Hamlet must penetrate to get to the truth. This pattern of deception provides an organizing principle around which Mack offers a reading of the entire play:

> Hamlet's problem, in its crudest form, is simply the problem of the avenger: he must carry out the injunction of the ghost and kill the king. But this

problem . . . is presented in terms of a certain kind of world. The ghost's injunction to act becomes so inextricably bound up for Hamlet with the character of the world in which the action must be taken—its mysteriousness, its baffling appearances, its deep consciousness of infection, frailty, and loss—that he cannot come to terms with either without coming to terms with both.

Although Mack places *Hamlet* in the tradition of revenge tragedy, his reading of the play emphasizes Shakespeare's arrangement of language rather than literary history as a means of providing an interpretation that accounts for various elements of the play. Mack's formalist strategy explores how diction reveals meaning and how repeated words and images evoke and reinforce important thematic significances.

For an example of a work in which the shape of the plot serves as the major organizing principle, let's examine Kate Chopin's "The Story of an Hour" (p. 46), a two-page short story that takes only a few minutes to read. With the story fresh in your mind, consider how you might approach it from a formalist perspective. A first reading probably results in surprise at the story's ending: a grieving wife "afflicted with a heart trouble" suddenly dies of a heart attack, not because she's learned that her kind and loving husband has been killed in a terrible train accident but because she discovers that he is very much alive. Clearly, we are faced with an ironic situation since there is such a powerful incongruity between what is expected to happen and what actually happens. A likely formalist strategy for analyzing this story would be to raise questions about the ironic ending. Is this merely a trick ending, or is it a carefully wrought culmination of other elements in the story so that in addition to creating surprise the ending snaps the story shut on an interesting and challenging theme? Formalists value such complexities over simple surprise effects.

A second, closer reading indicates that Chopin's third-person narrator presents the story in a manner similar to Josephine's gentle attempts to break the news about Brently Mallard's death. The story is told in "veiled hints that [reveal] in half concealing." But unlike Josephine, who tries to protect her sister's fragile heart from stress, the narrator seeks to reveal Mrs. Mallard's complex heart. A formalist would look back over the story for signs of the ending in the imagery. Although Mrs. Mallard grieves immediately and unreservedly when she hears about the train disaster, she soon begins to feel a different emotion as she looks out the window at "the tops of trees . . . all aquiver with the new spring life." This symbolic evocation of renewal and rebirth—along with "the delicious breath of rain," the sounds of life in the street, and the birds singing—causes her to feel, in spite of her own efforts to repress her thoughts and emotions, "free, free, free!" She feels alive with a sense of possibility, with a "clear and exalted perception" that she "would live for herself" instead of for and through her husband.

It is ironic that this ecstatic "self-assertion" is interpreted by Josephine as grief, but the crowning irony for this "goddess of Victory" is the doctors' assumption that she dies of joy rather than of the shock of having to abandon her newly discovered self once she realizes her husband is still alive. In the course of an hour, Mrs. Mallard's life is irretrievably changed: her husband's assumed accidental death frees her, but the fact that he lives and all the expectations imposed on her by his continued life kill her. She does, indeed, die of a broken heart, but only Chopin's readers know the real ironic meaning of that explanation.

Although this brief discussion of some of the formal elements of Chopin's story does not describe all there is to say about how they produce an effect and create meaning, it does suggest the kinds of questions, issues, and evidence that a formalist strategy might raise in providing a close reading of the text itself.

BIOGRAPHICAL STRATEGIES

A knowledge of an author's life can help readers understand his or her work more fully. Events in a work might follow actual events in a writer's life just as characters might be based on people known by the author. Ernest Hemingway's "Soldier's Home" is a short story about the difficulties of a World War I veteran named Krebs returning to his small hometown in Oklahoma, where he cannot adjust to the pious assumptions of his family and neighbors. He refuses to accept their innocent blindness to the horrors he has witnessed during the war. They have no sense of the brutality of modern life; instead they insist he resume his life as if nothing has happened. There is plenty of biographical evidence to indicate that Krebs's unwillingness to lie about his war experiences reflects Hemingway's own responses upon his return to Oak Park, Illinois, in 1919. Krebs, like Hemingway, finds he has to leave the sentimentality, repressiveness, and smug complacency that threaten to render his experiences unreal: "the world they were in was not the world he was in."

An awareness of Hemingway's own war experiences and subsequent disillusionment with his hometown can be readily developed through available biographies, letters, and other works he wrote. Consider, for example, this passage from *By Force of Will: The Life and Art of Ernest Hemingway*, in which Scott Donaldson describes Hemingway's response to World War I:

In poems, as in [*A Farewell to Arms*], Hemingway expressed his distaste for the first war. The men who had to fight the war did not die well:

Soldiers pitch and cough and twitch—
    All the world roars red and black;
Soldiers smother in a ditch,
    Choking through the whole attack.

And what did they die for? They were "sucked in" by empty words and phrases—

King and country,
Christ Almighty,
And the rest,
Patriotism,
Democracy,
Honor —

which spelled death. The bitterness of these outbursts derived from
the distinction Hemingway drew between the men on the line and
those who started the wars that others had to fight.

This kind of information can help to deepen our understanding of just
how empathetically Krebs is presented in the story. Relevant facts about
Hemingway's life will not make "Soldier's Home" a better written story than
it is, but such information can make clearer the source of Hemingway's
convictions and how his own experiences inform his major concerns as a
storyteller.

Some formalist critics—some New Critics, for example—argue that
interpretation should be based exclusively on internal evidence rather than
on any biographical information outside the work. They argue that it is not
possible to determine an author's intention and that the work must stand by
itself. Although this is a useful caveat for keeping the work in focus, a reader
who finds biography relevant would argue that biography can at the very
least serve as a control on interpretation. A reader who, for example, finds
Krebs at fault for not subscribing to the values of his hometown would be
misreading the story, given both its tone and the biographical information
available about the author. Although the narrator never *tells* the reader that
Krebs is right or wrong for leaving town, the story's tone sides with his view
of things. If, however, someone were to argue otherwise, insisting that the
tone is not decisive and that Krebs's position is problematic, a reader familiar
with Hemingway's own reactions could refute that argument with a powerful
confirmation of Krebs's instincts to withdraw. Hence, many readers find
biography useful for interpretation.

However, it is also worth noting that biographical information can complicate a work. Chopin's "Story of an Hour" presents a repressed wife's
momentary discovery of what freedom from her husband might mean to
her. She awakens to a new sense of herself when she learns of her husband's
death, only to collapse of a heart attack when she sees that he is alive.
Readers might be tempted to interpret this story as Chopin's fictionalized
commentary about her own marriage, because her husband died twelve
years before she wrote the story and seven years before she began writing
fiction seriously. Biographers seem to agree, however, that Chopin's marriage
was evidently satisfying to her and that she was not oppressed by her husband
and did not feel oppressed.

Moreover, consider this diary entry from only one month after Chopin
wrote the story (quoted by Per Seyersted in *Kate Chopin: A Critical Biography*):

If it were possible for my husband and my mother to come back to earth, I feel that I would unhesitatingly give up everything that has come into my life since they left it and join my existence again with theirs. To do that, I would have to forget the past ten years of my growth—my real growth. But I would take back a little wisdom with me; it would be the spirit of perfect acquiescence.

This passage raises provocative questions instead of resolving them. How does that "spirit of perfect acquiescence" relate to Mrs. Mallard's insistence that she "would live for herself"? Why would Chopin be willing to "forget the past ten years of . . . growth" given her protagonist's desire for "self-assertion"? Although these and other questions raised by the diary entry cannot be answered here, this kind of biographical perspective certainly adds to the possibilities of interpretation.

Sometimes biographical information does not change our understanding so much as it enriches our appreciation of a work. It matters, for instance, that much of John Milton's poetry, so rich in visual imagery, was written after he became blind; and it is just as significant—to shift to a musical example—that a number of Ludwig van Beethoven's greatest works, including the Ninth Symphony, were composed after he succumbed to total deafness.

PSYCHOLOGICAL STRATEGIES

Given the enormous influence that Sigmund Freud's psychoanalytic theories have had on twentieth-century interpretations of human behavior, it is nearly inevitable that most people have some familiarity with his ideas concerning dreams, unconscious desires, and sexual repression, as well as his terms for different aspects of the psyche—the id, ego, and superego. Psychological approaches to literature draw upon Freud's theories and other psychoanalytic theories to understand more fully the text, the writer, and the reader. Critics use such approaches to explore the motivations of characters and the symbolic meanings of events, while biographers speculate about a writer's own motivations—conscious or unconscious—in a literary work. Psychological approaches are also used to describe and analyze the reader's personal responses to a text.

Although it is not feasible to explain psychoanalytic terms and concepts in so brief a space as this, it is possible to suggest the nature of a psychological approach. It is a strategy based heavily on the idea of the existence of a human unconscious—those impulses, desires, and feelings about which a person is unaware but which influence emotions and behavior.

Central to a number of psychoanalytic critical readings is Freud's concept of what he called the Oedipus complex, a term derived from Sophocles' tragedy *Oedipus the King*. This complex is predicated on a boy's unconscious rivalry with his father for his mother's love and his desire to eliminate his father in order to take his father's place with his mother. The female version of the psychological conflict is known as the Electra complex, a term used to describe a daughter's unconscious rivalry for her father. The name comes from a Greek legend about Electra, who avenged the death of her father, Agamemnon, by killing her mother. In *The Interpretation of Dreams,* Freud explains why *Oedipus the King* "moves a modern audience no less than it did the contemporary Greek one." What unites their powerful attraction to the play is an unconscious response:

> There must be something which makes a voice within us ready to recognize the compelling force of destiny in the *Oedipus.* . . . His destiny moves us only because it might have been ours—because the oracle laid the same curse upon us before our birth as upon him. It is the fate of all of us, perhaps, to direct our first sexual impulse towards our mother and our first hatred and our first murderous wish against our father. Our dreams convince us that this is so. King Oedipus, who slew his father Laius and married his mother Jocasta, merely shows us the fulfillment of our own childhood wishes . . . and we shrink back from him with the whole force of the repression by which those wishes have since that time been held down within us.

In this passage Freud interprets the unconscious motives of Sophocles in writing the play, Oedipus in acting within it, and the audience in responding to it.

A further application of the Oedipus complex can be observed in a classic interpretation of *Hamlet* by Ernest Jones, who used this concept to explain why Hamlet delays in avenging his father's death. This reading has been tightly summarized by Norman Holland, a recent psychoanalytic critic, in *The Shakespearean Imagination.* Holland shapes the issues into four major components:

> One, people over the centuries have been unable to say why Hamlet delays in killing the man who murdered his father and married his mother. Two, psychoanalytic experience shows that every child wants to do just exactly that. Three, Hamlet delays because he cannot punish Claudius for doing what he himself wished to do as a child and, unconsciously, still wishes to do: he would be punishing himself. Four, the fact that this wish is unconscious explains why people could not explain Hamlet's delay.

Although the Oedipus complex is, of course, not relevant to all psychological interpretations of literature, interpretations involving this complex do offer a useful example of how psychoanalytic critics tend to approach a text.

The situation in which Mrs. Mallard finds herself in Chopin's "The Story of an Hour" is not related to an Oedipus complex, but it is clear that news of her husband's death has released powerful unconscious desires for freedom that she had previously suppressed. As she grieved, "something" was "coming to her and she was waiting for it, fearfully." What comes to her is what she senses about the life outside her window; that's the stimulus, but the true source of what was to "possess her," which she strove to "beat . . . back with her [conscious] will" is her desperate desire for the autonomy and fulfillment she had been unable to admit did not exist in her marriage. A psychological approach to her story amounts to a case study in the destructive nature of self-repression. Moreover, the story might reflect Chopin's own views of her marriage—despite her conscious statements about her loving husband. And what about the reader's response? How might a psychological approach account for different responses in female and male readers to Mrs. Mallard's death? One needn't be versed in psychoanalytic terms to entertain this question.

HISTORICAL STRATEGIES

Historians sometimes use literature as a window onto the past, because literature frequently provides the nuances of an historic period that cannot be readily perceived through other sources. The characters in Harriet Beecher Stowe's *Uncle Tom's Cabin* (1852) display, for example, a complex set of white attitudes toward blacks in mid-nineteenth-century America that is absent from more traditional historic documents, such as census statistics or state laws. Another way of approaching the relationship between literature and history, however, is to use history as a means of understanding a literary work more clearly. The plot pattern of pursuit, escape, and capture in nineteenth-century slave narratives had a significant influence on Stowe's plotting of action in *Uncle Tom's Cabin*. This relationship demonstrates that the writing contemporary to an author is an important element of the history that helps to shape a work.

Literary historians shift the emphasis from the period to the work. Hence a literary historian might also examine mid-nineteenth-century abolitionist attitudes toward blacks to determine whether Stowe's novel is representative of those views or significantly to the right or left of them. Such a study might even indicate how closely the book reflects racial attitudes of twentieth-century readers. A work of literature may transcend time to the extent that it addresses the concerns of readers over a span of decades or centuries, but it remains for the literary historian a part of the past in which it was composed, a past that can reveal more fully a work's language, ideas, and purposes.

Literary historians move beyond both the facts of an author's personal life and the text itself to the social and intellectual currents in which the author composed the work. They place the work in the context of its time (as do many critical biographers, who write "life and times" studies), and sometimes they make connections with other literary works that may have influenced the author. The basic strategy of literary historians is to illuminate the historic background in order to shed light on some aspect of the work itself.

In Hemingway's "Soldier's Home" we learn that Krebs had been at Belleau Wood, Soissons, the Champagne, St. Mihiel, and the Argonne. Although nothing is said of these battles in the story, they were among the most bloody battles of the war; the wholesale butchery and staggering casualties incurred by both sides make credible the way Krebs's unstated but lingering memories have turned him into a psychological prisoner of war. Knowing something about the ferocity of those battles helps us account for Krebs's response in the story. Moreover, we can more fully appreciate Hemingway's refusal to have Krebs lie about the realities of war for the folks back home if we are aware of the numerous poems, stories, and plays published during World War I that presented war as a glorious, manly, transcendent sacrifice for God and country. Juxtaposing those works with "Soldier's Home" brings the differences into sharp focus.

Similarly, a reading of William Blake's poem "London" is less complete if we do not know of the horrific social conditions—the poverty, disease, exploitation, and hypocrisy—that characterized the city Blake laments in the late eighteenth century.

One last example: The repression expressed in the lines on Mrs. Mallard's face is more distinctly seen if Chopin's "The Story of an Hour" is placed in the context of "the women's question" as it continued to develop in the 1890s. Mrs. Mallard's impulse toward "self-assertion" runs parallel with a growing women's movement away from the role of long-suffering housewife. This desire was widely regarded by traditionalists as a form of dangerous selfishness that was considered as unnatural as it was immoral. It is no wonder that Chopin raises the question of whether Mrs. Mallard's sense of freedom owing to her husband's death isn't a selfish, "monstrous joy." Mrs. Mallard, however, dismisses this question as "trivial" in the face of her new perception of life, a dismissal that Chopin endorses by way of the story's ironic ending. The larger social context of this story would have been more apparent to Chopin's readers in 1894 than it is to readers in the 1990s. That is why an historical reconstruction of the limitations placed on married women helps to explain the pressures, tensions, and momentary—only momentary—release that Mrs. Mallard experiences.

Since the 1960s a development in historical approaches to literature known as New Historicism has emphasized the interaction between the historic context of a work and a modern reader's understanding and interpretation of the work. In contrast to many traditional literary historians, however, New Historicists attempt to describe the culture of a period by reading many different kinds of texts that traditional historians might have previously left for sociologists and anthropologists. New Historicists attempt to read a period in all its dimensions, including political, economic, social, and aesthetic concerns. These considerations could be used to explain the pressures that destroy Mrs. Mallard. A New Historicist might examine not only the story and the public attitudes toward women contemporary to "The Story of an Hour" but also documents such as suffragette tracts and medical diagnoses in order to explore how the same forces—expectations about how women are supposed to feel, think, and behave—shape different kinds of texts and how these texts influence each other. A New Historicist might, for example, examine medical records for evidence of "nervousness" and "hysteria" as common diagnoses for women who led lives regarded as too independent by their contemporaries.

Without an awareness of just how selfish and self-destructive Mrs. Mallard's impulses would have been in the eyes of her contemporaries, twentieth-century readers might miss the pervasive pressures embedded not only in her marriage but in the social fabric surrounding her. Her death is made more understandable by such an awareness. The doctors who diagnose her as suffering from "the joy that kills" are not merely insensitive or stupid; they represent a contrasting set of assumptions and values that are as historic and real as Mrs. Mallard's yearnings.

New Historicist criticism acknowledges more fully than traditional historical approaches the competing nature of readings of the past and thereby tends to offer new emphases and perspectives. New Historicism reminds us that there is not only one historic context for "The Story of an Hour." Those doctors reveal additional dimensions of late-nineteenth-century social attitudes that warrant our attention, whether we agree with them or not. By emphasizing that historical perceptions are governed, at least in part, by our own concerns and preoccupations, New Historicists sensitize us to the fact that the history on which we choose to focus is colored by being reconstructed from our own present moment. This reconstructed history affects our reading of texts.

SOCIOLOGICAL STRATEGIES, INCLUDING MARXIST AND FEMINIST STRATEGIES

Sociological approaches examine social groups, relationships, and values as they are manifested in literature. These approaches necessarily overlap historical analyses, but sociological approaches to a work emphasize more specifically the nature and effect of the social forces that shape power relationships between groups or classes of people. Such readings treat literature as either a document reflecting social conditions or a product of those conditions. The former view brings into focus the social milieu; the latter emphasizes the work. A sociological reading of Arthur Miller's *Death of a Salesman* might, for instance, discuss how the characters' efforts to succeed reflect an increasingly competitive twentieth-century urban sensibility in America. Or it might emphasize how the "American Dream" of success shapes Willy Loman's aspirations and behavior. Clearly, there are numerous ways to talk about the societal aspects of a work. Two sociological strategies that have been especially influential are Marxist and feminist approaches.

Marxist Criticism

Marxist readings developed from the heightened interest in radical reform during the 1930s, when many critics looked to literature as a means of furthering proletarian social and economic goals, based largely on the writings of Karl Marx. Marxist critics focus on the ideological content of a work—its explicit and implicit assumptions and values about matters such as culture, race, class, and power. Marxist studies typically aim at not only revealing and clarifying ideological issues but also correcting social injustices. Some Marxist critics have used literature to describe the competing socioeconomic interests that too often advance capitalist money and power rather than socialist morality and justice. They argue that criticism, like literature, is essentially political because it either challenges or supports economic oppression. Even if criticism attempts to ignore class conflicts, it is politicized, according to Marxists, because it supports the status quo.

It is not surprising that Marxist critics pay more attention to the content and themes of literature than to its form. A Marxist critic would more likely be concerned with the exploitive economic forces that cause Willy Loman to feel trapped in Miller's *Death of a Salesman* than with the playwright's use of nonrealistic dramatic techniques to reveal Loman's inner thoughts. Similarly, a Marxist reading of Chopin's "The Story of an Hour" might draw on the evidence made available in a book published only a few years after the story by Charlotte Perkins Gilman titled *Women and Economics: A Study of the Economic Relation between Men and Women as a Factor in Social Evolution* (1898). An examination of this study could help explain how some of the "repression" Mrs. Mallard experiences was generated by the socioeconomic structure contemporary to her and how Chopin challenges the validity of that structure by having Mrs. Mallard resist it with her very life. A Marxist reading would see the protagonist's conflict as not only an individual issue but part of a larger class struggle.

Feminist Criticism

Feminist critics would also be interested in Gilman's study of *Women and Economics,* because they seek to correct or supplement what they regard as a predominantly male-dominated critical perspective with a feminine consciousness. Like other forms of sociological criticism, feminist criticism places literature in a social context, and, like those of Marxist criticism, its analyses often have sociopolitical purposes, purposes that might explain, for example, how images of women in literature reflect the patriarchal social forces that have impeded women's efforts to achieve full equality with men.

Feminists have analyzed literature by both men and women in an effort to understand literary representations of women as well as the writers and cultures that create them. Related to concerns about how gender affects the way men and women write about each other is an interest in whether women use language differently from the way men do. Consequently, feminist critics' approach to literature is characterized by the use of a broad range of disciplines, including history, sociology, psychology, and linguistics, to provide a perspective sensitive to feminist issues.

A feminist approach to Chopin's "The Story of an Hour" might explore the psychological stress created by the expectations that marriage imposes on Mrs. Mallard, expectations that literally and figuratively break her heart. Given that her husband is kind and loving, the issue is not her being married to Brently but her being married at all. Chopin presents marriage as an institution that creates in both men and women the assumed "right to impose a private will upon a fellow-creature." That "right," however, is seen, especially from a feminist perspective, as primarily imposed on women by men. A feminist critic might note, for instance, that the protagonist is introduced as "Mrs. Mallard" (we learn that her first name is Louise only later); she is defined by her marital status and her husband's name, a name whose origin from the Old French is related to the word *masle*, which means "male." The appropriateness of her name points up the fact that her emotions and the cause of her death are interpreted in male terms by the doctors. The value of a feminist perspective on this work can be readily discerned if a reader imagines Mrs. Mallard's story being told from the point of view of one of the doctors who diagnoses the cause of her death as a weak heart rather than as a fierce struggle.

MYTHOLOGICAL STRATEGIES

Mythological approaches to literature attempt to identify what in a work creates deep universal responses in readers. Whereas psychological critics interpret the symbolic meanings of characters and actions in order to understand more fully the unconscious dimensions of an author's mind, a character's motivation, or a reader's response, mythological critics (also frequently referred to as archetypal critics) interpret the hopes, fears, and expectations of entire cultures.

In this context myth is not to be understood simply as referring to stories about imaginary gods who perform astonishing feats in the causes of love, jealousy, or hatred. Nor are myths to be judged as merely erroneous, primitive accounts of how nature runs its course and humanity its affairs. Instead, literary critics use myths as a strategy for understanding how human beings try to account for their lives symbolically. Myths can be a window onto a culture's deepest perceptions about itself, because myths attempt to explain what otherwise seems unexplainable: a people's origin, purpose, and destiny.

All human beings have a need to make sense of their lives, whether they are concerned about their natural surroundings, the seasons, sexuality, birth, death, or the very meaning of existence. Myths help people organize their experiences; these systems of belief (less formally held than religious or political tenets but no less important) embody a culture's assumptions and values. What is important to the mythological critic is not the validity or truth of those assumptions and values; what matters is that they reveal common human concerns.

It is not surprising that although the details of mythic stories vary enormously, the essential patterns are often similar, because these myths attempt to explain universal experiences. There are, for example, numerous myths that redeem humanity from permanent death through a hero's resurrection and rebirth. The resurrection of Jesus for Christians symbolizes the ultimate defeat of death and coincides with the rebirth of nature's fertility in spring. Features of this rebirth parallel the Greek myths of Adonis and Hyacinth, who die but are subsequently transformed into living flowers; there are also similarities that connect these stories to the reincarnation of the Indian Buddha or the rebirth of the Egyptian Osiris. To be sure, important differences exist among these stories, but each reflects a basic human need to limit the power of death and to hope for eternal life.

Mythological critics look for underlying, recurrent patterns in literature that reveal universal meanings and basic human experiences for readers regardless of when or where they live. The characters, images, and themes that symbolically embody these meanings and experiences are called archetypes. This term designates universal symbols, which evoke deep and perhaps unconscious responses in a reader because archetypes bring with them the heft of our hopes and fears since the beginning of human time. Surely one of the most powerfully compelling archetypes is the death/rebirth theme that relates the human life cycle to the cycle of the seasons. Many others could be cited and would be exhausted only after all human concerns were catalogued, but a few examples can suggest some of the range of plots, images, and characters addressed.

Among the most common literary archetypes are stories of quests, initiations, scapegoats, meditative withdrawals, descents to the underworld, and heavenly ascents. These stories are often filled with archetypal images: bodies of water that may symbolize the unconscious or eternity or baptismal rebirth; rising suns, suggesting reawakening and enlightenment; setting suns, pointing toward death; colors such as green, evocative of growth and fertility, or black, indicating chaos, evil, and death. Along the way are earth mothers, fatal women, wise old men, desert places, and paradisal gardens. No doubt your own reading has introduced you to any number of archetypal plots, images, and characters.

Mythological critics attempt to explain how archetypes are embodied in literary works. Employing various disciplines, these critics articulate the power a literary work has over us. Some critics are deeply grounded in classical literature, whereas others are more conversant with philology, anthropology, psychology, or cultural history. Whatever their emphases, however, mythological critics examine the elements of a work in order to make larger connections that explain the work's lasting appeal.

A mythological reading of Sophocles' *Oedipus the King,* for example, might focus on the relationship between Oedipus's role as a scapegoat and the plague and drought that threaten to destroy Thebes. The city is saved and the fertility of its fields restored only after the corruption is located in Oedipus. His subsequent atonement symbolically provides a kind of rebirth for the city. Thus, the plot recapitulates ancient rites in which the well-being of a king was directly linked to the welfare of his people. If a leader were sick or corrupt, he had to be replaced in order to guarantee the health of the community.

A similar pattern can be seen in the rottenness that Shakespeare exposes in Hamlet's Denmark. *Hamlet* reveals an archetypal pattern similar to that of *Oedipus the King:* not until the hero sorts out the corruption in his world and in himself can vitality and health be restored in his world. Hamlet avenges his father's death and becomes a scapegoat in the process. When he fully accepts his responsibility to set things right, he is swept away along with the tide of intrigue and corruption that has polluted life in Denmark. The new order—established by Fortinbras at the play's end—is achieved precisely because Hamlet is willing and finally able to sacrifice himself in a necessary purgation of the diseased state.

These kinds of archetypal patterns exist potentially in any literary period. Consider how in Chopin's "The Story of an Hour" Mrs. Mallard's life parallels the end of winter and the earth's renewal in spring. When she feels a surge of new life after grieving over her husband's death, her own sensibilities are closely aligned with the "new spring life" that is "all aquiver" outside her window. Although she initially tries to resist that renewal by "beat[ing] it back with her will," she cannot control the life force that surges within her and all around her. When she finally gives herself to the energy and life she experiences, she feels triumphant—like a "goddess of Victory." But this victory is short-lived when she learns that her husband is still alive and with him all the obligations that made her marriage feel like a wasteland. Her death is an ironic version of a rebirth ritual. The coming of spring is an ironic contrast to her own discovery that she can no longer live a repressed, circumscribed life with her husband. Death turns out to be preferable to the living death that her marriage means to her. Although spring will go on, this "goddess of Victory" is defeated by a devastating social contract. The old, corrupt order continues, and that for Chopin is a cruel irony that mythological critics would see as an unnatural disruption of the nature of things.

READER-RESPONSE STRATEGIES

Reader-response criticism, as its name implies, focuses its attention on the reader rather than the work itself. This approach to literature describes what goes on in the reader's mind during the process of reading a text. In a sense, all critical approaches (especially psychological and mythological criticism) concern themselves with a reader's response to literature, but there is a stronger emphasis in reader-response criticism on the reader's active construction of the text. Although many critical theories inform reader-response criticism, all reader-response critics aim to describe the reader's experience of a work: in effect we get a reading of the reader, who comes to the work with certain expectations and assumptions, which are either met or not met. Hence the consciousness of the reader—produced by reading the work—is the subject matter of reader-response critics. Just as writing is a creative act, reading is, since it also produces a text.

Reader-response critics do not assume that a literary work is a finished product with fixed formal properties, as, for example, formalist critics do. Instead, the literary work is seen as an evolving creation of the reader's as he or she processes characters, plots, images, and other elements while reading. Some reader-response critics argue that this act of creative reading is, to a degree, controlled by the text, but it can produce many interpretations of the same text by different readers. There is no single definitive reading of a work, because the crucial assumption is that readers create rather than discover meanings in texts. Readers who have gone back to works they had read earlier in their lives often find that a later reading draws very different responses from them. What earlier seemed unimportant is now crucial; what at first seemed central is now barely worth noting. The reason, put simply, is that two different people have read the same text. Reader-response critics are not after the "correct" reading of the text or what the author presumably intended; instead they are interested in the reader's experience with the text.

These experiences change with readers; although the text remains the same, the readers do not. Social and cultural values influence readings, so that, for example, an avowed Marxist would be likely to come away from Miller's *Death of a Salesman* with a very different view of American capitalism than that of, say, a successful sales representative, who might attribute Willy Loman's fall more to his character than to the American economic system. Moreover, readers from different time periods respond differently to texts. An Elizabethan—concerned perhaps with the stability of monarchical rule— might respond differently to Hamlet's problems than would a twentieth-century reader well versed in psychology and concepts of what Freud called the Oedipus complex. This is not to say that anything goes, that Miller's play can be read as an amoral defense of cheating and rapacious business practices or that *Hamlet* is about the dangers of living away from home. The text does, after all, establish some limits that allow us to reject certain readings as erroneous. But reader-response critics do reject formalist approaches that describe a literary work as a self-contained object, the meaning of which can be determined without reference to any extrinsic matters, such as the social and cultural values assumed by either the author or the reader.

Reader-response criticism calls attention to how we read and what influences our readings. It does not attempt to define what a literary work means on the page but rather what it does to an informed reader, a reader who understands the language and conventions used in a given work. Reader-response criticism is not a rationale for mistaken or bizarre readings of works but an exploration of the possibilities for a plurality of readings shaped by the readers' experience with the text. This kind of strategy can help us understand how our responses are shaped by both the text and ourselves.

Chopin's "The Story of an Hour" illustrates how reader-response critical strategies read the reader. Chopin doesn't say that Mrs. Mallard's marriage is repressive; instead, that troubling fact dawns on the reader at the same time that the recognition forces its way into Mrs. Mallard's consciousness. Her surprise is also the reader's, because although she remains in the midst of intense grief, she is on the threshold of a startling discovery about the new possibilities life offers. How the reader responds to that discovery, however, is not entirely controlled by Chopin. One reader, perhaps someone who has recently lost a spouse, might find Mrs. Mallard's "joy" indeed "monstrous" and selfish. Certainly that's how Mrs. Mallard's doctors—the seemingly authoritative diagnosticians in the story—would very likely read her. But for other readers—especially late-twentieth-century readers steeped in feminist values—Mrs. Mallard's feelings require no justification. Such readers might find Chopin's ending to the story more ironic than she seems to have intended, because Mrs. Mallard's death could be read as Chopin's inability to envision a protagonist who has the strength of her convictions. In contrast, a reader in 1894 might have seen the ending as Mrs. Mallard's only escape from the repressive marriage her husband's assumed death suddenly allowed her to see. A late-twentieth-century reader probably would argue that it was the marriage that should have died rather than Mrs. Mallard, that she had other alternatives, not just obligations (as the doctors would have insisted), to consider.

By imagining different readers we can imagine a variety of responses to the story that are influenced by the readers' own impressions, memories, or experiences with marriage. Such imagining suggests the ways in which reader-response criticism opens up texts to a number of interpretations. As one final example, consider how readers' responses to "The Story of an Hour" would be affected if it were printed in two different magazines, read in the context of either *Ms.* or *Good Housekeeping*. What assumptions and beliefs would each magazine's readership be likely to bring to the story? How do you think the respective experiences and values of each magazine's readers would influence their readings? (For a student's reader-response approach to "The Story of an Hour," see the sample paper on p. 133.)

DECONSTRUCTIONIST STRATEGIES

Deconstructionist critics insist that literary works do not yield fixed, single meanings. They argue that there can be no absolute knowledge about anything because language can never say what we intend it to mean. Anything we write conveys meanings we did not intend, so the deconstructionist argument goes. Language is not a precise instrument but a power whose meanings are caught in an endless web of possibilities that cannot be limited or reduced to a single strand of meaning. Accordingly, any idea or statement that insists on being understood separately can ultimately be "deconstructed" to reveal its relations and connections to contradictory and opposite meanings.

Unlike other forms of criticism, deconstructionism seeks to destabilize meanings instead of establishing them. In contrast to formalists such as the New Critics, who closely examine a work in order to call attention to how its various components interact to establish a unified whole, deconstructionists try to show how a close examination of the language in a text inevitably reveals conflicting, contradictory impulses that "deconstruct" or break down its apparent unity.

Although deconstructionists and New Critics both examine the language of a text closely, deconstructionists focus on the gaps and ambiguities that reveal a text's instability and indeterminacy, whereas New Critics look for patterns that explain how the text's fixed meaning is structured. Deconstructionists painstakingly examine the competing meanings within the text rather than attempting to resolve them into a unified whole.

The questions deconstructionists ask are aimed at discovering and describing how a variety of possible readings are generated by the elements of a text. In contrast to a New Critic's concerns about the ultimate meaning of a work, a deconstructionist is primarily interested in how the use of language—diction, tone, metaphor, symbol, and so on—yields only provisional, not definitive, meanings. Consider, for example, the following excerpt from an American Puritan poet, Anne Bradstreet. The excerpt is from "The Flesh and the Spirit" (1678), which consists of an allegorical debate between two sisters, the body and the soul. During the course of the debate, Flesh, a consummate materialist, insists that Spirit values ideas that do not exist and that her faith in idealism is both unwarranted and insubstantial in the face of the material values that earth has to offer—riches, fame, and physical pleasure. Spirit, however, rejects the materialistic worldly argument that the only ultimate reality is physical reality and pledges her faith in God:

> Mine eye doth pierce the heavens and see
> What is invisible to thee.
> My garments are not silk nor gold,
> Nor such like trash which earth doth hold,
> But royal robes I shall have on,   5
> More glorious than the glist'ring sun;
> My crown not diamonds, pearls, and gold,
> But such as angels' heads enfold
> The city where I hope to dwell,
> There's none on earth can parallel;   10
> The stately walls both high and strong,
> Are made of precious jasper stone;

The gates of pearl, both rich and clear,
And angels are for porters there;
The streets thereof transparent gold,   15
Such as no eye did e'er behold;
A crystal river there doth run,
Which doth proceed from the Lamb's throne.

A deconstructionist would point out that Spirit's language—her use of
material images such as jasper stone, pearl, gold, and crystal—cancels
the explicit meaning of the passage by offering a supermaterialistic reward
to the spiritually faithful. Her language, in short, deconstructs her intended
meaning by employing the same images that Flesh would use to describe
the rewards of the physical world. A deconstructionist reading, then,
reveals the impossibility of talking about the invisible and spiritual worlds
without using materialistic (that is, metaphoric) language. Thus Spirit's
very language demonstrates a contradiction and conflict in her conviction
that the world of here and now must be rejected for the hereafter. Her
language deconstructs her meaning.

Deconstructionists look for ways to question and extend the meanings
of a text. A deconstructionist might find, for example, the ironic ending of
Chopin's "The Story of an Hour" less tidy and conclusive than would a New
Critic, who might attribute Mrs. Mallard's death to her sense of lost personal
freedom. A deconstructionist might use the story's ending to suggest that
the narrative shares the doctors' inability to imagine a life for Mrs. Mallard
apart from her husband.

As difficult as it is controversial, deconstructionism is not easily summarized or paraphrased. For an example of deconstructionism in practice and
how it differs from New Criticism, see Andrew P. Debicki's "New Criticism
and Deconstructionism: Two Attitudes in Teaching Poetry" in "Perspectives
on Critical Reading," (p. 122).

SELECTED BIBLIOGRAPHY

Canonical Issues

"The Changing Culture of the University." Special Issue. *Partisan Review*
58 (Spring 1991): 185–410.
Gates, Henry Louis, Jr. *The Signifying Monkey*. New York: Oxford UP,
1988.
Lauter, Paul. *Canons and Contexts*. New York: Oxford UP, 1991.
"The Politics of Liberal Education." Special Issue. *South Atlantic Quar-
terly* 89 (Winter 1990): 1–234.
Sykes, Charles J. *The Hollow Men: Politics and Corruption in Higher
Education*. Washington, D.C.: Regnery Gateway, 1990.

Formalist Strategies

Brooks, Cleanth. *The Well Wrought Urn: Studies in the Structure of Poetry.* New York: Reynal and Hitchcock, 1947.

Crane, Ronald Salmon. *The Languages of Criticism and the Structure of Poetry.* Toronto: U of Toronto P, 1953.

Eliot, Thomas Stearns. *The Sacred Wood: Essays in Poetry and Criticism.* London: Methuen, 1920.

Fekete, John. *The Critical Twilight: Explorations in the Ideology of Anglo-American Literary Theory from Eliot to McLuhan.* London: Routledge, 1977.

Lemon, Lee T., and Marion J. Reis, eds. *Russian Formalist Criticism: Four Essays.* Lincoln: U of Nebraska P, 1965.

Ransom, John Crowe. *The New Criticism.* Norfolk, CT: New Directions, 1941.

Wellek, Rene, and Austin Warren. *Theory of Literature.* New York: Harcourt, Brace and World, 1949.

Biographical and Psychological Strategies

Bleich, David. *Subjective Criticism.* Baltimore: Johns Hopkins UP, 1978.

Bloom, Harold. *The Anxiety of Influence.* New York: Oxford UP, 1975.

Crews, Frederick. *Out of My System: Psychoanalysis, Ideology, and Critical Method.* New York: Oxford UP, 1975.

———. *The Sins of the Fathers: Hawthorne's Psychological Themes.* New York: Oxford UP, 1966.

Felman, Shoshana. *Writing and Madness (Literature/Philosophy/Psychoanalysis).* Ithaca: Cornell UP, 1985.

Felman, Shoshana, ed. *Literature and Psychoanalysis: The Question of Reading: Otherwise.* Baltimore: Johns Hopkins UP, 1981.

Freud, Sigmund. *The Standard Edition of the Complete Psychological Works.* 24 vols. 1940–1968. London: Hogarth Press and the Institute of Psychoanalysis, 1953.

Holland, Norman. *The Dynamics of Literary Response.* New York: Oxford UP, 1968.

Jones, Ernest. *Hamlet and Oedipus.* New York: Doubleday, 1949.

Lacan, Jacques. *Écrits: A Selection.* Trans. Alan Sheridan. New York: Norton, 1977.

———. *The Four Fundamental Concepts of Psychoanalysis.* Trans. Alan Sheridan. London: Penguin, 1980.

Lesser, Simon O. *Fiction and the Unconscious.* Chicago: U of Chicago P, 1957.

Skura, Meredith Anne. *The Literary Use of the Psychoanalytic Process.* New Haven: Yale UP, 1981.

Weiss, Daniel. *The Critic Agonistes: Psychology, Myth, and the Art of Fiction.* Ed. Stephen Arkin and Eric Solomon. Seattle: U of Washington P, 1985.

Historical and New Historicist Strategies

Armstrong, Nancy. *Desire and Domestic Fiction*. New York: Oxford UP, 1987.

Dollimore, Jonathan. *Radical Tragedy: Religion, Ideology and Power in the Drama of Shakespeare and His Contemporaries*. Brighton, Eng.: Harvester Press, 1984.

Geertz, Clifford. *The Interpretation of Cultures: Selected Essays*. New York: Basic Books, 1973.

Greenblatt, Stephen. *Renaissance Self-Fashioning: From More to Shakespeare*. Chicago: U of Chicago P, 1980.

———. *Shakespearean Negotiations: The Circulation of Social Energy in Renaissance England*. Berkeley: U of California P, 1985.

Lindenberger, Herbert. *Historical Drama: The Relation of Literature and Reality*. Chicago: U of Chicago P, 1975.

McGann, Jerome. *The Beauty of Inflections: Literary Investigations in Historical Method and Theory*. Oxford: Clarendon P, 1985.

Tennenhouse, Leonard. *Power on Display: The Politics of Shakespeare's Genres*. New York: Methuen, 1986.

White, Hayden. *Tropics of Discourse: Essays in Cultural Criticism*. Baltimore: Johns Hopkins UP, 1978.

Sociological Strategies (Including Marxist and Feminist Strategies)

Adorno, Theodor. *Prisms: Cultural Criticism and Society*. 1955. London: Neville Spearman, 1967.

Beauvoir, Simone de. *The Second Sex*. Trans. H. M. Parshley. New York: Knopf, 1972. Trans. of *Le deuxième sexe*. Paris: Gallimard, 1949.

Benjamin, Walter. *Illuminations*. New York: Harcourt, Brace and World, 1968.

Benstock, Shari, ed. *Feminist Issues and Literary Scholarship*. Bloomington: Indiana UP, 1987.

Cixous, Hélène, and Catherine Clément. *The Newly Born Woman*. Trans. Betsy Wing. Minneapolis: U of Minnesota P, 1986.

Eagleton, Terry. *Criticism and Ideology: A Study in Marxist Literary Theory*. London: New Left Books, 1976.

Fetterley, Judith. *The Resisting Reader: A Feminist Approach to American Fiction*. Bloomington: Indiana UP, 1978.

Frow, John. *Marxist and Literary History*. Cambridge: Harvard UP, 1986.

Gilbert, Sandra M., and Susan Gubar. *The Madwoman in the Attic: The Woman Writer and the Nineteenth-Century Literary Imagination*. New Haven: Yale UP, 1979.

Irigaray, Luce. *This Sex Which Is Not One*. Ithaca: Cornell UP, 1985. Trans. of *Ce sexe qui n'en est pas un*. Paris: Éditions de Minuit, 1977.

Jameson, Fredric. *The Political Unconscious: Studies in the Ideology of Form*. Ithaca: Cornell UP, 1979.

Kolodny, Annette. "Some Notes on Defining a 'Feminist Literary Criticism.' " *Critical Inquiry* 2 (1975): 75–92.

Lukács, Georg. *Realism in Our Time: Literature and the Class Struggle*. 1957. New York: Harper and Row, 1964.

Marx, Karl, and Friedrich Engels. *Marx and Engels on Literature and Art*. St. Louis: Telos, 1973.

Millet, Kate. *Sexual Politics*. New York: Avon, 1970.

Showalter, Elaine. *A Literature of Their Own: British Women Novelists from Brontë to Lessing*. Princeton: Princeton UP, 1977.

Smith, Barbara. *Toward a Black Feminist Criticism*. New York: Out and Out, 1977.

Trotsky, Leon. *Literature and the Revolution*. 1924. Ann Arbor: U of Michigan P, 1960.

Williams, Raymond. *Marxism and Literature*. Oxford: Oxford UP, 1977.

Mythological Strategies

Bodkin, Maud. *Archetypal Patterns in Poetry*. London: Oxford UP, 1934.

Frye, Northrop. *Anatomy of Criticism: Four Essays*. Princeton: Princeton UP, 1957.

Jung, Carl Gustav. *Complete Works*. Eds. Herbert Read, Michael Fordham, and Gerhard Adler. 17 vols. New York: Pantheon, 1953–.

Reader-Response Strategies

Booth, Wayne, C. *The Rhetoric of Fiction*. 2nd ed. Chicago: U of Chicago P, 1983.

Eco, Umberto. *The Role of the Reader: Explorations in the Semiotics of Texts*. Bloomington: Indiana UP, 1979.

Escarpit, Robert. *Sociology of Literature*. Painesville, Ohio: Lake Erie College P, 1965.

Fish, Stanley. *Is There a Text in This Class? The Authority of Interpretive Communities*. Cambridge: Harvard UP, 1980.

Freund, Elizabeth. *The Return of the Reader: Reader-Response Criticism*. London: Methuen, 1987.

Holland, Norman N. *5 Readers Reading*. New Haven: Yale UP, 1975.

Iser, Wolfgang. *The Implied Reader: Patterns of Communication in Prose Fiction from Bunyan to Beckett*. Baltimore: Johns Hopkins UP, 1974.

Jauss, Hans Robert. "Literary History as a Challenge to Literary Theory." *Toward an Aesthetics of Reception*. Trans. Timothy Bahti. Minneapolis: U of Minnesota P, 1982. Pp. 3–46.

Rosenblatt, Louise. *Literature as Exploration*. 1938. New York: MLA, 1983.

Suleiman, Susan, and Inge Crosman, eds. *The Reader in the Text: Essays on Audience and Interpretation*. Princeton: Princeton UP, 1980.

Tompkins, Jane P., ed. *Reader-Response Criticism: From Formalism to Post-Structuralism*. Baltimore: Johns Hopkins UP, 1980.

Deconstructionist and Other Poststructuralist Strategies

Culler, Jonathan. *On Deconstruction: Theory and Criticism after Structuralism*. Ithaca: Cornell UP, 1982.

de Man, Paul. *Blindness and Insight*. New York: Oxford UP, 1971.

Derrida, Jacques. *Of Grammatology*. 1967. Baltimore: Johns Hopkins UP, 1976.

———. *Writing and Difference*. 1967. Chicago: U of Chicago P, 1978.

Foucault, Michel. *Language, Counter-Memory, Practice*. Ithaca: Cornell UP, 1977.

———. *The Order of Things: An Archaeology of the Human Sciences*. 1966. London: Tavistock, 1970.

Gasche, Rodolphe. "Deconstruction as Criticism." *Glyph* 6 (1979): 177–216.

Hartman, Geoffrey H. *Criticism in the Wilderness*. New Haven: Yale UP, 1980.

Johnson, Barbara. *The Critical Difference: Essays in the Contemporary Rhetoric of Reading*. Baltimore: Johns Hopkins UP, 1980.

Melville, Stephen W. *Philosophy Beside Itself: On Deconstruction and Modernism*. Theory and History of Literature 27. Minneapolis: U of Minnesota P, 1986.

Said, Edward W. *The World, the Text, and the Critic*. Cambridge: Harvard UP, 1983.

Smith, Barbara Hernstein. *On the Margins of Discourse: The Relation of Literature to Language*. Chicago: U of Chicago P, 1979.

PERSPECTIVES ON CRITICAL READING

SUSAN SONTAG (b. 1933)
Against Interpretation 1964

Like the fumes of the automobile and of heavy industry which befoul the urban atmosphere, the effusion of interpretations of art today poisons our sensibilities. In a culture whose already classical dilemma is the hypertrophy of the intellect at the expense of energy and sensual capability, interpretation is the revenge of the intellect upon art.

Even more. It is the revenge of the intellect upon the world. To interpret is to impoverish, to deplete the world—in order to set up a shadow world of "meanings." It is to turn *the* world into *this* world. ("This world"! As if there were any other.)

The world, our world, is depleted, impoverished enough. Away with all duplicates of it, until we again experience more immediately what we have. . . .

In most modern instances, interpretation amounts to the philistine refusal to leave the work of art alone. Real art has the capacity to make us nervous. By reducing the work of art to its content and then interpreting *that,* one tames the work of art. Interpretation makes art manageable, conformable.

This philistinism of interpretation is more rife in literature than in any other art. For decades now, literary critics have understood it to be their task to translate the elements of the poem or play or novel or story into something else.

From *Against Interpretation*

Considerations for Critical Thinking and Writing

1. What are Sontag's objections to "interpretation"? Explain whether you agree or disagree with them.
2. In what sense does interpretation make art "manageable" and "conformable"?
3. In an essay explore what you take to be both the dangers of interpretation and its contributions to your understanding of literature.

STANLEY FISH (b. 1938)
On What Makes an Interpretation Acceptable   1980

. . . After all, while [William Blake's] "The Tyger" is obviously open to more than one interpretation, it is not open to an infinite number of interpretations. There may be disagreements as to whether the tiger is good or evil, or whether the speaker is Blake or a persona, and so on, but no one is suggesting that the poem is an allegory of the digestive processes or that it predicts the Second World War, and its limited plurality is simply a testimony to the capacity of a great work of art to generate multiple readings. The point is one that Wayne Booth makes when he asks, "Are we *right* to rule out at least some readings?" and then answers his own question with a resounding yes. It would be my answer too; but the real question is what gives us the right so to be right. A pluralist is committed to saying that there is something in the text which rules out some readings and allows others (even though no one reading can ever capture the text's "inexhaustible richness and complexity"). His best evidence is that in practice "we all in fact" do reject unacceptable readings and that more often than not we agree on the readings that are not rejected. . . . Booth concludes that there are justified limits to what we can legitimately do with a text, for "surely we could not go on disputing at all if a core of agreement did not exist." Again, I agree, but if, as I have argued, the text is always a function of interpretation, then the text cannot be the location of the core of agreement by means of which we reject interpretations. We seem to be at an impasse: on the one hand there would seem to be no basis for labeling an interpretation unacceptable, but on the other we do it all the time.

This, however, is an impasse only if one assumes that the activity of interpretation is itself unconstrained; but in fact the shape of that activity is determined by the literary institution which at any one time will authorize only a finite number of interpretive strategies. Thus, while there is no core of agreement *in* the text, there is a core of agreement (although one subject to change) concerning the ways of *producing* the text. Nowhere is this set of acceptable ways written down, but it is a part of everyone's knowledge of what it means to be operating within the literary institution as it is now constituted. A student of mine recently demonstrated this knowledge when, with an air of giving away a trade secret, she confided that she could go into any classroom, no matter what the subject of the course, and win approval for running one of a number of well-defined interpretive routines: she could view the assigned text as an instance of the tension between nature and culture; she could look in the text for evidence of large mythological oppositions; she could argue that the true subject of the text was its own composition, or that in the guise of fashioning a narrative the speaker was fragmenting and displacing his own anxieties and fears. She could not . . . argue that the text was a prophetic message inspired by the ghost of her Aunt Tilly.

My student's understanding of what she could and could not get away with, of the unwritten rules of the literary game, is shared by everyone who plays that game, by those who write and judge articles for publication in learned journals, by those who read and listen to papers at professional meetings, by those who seek and award tenure in innumerable departments of English and comparative literature, by the armies of graduate students for whom knowledge of the rules is the real mark of professional initiation. This does not mean that these rules and the practices they authorize are either monolithic or stable. Within the literary community there are subcommunities. . . . In a classroom whose authority figures include David Bleich and Norman Holland, a student might very well relate a text to her memories of a favorite aunt, while in other classrooms, dominated by the spirit of [Cleanth] Brooks and [Robert Penn] Warren, any such activity would immediately be dismissed as nonliterary, as something that isn't done.

The point is that while there is always a category of things that are not done (it is simply the reverse or flip side of the category of things that *are* done), the membership in that category is continually changing. It changes laterally as one moves from subcommunity to subcommunity, and it changes through time when once interdicted interpretive strategies are admitted into the ranks of the acceptable. Twenty years ago one of the things that literary critics didn't do was talk about the reader, at least in a way that made his experience the focus of the critical act. The prohibition on such talk was largely the result of [W. K.] Wimsatt's and [Monroe] Beardsley's famous essay "The Affective Fallacy," which argued that the variability of readers renders any investigation of their responses ad-hoc and relativistic: "The poem itself," the authors complained, "as an object of specifically critical judgment, tends to disappear." So influential was this essay that it was possible for a reviewer to dismiss a book merely by finding in it evidence that the affective fallacy had been committed. The use of a juridical terminology is not accidental; this was in a very real sense a *legal* finding of activity in violation of understood and institutionalized decorums. Today, however, the affective fallacy, no longer a fallacy but a methodology, is committed all the time, and its practitioners have behind them the full and authorizing weight of a fully articulated institutional apparatus. The "reader in literature" is regularly the subject of forums and workshops at the convention of the Modern Language Association; there is a reader newsletter which reports on the multitudinous labors of a reader industry; any list of currently active schools of literary criticism includes the school of "reader response," and two major university presses have published collections of essays designed both to display the variety of reader-centered criticism (the emergence of factions within a once interdicted activity is a sure sign of its having achieved the status of an orthodoxy) and to detail its history. None of this of course means that a reader-centered criticism is now invulnerable to challenge or attack, merely that it is now recognized as a competing literary strategy that cannot be dismissed simply by being named. It is acceptable not because everyone accepts it but because those who do not are now obliged to argue against it.

From *Is There a Text in This Class?*

Considerations for Critical Thinking and Writing

1. What kinds of strategies for reading have you encountered in your classroom experiences? Which have you found to be the most useful? Explain why.
2. Write an essay that describes what you "could and could not get away with" in the literature courses you have taken in high school and college.

ANNETTE KOLODNY (b. 1941)
On the Commitments of Feminist Criticism 1980

If feminist criticism calls anything into question, it must be that dog-eared myth of intellectual neutrality. For what I take to be the underlying spirit or message of any consciously ideologically premised criticism—that is, that ideas are important *because* they determine the ways we live, or want to live, in the world—is vitiated by confining those ideas to the study, the classroom, or the pages of our books. To write chapters decrying the sexual stereotyping of women in our literature, while closing our eyes to the sexual harassment of our women students and colleagues; to display Katharine Hepburn and Rosalind Russell in our courses on "The Image of the Independent Career Women in Film," while managing not to notice the paucity of female administrators on our own campus; to study the women who helped make universal enfranchisement a political reality, while keeping silent about our activist colleagues who are denied promotion or tenure; to include segments on "Women in the Labor Movement" in our American studies or women's studies courses, while remaining willfully ignorant of the department secretary fired for efforts to organize a clerical workers' union; to glory in the delusions of "merit," "privilege," and "status" which accompany campus life in order to insulate ourselves from the millions of women who labor in poverty—all this is not merely hypocritical; it destroys both the spirit and the meaning of what we are about.

From "Dancing through the Minefield:
Some Observations on the Theory, Practice, and Politics
of a Feminist Literary Criticism," <i>Feminist Studies</i>, 6, 1980

Considerations for Critical Thinking and Writing

1. Why does Kolodny reject "intellectual neutrality" as a "myth"? Explain whether you agree or disagree with her point of view.
2. Kolodny argues that feminist criticism can be used as an instrument for social reform. Discuss the possibility and desirability of her position. Do you think other kinds of criticism can and should be used to create social change?

ANDREW P. DEBICKI (b. 1934)
New Criticism and Deconstructionism: Two Attitudes in Teaching Poetry   1985

[Let's] look at the ways in which a New Critic and a deconstructivist might handle a poem. My first example, untitled, is a work by Pedro Salinas, which I first analyzed many years ago and which I have recently taught to a group of students influenced by deconstruction:

Sand: sleeping on the beach today
and tomorrow caressed
in the bosom of the sea:
the sun's today, water's prize tomorrow.
Softly you yield
to the hand that presses you
and go away with the first
courting wind that appears.
Pure and fickle sand,
changing and clear beloved,
I wanted you for my own,
and held you against my chest and soul.
But you escaped with the waves, the wind, the sun,
and I remained without a beloved,

my face turned to the wind which robbed her,
and my eyes to the far-off sea in which she had
green loves in a green shelter.

My original study of this poem, written very much in the New Critical
tradition, focused on the unusual personification of sand as beloved and on
the metaphorical pattern that it engendered. In the first part of the work,
the physical elusiveness of sand (which slips through one's hand, flies
with the wind, moves from shore to sea) evokes a coquettish woman, yielding
to her lover and then escaping, running off with a personified wind, moving
from one being to another. Watching these images, the reader gradually
forgets that the poem is metaphorically describing sand and becomes taken
up by the unusual correspondences with the figure of a flirting woman.
When in the last part of the poem the speaker laments his loss, the reader
is drawn into his lament for a fickle lover who has abandoned him.

Continuing a traditional analysis of this poem, we would conclude that
its unusual personification/metaphor takes us beyond a literal level and leads
us to a wider vision. The true subject of this poem is not sand, nor is it a
flirt who tricks a man. The comparison between sand and woman, however,
has made us feel the elusiveness of both, as well as the effect that this
elusiveness has had on the speaker, who is left sadly contemplating it at the
end of the poem. The poem has used its main image to embody a general
vision of fleetingness and its effects.

My analysis, as developed thus far, is representative of a New Critical
study. It focuses on the text and its central image, it describes a tension
produced within the text, and it suggests a way in which this tension is
resolved so as to move the poem beyond its literal level. In keeping with
the tenets of traditional analytic criticism, it shows how the poem conveys
a meaning that is far richer than its plot or any possible conceptual message.
But while it is careful not to reduce the poem to a simple idea or to an
equivalent of its prose summary, it does attempt to work all of its elements
into a single interpretation which would satisfy every reader . . . . : it makes
all of the poem's meanings reside in its verbal structures, and it suggests that
those meanings can be discovered and combined into a single cohesive
vision as we systematically analyze those structures.

By attempting to find a pattern that will incorporate and resolve the
poem's tensions, however, this reading leaves some loose ends, which I
noticed even in my New Critical perspective—and which I found difficult
to explain. To see the poem as the discovery of the theme of fleetingness
by an insightful speaker, we have to ignore the fanciful nature of the comparison, the whimsical attitude to reality that it suggests, and the excessively
serious lament of the speaker, which is difficult to take at face value—he
laments the loss of *sand* with the excessive emotion of a romantic lover!
The last lines, with their evocation of the beloved/sand in an archetypal
kingdom of the sea, ring a bit hollow. Once we notice all of this, we see
the speaker as being somehow unreliable in his strong response to the

situation. He tries too hard to equate the loss of sand with the loss of love, he paints himself as too much of a romantic, and he loses our assent when we realize that his rather cliché declarations are not very fitting. Once we become aware of the speaker's limitations, our perspective about the poem changes: we come to see its "meaning" as centered, not on the theme of fleetingness as such, but on a portrayal of the speaker's exaggerated efforts to embody this theme in the image of sand.

For the traditional New Critic, this would pose a dilemma. The reading of the poem as a serious embodiment of the theme of evanescence is undercut by an awareness of the speaker's unreliability. One can account for the conflict between readings, to some extent, by speaking of the poem's use of irony and by seeing a tension between the theme of evanescence and the speaker's excessive concern with an imaginary beloved (which blinds him to the larger issues presented by the poem). That still leaves unresolved, however, the poem's final meaning and effect. In class discussions, in fact, a debate between those students who asserted that the importance of the poem lay in its engendering the theme of fleetingness and those who noted the absurdity of the speaker often ended in an agreement that this was a "problem poem" which never resolved or integrated its "stresses" and its double vision. . . .

The deconstructive critic, however, would not be disturbed by a lack of resolution in the meanings of the poem and would use the conflict between interpretations as the starting point for further study. Noting that the view of evanescence produced by the poem's central metaphor is undercut by the speaker's unreliability, the deconstructive critic would explore the play of signification that the undercutting engenders. Calling into question the attempt to neatly define evanescence, on the one hand, and the speaker's excessive romanticism on the other, the poem would represent, for this critic, a creative confrontation of irresoluble visions. The image of the sand as woman, as well as the portrayal of the speaker, would represent a sort of "seam" in the text, an area of indeterminacy that would open the way to further readings. This image lets us see the speaker as a sentimental poet, attempting unsuccessfully to define evanescence by means of a novel metaphor but getting trapped in the theme of lost love, which he himself has engendered; it makes us think of the inadequacy of language, of the ways in which metaphorical expression and the clichés of a love lament can undercut each other.

Once we adopt such a deconstructivist perspective, we will find in the text details that will carry forward our reading. The speaker's statement that he held "her" against his "chest and his soul" underlines the conflict in his perspective: it juggles a literal perspective (he rubs sand against himself) and a metaphorical one (he reaches for his beloved), but it cannot fully combine them—"soul" is ludicrously inappropriate in reference to the former. The reader, noting the inappropriateness, has to pay attention to the inadequacy of language as used here. All in all, by engendering a conflict between various levels and perspectives, the poem makes us feel the incompleteness of any one reading, the way in which each one is a "misreading" (not because it is wrong, but because it is incomplete), and the creative lack of closure in the poem. By not being subject to closure, in fact, this text becomes all the more exciting: its view of the possibilities and limitations of metaphor, language, and perspective seems more valuable than any static portrayal of "evanescence."

The analyses I have offered of this poem exemplify the different classroom approaches that would be taken by a stereotypical New Critic, on the one hand, and a deconstructive critic on the other. Imbued with the desire to come to an overview of the literary work, the former will attempt to resolve its tensions (and probably remain unsatisfied with the poem). Skeptical of such a possibility and of the very existence of a definable "work," the latter will focus on the tensions that can be found in the text as vehicles for multiple readings. Given his or her attitude to the text, the deconstructive critic will not worry about going beyond its "limits" (which really do not exist). This will allow, of course, for more speculative readings; it will also lead to a discussion of ways in which the text can be extended and "cured" in successive readings, to the fact that it reflects on the process of its own creation, and to ways in which it will relate to other texts.

From *Writing and Reading DIFFERENTLY: Deconstruction
and the Teaching of Composition and Literature,*
edited by G. Douglas Atkins and Michael L. Johnson

Considerations for Critical Thinking and Writing

1. Explain how the New Critical and deconstructionist approaches to the Salinas poem differ. What kinds of questions are raised by each? What elements of the poem are focused on in each approach?
2. Write an essay explaining which reading of the poem you find more interesting. In your opening paragraph define what you mean by "interesting."
3. Choose one of the critical strategies for reading discussed in this chapter and discuss Salinas's poem from that perspective.

HARRIET HAWKINS (b. 1939)
Should We Study King Kong or King Lear?   1988

> *There is nothing either good or bad, but thinking makes it so.*
> — *Hamlet*

> Troilus: *What's aught but as 'tis valued?*
> Hector: *But value dwells not in particular will:*
> *It holds its estimate and dignity*
> *As well wherein 'tis precious of itself*
> *As in the prizer.*
> — *Troilus and Cressida*

To what degree is great literature—or bad literature—an artificial category? Are there any good—or bad—reasons why most societies have given high status to certain works of art and not to others? Could Hamlet be right in concluding that there is *nothing* either good or bad but thinking—or critical or ideological discourse—makes it so? Or are certain works of art so precious, so magnificent—or so trashy—that they obviously ought to be included in the canon or expelled from the classroom? So far as I know, there is not now any sign of a critical consensus on the correct answer to these questions either in England or in the United States.

In England there are, on the one hand, eloquent cases for the defense of the value of traditional literary studies, like Dame Helen Gardner's last book, *In Defence of the Imagination*. On the other hand, there are critical arguments insisting that what really counts is not what you read, but the way that you read it. You might as well study *King Kong* as *King Lear,* because what matters is not the script involved, but the critical or ideological virtues manifested in your own "reading" of whatever it is that you are reading. Reviewing a controversial book entitled *Re-Reading English,* the poet Tom Paulin gives the following account of the issues involved in the debate:

> The contributors are collectively of the opinion that English literature is a dying subject and they argue that it can be revived by adopting a "socialist pedagogy" and introducing into the syllabus "other forms of writing and cultural production than the canon of literature" . . . it is now time to challenge "hierarchical" and "elitist" conceptions of literature and to demolish the bourgeois ideology which has been "naturalised" as literary value. . . . They wish to develop "a politics of reading" and to redefine the term "text" in order to admit newspaper reports, songs, and even mass demonstrations as subjects for tutorial discussion. Texts no longer have to be books: indeed, "it may be more democratic to study *Coronation Street* [England's most popular soap opera] than *Middlemarch*."

However one looks at these arguments, it seems indisputably true that the issues involved are of paramount critical, pedagogical, and social importance. There are, however, any number of different ways to look at the various arguments. So far as I am, professionally, concerned, they raise the central question, "Why should any of us still study, or teach, Shakespeare's plays (or *Paradise Lost* or *The Canterbury Tales*)?" After all, there are quite enough films, plays, novels, and poems being produced today (to say nothing of all those "other forms of writing," including literary criticism, that are clamoring for our attention) to satisfy anyone interested in high literature, or popular genres, or any form of "cultural production" whatsoever. They also raise the obviously reflexive question: "Assuming that all traditionally 'canonized' works were eliminated, overnight, from the syllabus of every English department in the world, would not comparable problems of priority, value, elitism, ideological pressure, authoritarianism, and arbitrariness almost(?) immediately arise with reference to *whatever* works—of whatsoever kind and nature—were substituted for them?"

If, say, the place on the syllabus currently assigned to *King Lear* were reassigned to *King Kong,* those of us currently debating the relative merits of the Quarto, the Folio, or a conflated version of *King Lear* would, *mutatis mutandis,*° have to decide whether to concentrate classroom attention on the "classic" version of *King Kong,* originally produced in 1933, or to focus on the 1974 remake (which by now has many ardent admirers of its own). Although classroom time might not allow the inclusion of both, a decision to exclude either version might well seem arbitrary or authoritarian and so give rise to grumbles about the "canon." Moreover, comparable questions of "canonization" might well arise with reference to other films excluded from a syllabus that included either version (or both versions) of *King Kong.* For example: why assign class time to *King Kong* and not to (say) *Slave Girls of the White Rhinoceros?* Who, if any, of us has the right to decide whether *King Lear* or *King Kong* or the *Slave Girls* should, or should not, be included on, or excluded from, the syllabus? And can the decision to include, or exclude, any one of them be made, by any one of us, on any grounds whatsoever that do *not* have to do with comparative merit, or comparative value judgments, or with special interests—that is, with the aesthetic or ideological priorities, preferences, and prejudices of the assigners of positions on whatever syllabus there is? And insofar as most, if not all, of our judgments and preferences are comparative, are they not, inevitably, hierarchical?

Is there, in fact, any form of endeavor or accomplishment known to the human race—from sport to ballet to jazz to cooking—wherein comparative standards of excellence comparable to certain "hierarchical" and "elitist" conceptions of literature are nonexistent? Even bad-film buffs find certain bad films more gloriously bad than others. And, perhaps significantly given its comparatively short lifetime, the avant-garde cinema has, by now, produced snobs to rival the most elitist literary critic who ever lived, such as the one who thus puts down a friend who likes ordinary Hollywood films:

> Ah that's all right for you, I know the sort you are, but give me a private job that's shot on faded sepia sixteen millimetre stock with non-professional actors . . . no story and dialogue in French *any day of the week.*

What is striking about this snob's assumption is how characteristic it is of a long tradition of critical elitism that has consistently sneered at popular genres (e.g., romance fiction, soap operas, horror films, westerns, etc.) that are tainted by the profit motive and so tend to "give the public what it wants" in the way of sentimentality, sensationalism, sex, violence, romanticism, and the like.

From "*King Lear* to *King Kong* and Back: Shakespeare and Popular Modern Genres" in *"Bad" Shakespeare: Revaluations of the Shakespeare Canon,* edited by Maurice Charney

---

mutatis mutandis: Substituting different terms (Latin).

1. Do you agree or disagree that "great literature—or bad literature—[is] an artificial category"? Explain why.
2. Why would problems of "priority, value, elitism, ideological pressure, authoritarianism, and arbitrariness" probably become issues for evaluating any new works that replaced canonized works?
3. Write an essay in which you argue for (or against) studying popular arts (for example, popular song lyrics) alongside the works of classic writers such as Shakespeare.

HENRY A. GIROUX (b. 1943)
The Canon and Liberal Arts Education   1990

In the current debate about the importance of constructing a particular canon, the notion of naming and transmitting from one generation to the next what can be defined as "cultural treasure" specifies what has become the central argument for reforming the liberal arts. For that reason, perhaps, it appears as though the debate were reducible to the question of the contents of course syllabi. The notion of critical pedagogy for which I am arguing provides a fundamental challenge to this position: it calls for an argument that transcends the limited focus on the canon, that recognizes the crisis in liberal arts education to be one of historical purpose and meaning, a crisis that challenges us to rethink in a critical fashion the relationship between the role of the university and the imperatives of a democracy in a mass society.

Historically, education in the liberal arts was conceived of as the essential preparation for governing, for ruling—more specifically, the preparation and outfitting of the governing *elite*. The liberal arts curriculum, composed of the "best" that had been said or written, was intended, as Elizabeth Fox-Genovese has observed, "to provide selected individuals with a collective history, culture, and epistemology so that they could run the world effectively."[1] In this context the canon was considered to be a possession of the dominant classes or groups. Indeed, the canon was fashioned as a safeguard to insure that the cultural property of such groups was passed on from generation to generation along with the family estates. Thus, in these terms it seems most appropriate that the literary canon should be subject to revision—as it has been before in the course of the expansion of democracy—such that it might also incorporate and reflect the experience and aspirations of the women, minorities, and children of the working class who have been entering the academy.

Conceived of in this way, a radical vision of liberal arts education is to be found within its elite social origins and purpose. But this does not suggest

[1]Elizabeth Fox-Genovese, "The Claims of a Common Culture: Gender, Race, Class and the Canon," *Salmagundi* 72 (Fall 1986): 133.

that the most important questions confronting liberal arts reform lie in merely establishing the content of the liberal arts canon on the model of the elite universities. Instead, the most important questions become [those] of reformulating the meaning and purpose of higher education in ways that contribute to the cultivation and regeneration of an informed citizenry capable of actively participating in the shaping and governing of a democratic society. Within this discourse, the pedagogical becomes political and the notion of a liberal arts canon commands a more historically grounded and critical reading. The pedagogical becomes more political in that it proposes that the way in which students engage and examine knowledge is just as important an issue as the choosing of texts to be used in a class or program. That is, a democratic notion of liberal education rejects those views of the humanities which would treat texts as sacred and instruction as merely transmission. This notion of the canon undermines the possibility for dialogue, argument, and critical thinking; it treats knowledge as a form of cultural inheritance that is beyond considerations regarding how it might be implicated in social practices that exploit, infantilize, and oppress. The canons we have inherited, in their varied forms, cannot be dismissed as simply part of the ideology of privilege and domination. Instead, the privileged texts of the dominant or official canons should be explored with respect to the important role they have played in shaping, for better or worse, the major events of our time. But there are also forms of knowledge that have been marginalized by the official canons. There are noble traditions, histories, and narratives that speak to important struggles by women, blacks, minorities, and other subordinate groups that need to be heard so that such groups can lay claim to their own voices as part of a process of both affirmation and inquiry. At issue here is a notion of pedagogy as a form of cultural politics that rejects a facile restoration of the past, that rejects history as a monologue. A critical pedagogy recognizes that history is constituted in dialogue and that some of the voices that make up that dialogue have been eliminated. Such a pedagogy calls for a public debate regarding the dominant memories and repressed stories that constitute the historical narratives of a social order: in effect, canon formation becomes a matter of both rewriting and reinterpreting the past; canon formation embodies the ongoing "process of reconstructing the 'collective reflexivity' of lived cultural experience . . . which recognizes that the 'notions of the past and future are essentially notions of the present.' "[2] In this case, such notions are central to the politics of identity and power, and to the memories that structure how experience is individually and collectively authorized and experienced as a form of cultural identity. . . .

A critical pedagogy also rejects a discourse of value neutrality. Without subscribing to a language that polices behavior and desire, it aims at devel-

---

[2]Gail Guthrie Valaskakis, "The Chippewa and the Other: Living the Heritage of Lac Du Flambeau," *Cultural Studies* 2 (October 1988): 268.

oping pedagogical practices informed by an ethical stance that contests racism, sexism, class exploitation, and other dehumanizing and exploitative social relations as ideologies and social practices that disrupt and devalue public life. This is a pedagogy that rejects detachment, though it does not silence in the name of its own ideological fervor or correctness. It acknowledges social injustices, but examines with care and in dialogue with itself and others how such injustices work through the discourses, experiences, and desires that constitute daily life and the subjectivities of the students who invest in them. It is a pedagogy guided by ethical principles that correspond to a radical practice rooted in historical experience. And it is a pedagogy that comprehends the historical consequences of what it means to take a moral and political position with respect to the horror and suffering of, for example, the Gulag, the Nazi Holocaust, or the Pol Pot regime. Such events not only summon up images of terror, domination, and resistance, but also provide a priori examples of what principles have to be both defended and fought against in the interest of freedom and life. Within this perspective, ethics becomes more than the discourse of moral relativism or a static transmission of reified history. Ethics becomes, instead, a continued engagement in which the social practices of everyday life are interrogated in relation to the principles of individual autonomy and democratic public life—not as a matter of received truth but as a constant engagement. This represents an ethical stance which provides the opportunity for individual capacities to be questioned and examined so that they can serve both to analyze and advance the possibilities inherent in all social forms. At issue is an ethical stance in which community, difference, remembrance, and historical consciousness become central categories as part of the language of public life.

From "Liberal Arts Education and the Struggle
for Public Life: Dreaming about Democracy,"
South Atlantic Quarterly, 89, 1990

Considerations for Critical Thinking and Writing

1. Why does Giroux take debates about canonical issues beyond course reading lists? Upon what historical conditions does he base his argument?
2. What kind of teaching—"critical pedagogy"—does Giroux call for? Why?
3. According to Giroux, why should "value neutrality" be rejected by teachers and students?
4. Write an essay in which you agree or disagree that literature should be used to help create an "ethical stance" for its readers.

QUESTIONS FOR CRITICAL READING AND WRITING

The following lists of questions for the critical approaches covered in this chapter should be useful for discovering arguments you might make for writing about a short story, poem, or play. The page number that follows each heading refers to the discussion in the text for that particular approach.

Formalist Questions (p. 98)

1. How do various elements of the work—plot, character, point of view, setting, tone, diction, images, symbol, etc.—reinforce its meanings?
2. How are the elements related to the whole?
3. What is the work's major organizing principle? How is its structure unified?
4. What issues does the work raise? How does the work's structure resolve those issues?

Biographical Questions (p. 100)

1. Are there facts about the writer's life relevant to your understanding of the work?
2. Are characters and incidents in the work versions of the writer's own experiences? Are they treated factually or imaginatively?
3. How do you think the writer's values are reflected in the work?
4. Does the writer challenge or reflect the values contemporary to him or her?

Psychological Questions (p. 102)

1. How does the work reflect the author's personal psychology?
2. What do the characters' emotions and behavior reveal about their psychological states? What types of personalities are they?
3. Are psychological matters such as repression, dreams, and desire presented consciously or unconsciously by the author?
4. How does your own psychology affect your response to the work?

Historical Questions (p. 104)

1. How does the work reflect the period in which it is written?
2. How does the work reflect the period it represents?
3. What literary or historical influences helped to shape the form and content of the work?
4. How important is the historical context (both the work's and your own) to interpreting the work?

Marxist Questions (p. 107)

1. How are class differences presented in the work? Are characters aware or unaware of the economic and social forces that affect their lives?
2. How do economic conditions determine the characters' lives?
3. What ideological values are explicit or implicit?
4. Does the work challenge or affirm the social order it describes?

Feminist Questions (p. 107)

1. How are women's lives portrayed in the work? Do the women in the work accept or reject these roles?
2. Is the form and content of the work influenced by the author's gender?
3. What are the relationships between men and women? Are these relationships sources of conflict? Do they provide resolutions to conflicts?
4. Does the work challenge or affirm traditional ideas about women?

Mythological Questions (p. 108)

1. How does the story resemble other stories in plot, character, setting, or use of symbols?
2. Are archetypes presented, such as quests, initiations, scapegoats, or withdrawals and returns?
3. Does the protagonist undergo any kind of transformation such as a movement from innocence to experience that seems archetypal?
4. Are there any specific allusions to myths that shed light on the text?

Reader-Response Questions (p. 110)

1. How do you respond to the work?
2. How do your own experiences and expectations affect your reading and interpretation?
3. What is the work's original or intended audience? To what extent are you similar to or different from that audience?
4. Do you respond in the same way to the work after more than one reading?

Deconstructionist Questions (p. 112)

1. How are contradictory and opposing meanings expressed in the work?
2. How does meaning break down or deconstruct itself in the language of the text?
3. Would you say that ultimate definitive meanings are impossible to determine and establish in the text? Why? How does that affect your interpretation?
4. How are implicit ideological values revealed in the work?

These questions will not apply to all texts; and they are not mutually exclusive. They can be combined to explore a text from several critical perspectives simultaneously. A feminist approach to Kate Chopin's "The Story of an Hour" could also use Marxist concerns about class to make observations about the oppression of women's lives in the historical context of the nineteenth century. Your use of these questions should allow you to discover significant issues from which you can develop an argumentative essay that is organized around clearly defined terms, relevant evidence, and a persuasive analysis.

A SAMPLE READER-RESPONSE ANALYSIS: DIFFERENCES IN RESPONSES TO KATE CHOPIN'S "THE STORY OF AN HOUR"

The following paper was an assigned topic of three to four pages that required a reader-response approach to Chopin's story (p. 46) that described how different readers might interpret Mrs. Mallard's character.

Wally Villa

Professor Brian

English 210

March 12, 19--

Differences in Responses to

Kate Chopin's "The Story of an Hour"

Kate Chopin's "The Story of an Hour" appears merely to explore a woman's unpredictable reaction to her husband's assumed death and reappearance, but actually Chopin offers Mrs. Mallard's bizarre story to reveal problems that are inherent in the institution of marriage. By offering this depiction of a marriage that stifles the woman to the point that she celebrates the death of her kind and loving husband, Chopin challenges her readers to examine their own views of marriage and relationships between men and women. Each reader's judgment of Mrs. Mallard and her behavior inevitably stems from his or her own personal feelings about marriage and the influences of societal expectations. Readers of differing genders, ages, and marital experiences are, therefore, likely to react differently to Chopin's startling portrayal of the Mallards' marriage, and that certainly is true of my response to the story compared with my father's and grandmother's responses.

Marriage often establishes boundaries between people that make them unable to communicate with each other. The Mallards' marriage was evidently crippled both by their inability to talk to one another and by Mrs. Mallard's conviction that her marriage was defined by "a powerful will bending hers in that blind persistence with which men and women believe they have a right to impose a private will upon a fellow-creature."

Yet she does not recognize that it is not just men who impose
their will upon women, and that the problems inherent in marriage affect men and women equally. To me, Mrs. Mallard is a
somewhat sympathetic character, and I appreciate her longing
to live out the "years to come that would belong to her absolutely." However, I also believe that she could have tried to
improve her own situation somehow, by either reaching out to
her husband or by abandoning the marriage altogether. Chopin
uses Mrs. Mallard's tragedy to illuminate aspects of marriage
that are harmful and, in this case, even deadly. Perhaps the
Mallards' relationship should be taken as a warning to others,
that sacrificing one's own happiness in order to satisfy societal expectations can poison one's life and even destroy entire families.

When my father read "The Story of an Hour," his reaction
to Mrs. Mallard was more antagonistic than my own. He saw
Chopin's story as a timeless "battle of the sexes," serving as
further proof that men will never really be able to understand
what it is that women want. Mrs. Mallard endured an obviously
unsatisfying marriage, without ever explaining to her husband
that she felt trapped and unfulfilled. Mrs. Mallard dismissed
the question of whether or not she was experiencing a "monstrous joy" as trivial, but my father does not think that this
is a trivial question. He believes it was a monstrous joy,
because she selfishly celebrated the death of her husband
without ever allowing him the opportunity to understand her
feelings. He believes that above all, Brently Mallard should
be seen as the most victimized character in the story. He
was a good, kind man, with friends who cared about

him and a marriage that he thought he could depend upon. He "never looked save with love" upon his wife, his only "crime" was coming home from work one day, and yet he is the one who is bereaved at the end of the story, for reasons he will never understand. Mrs. Mallard's passion for her newly discovered freedom is perhaps understandable, but according to my father, Mr. Mallard is the character most deserving of sympathy.

Maybe not surprisingly, my grandmother's interpretation of "The Story of an Hour" was radically different from both mine and my father's. My grandmother was married in 1936 and widowed in 1959, and therefore has the closest personal relationship to Chopin's characters living at the turn of the century. Her first reaction, aside from her unwavering support for Mrs. Mallard and her predicament, was that this story demonstrates the differences between the ways men and women related to each other a century ago and the way they relate today. Unlike my father, who thought Mrs. Mallard was too passive, my grandmother believed that Mrs. Mallard didn't even know that she was feeling repressed until after she was told that Brently was dead. In 1894, divorce was so scandalous and stigmatized that it simply wouldn't have been an option for Mrs. Mallard, and so her only "out" of the marriage would have to be one of their deaths. Being rather young, Mrs. Mallard probably considered herself doomed to a long life and an equally long marriage. Another interesting point that my grandmother made was that in spite of all we know about Mrs. Mallard's feelings about her husband and her marriage, she still managed to live up to everyone's expectations of her as a woman both in life and in death. She was a dutiful wife to Brently, as she was expected to be, she wept "with sudden, wild abandonment" when she heard the news of his death, she locked herself in her room to cope with her new situation, and she had a fatal heart attack upon seeing her husband arrive home. Naturally the male doctors would think that she died of the "joy that kills"; nobody could have guessed that she was unhappy with her life, and she would never have wanted them to know.

Interpretations of "The Story of an Hour" seem to vary according to the gender, age, and experience of the reader. While both male and female readers can certainly sympathize with Mrs. Mallard's plight, female readers--as was evident in our class discussions--seem to relate more easily to her pre-dicament and are quicker to exonerate her of any responsibil-ity for her unhappy situation. Conversely, male readers are more likely to feel compassion for Mr. Mallard, who lost his wife for reasons that will always remain entirely unknown to him. Older readers probably understand more readily the strength of social forces and the difficulty of trying to deny societal expectations concerning gender roles in general and marriage in particular. Younger readers seem to feel that Mrs. Mallard was too passive a character, and that she could have improved her domestic life immeasurably if she had taken the initiative to either improve or end her relationship with her husband. Ultimately, how each individual reader responds to Mrs. Mallard's story reveals his or her own ideas about marriage, society, and how men and women communicate with each other.

7. Studying an Author in Depth

This chapter includes four poems by Emily Dickinson, as the subject of a sample in-depth study of her poetry. These poems are not wholly representative of the poet's work, but they suggest some of the techniques and concerns that characterize the poet's writings. The poems speak not only to readers but to one another. That's natural enough: the more familiar you are with a writer's work, the easier it is to perceive and enjoy the strategies and themes he or she employs. The sample paper (p. 145) discusses Dickinson's attitudes toward religious faith in these poems.

EMILY DICKINSON (1830–1886)

Emily Dickinson grew up in a prominent and prosperous household in Amherst, Massachusetts. Along with her younger sister Lavinia and older brother Austin, she experienced a quiet and reserved family life headed by her father Edward Dickinson. In a letter to Austin at law school, she once described the atmosphere in her father's house as "pretty much all sobriety." Her mother, Emily Norcross Dickinson, was not as powerful a presence in her life; she seems not to have been as emotionally accessible as Dickinson would have liked. Her daughter is said to have characterized her as not the sort of mother "to whom you hurry when you are troubled." Both parents raised Dickinson to be a cultured Christian woman who would one day be responsible for a family of her own. Her father attempted to protect her from reading books that might "joggle" her mind, particularly her religious faith, but Dickinson's individualistic instincts and irreverent sensibilities created conflicts that did not allow her to fall into step with the conventional piety, domesticity, and social duty prescribed by her father and the orthodox Congregationalism of Amherst.

The Dickinsons were well known in Massachusetts. Her father was a lawyer and served as the treasurer of Amherst College (a position Austin eventually took up as well), and her grandfather was one of the college's founders. Although nineteenth-century politics, economics, and social issues do not appear in the foreground of her poetry, Dickinson lived in a family environment that was steeped in them: her father was an active town official and served in the General Court of Massachusetts, the State Senate, and the United States House of Representatives.

Dickinson, however, withdrew not only from her father's public world but also from almost all social life in Amherst. She refused to see most people, and aside from a single year at South Hadley Female Seminary (now Mount Holyoke College), one excursion to Philadelphia and Washington, and several brief trips to Boston to see a doctor about eye problems, she lived all her life in her father's house. She dressed only in white and developed a reputation as a reclusive eccentric. Dickinson selected her own society carefully and frugally. Like her poetry, her relationship to the world was intensely reticent. Indeed, during the last twenty years of her life she rarely left the house.

Though Dickinson never married, she had significant relationships with several men who were friends, confidantes, and mentors. She also enjoyed an intimate relationship with her friend Susan Huntington Gilbert, who became her sister-in-law by marrying Austin. Susan and her husband lived next door and were extremely close with Dickinson. Biographers have attempted to find in a number of her relationships the source for the passion of some of her love poems and letters, but no biographer has been able to identify definitively the object of Dickinson's love. What matters, of course, is not with whom she was in love—if, in fact, there was any single person—but that she wrote about such passions so intensely and convincingly in her poetry.

Choosing to live life internally within the confines of her home, Dickinson brought her life into sharp focus. For she also chose to live within the limitless expanses of her imagination, a choice she was keenly aware of and which she described in one of her poems this way: "I dwell in Possibility." Her small circle of domestic life did not impinge upon her creative sensibilities. Like Henry David Thoreau, she simplified her life so that doing without was a means of being within. In a sense she redefined the meaning of deprivation because being denied something—whether it was faith, love, literary recognition, or some other desire—provided a sharper, more intense understanding than she would have experienced had she achieved what she wanted: " 'Heaven,' " she wrote, "is what I cannot reach!" This line, along with many others, such as "Water, is taught by thirst" and "Success is counted sweetest / By those who ne'er succeed," suggest just how persistently she saw deprivation as a way of sensitizing herself to the value of what she was missing. For Dickinson hopeful expectation was always more satisfying than achieving a golden moment.

Writers contemporary to her had little or no effect upon the style of her writing. In her own work she was original and innovative, but she did draw upon her knowledge of the Bible, classical myths, and Shakespeare for allusions and references in her poetry. She also used contemporary popular church hymns, transforming their standard rhythms into free-form hymn meters.

Today, Dickinson is regarded as one of America's greatest poets, but when she died at the age of fifty-six after devoting most of her life to writing poetry, her nearly 2,000 poems—only a dozen of which were published anonymously during her lifetime—were unknown except to a small number of friends and relatives. Dickinson was not recognized as a major poet until the twentieth century, when modern readers ranked her as a major new voice whose literary innovations were unmatched by any other nineteenth-century poet in the United States.

Dickinson neither completed many poems nor prepared them for publication. She wrote her drafts on scraps of paper, grocery lists, and the backs of recipes and used envelopes. Early editors of her poems took the liberty of making them more accessible to nineteenth-century readers when several volumes of selected poems were published in the 1890s. The poems were made to appear like traditional nineteenth-century verse by assigning them titles, rearranging their syntax, normalizing their grammar, and regularizing their capitalizations. Instead of dashes editors used standard punctuation; instead of the highly elliptical telegraphic lines so characteristic of her poems editors added articles, conjunctions, and prepositions to make them more readable and in line with conventional expectations. In addition, the poems were made more predictable by organizing them into categories such as friendship, nature, love, and death. Not until 1955, when Thomas Johnson published Dickinson's complete works in a form that attempted to be true to her manuscript versions, did readers have an opportunity to see the full range of her style and themes.

Dickinson's popular reputation has sometimes relegated her to the role of a New England regionalist who writes quaint uplifting verses that touch the heart. In 1971 that image was mailed first class all over the country by the United States Postal Service. In addition to issuing a commemorative stamp featuring a portrait of Dickinson, the Postal Service affixed the stamp to a first-day-of-issue envelope that included an engraved rose and one of her poems. The one chosen from among the nearly 2,000 she wrote is a seven-line poem that has the speaker assert, "If I can stop one Heart from breaking . . . I shall not live in vain." The major image that supports this claim consists of the speaker helping a robin back into its nest after it has fainted.

This sort of poetry is typical not only of many nineteenth-century popular poems, but of the kind of verse that can be found in contemporary greeting cards. The speaker tells us what we imagine we should think about and makes the point simply with a sentimental image of a "fainting Robin." To point out that robins don't faint or that altruism isn't necessarily the only rule of conduct by which one should live one's life is to make trouble for this poem. Moreover, its use of language is unexceptional; the metaphors used, like that robin, are a bit weary. If this poem were characteristic of Dickinson's poetry, the Postal Service probably would not have been urged to issue a stamp in her honor nor would you be reading her poems in this book or many others. Another poem by Dickinson that is more typical of her writing is also about robins. It begins with a conventional concern expressed by the speaker about whether or not she will "be alive / When the Robins come." If she isn't, she asks that she be remembered by feeding the robins. The second stanza of this eight-line poem, however, shifts from a light tone to something darker when she apologizes for not thanking her friend for feeding the robins: "You will know I'm trying / With my Granite lip!"

This poem is more representative of Dickinson's sensibilities and techniques. The sentimental expectations of the first six lines—lines that could have been written by any number of popular nineteenth-century writers—are dashed by the penultimate word of the last line. "Granite" is the perfect word here because it forces us to reread the poem and to recognize that it's not about feeding robins or offering a cosmetic treatment of death; rather it's a bone-chilling description of a corpse's lip that evokes the cold, hard texture and grayish color of tombstones. These lips will never say "Thank you" or anything else.

Instead of the predictable sentiments of "If I can stop one Heart from breaking," this poem is unnervingly precise in its use of language and tidily points out how much emphasis Dickinson places on an individual word. This is a better poem, not because it's grim or about death, but because it demonstrates Dickinson's skillful use of language to produce a shocking irony.

Dickinson found irony, ambiguity, and paradox lurking in the simplest and commonest experiences. The materials and subject matter of her poetry are quite conventional. Her poems are filled with robins, bees, winter light, household items, and domestic duties. These materials represent the range of what she experienced in and around her father's house. She used them because they constituted so much of her life and, more importantly, because she found meanings latent in them. Though her world was simple, it was also complex in its beauties and its terrors. Her lyric poems capture impressions of particular moments, scenes, or moods, and she characteristically focuses upon topics such as nature, love, immorality, death, faith, doubt, pain, and the self.

Though her materials were conventional, her treatment of them was innovative, because she was willing to break whatever poetic conventions stood in the way of the intensity of her thought and images. Her conciseness, brevity, and wit are tightly packed. Typically she offers her observations via one or two images that reveal her thought in a powerful manner. She once characterized her literary art by writing "My business is circumference." Her method is to reveal the inadequacy of declarative statements by evoking qualifications and questions with images that complicate firm assertions and affirmations. In one of her poems she describes her strategies this way: "Tell all the Truth but tell it slant—/ Success in Circuit lies." This might well stand as a working definition of Dickinson's aesthetics.

Dickinson's poetry is challenging because it is radical and original in its rejection of most traditional nineteenth-century themes and techniques. Her poems require active engagement from the reader, because she seems to leave out so much with her elliptical style and remarkable contracting metaphors. But these apparent gaps are filled with meaning if we are sensitive to her use of devices such as personification, allusion, symbolism, and startling syntax and grammar. Since her use of dashes is sometimes puzzling, it helps to read her poems aloud to hear how carefully the words are arranged. What might initially seem intimidating on a silent page can surprise the reader with meaning when heard. It's also worth keeping in mind that Dickinson was not always consistent in her views and that they can change from poem to poem, depending upon how she felt at a given moment: Dickinson was less interested in absolute answers to questions than she was in examining and exploring their "circumference."

"Faith" is a fine invention   c. 1860

"Faith" is a fine invention
When Gentlemen can *see*—
But *Microscopes* are prudent
In an Emergency.

I know that He exists   c. 1862

I know that He exists.
Somewhere—in Silence—
He has hid his rare life
From our gross eyes.

'Tis an instant's play.   5
'Tis a fond Ambush—
Just to make Bliss
Earn her own surprise!

But—should the play
Prove piercing earnest —   10
Should the glee-glaze —
In Death's—stiff—stare—

Would not the fun
Look too expensive!
Would not the jest—
Have crawled too far!

15

I never saw a Moor— c. 1865

I never saw a Moor—
I never saw the Sea—
Yet know I how the Heather looks
And what a Billow be.

I never spoke with God
Nor visited in Heaven—
Yet certain am I of the spot
As if the Checks were given—

Apparently with no surprise c. 1884

Apparently with no surprise
To any happy Flower
The Frost beheads it at its play—
In accidental power—
The blond Assassin passes on—
The Sun proceeds unmoved
To measure off another Day
For an Approving God.

QUESTIONS FOR WRITING ABOUT
AN AUTHOR IN DEPTH

The following questions can help you to respond to multiple works by the same author. Whether the works are fiction, poetry, or drama, you're likely to be struck by the similarities and differences in works by the same author. Previous knowledge of a writer's work can set up useful expectations in a reader. If you've read Nathaniel Hawthorne's "Young Goodman Brown" you're likely to find the content and style of *The Scarlet Letter* familiar to you. That's not to say, however, that writers don't qualify their ideas or techniques as they develop as artists. For all of Hawthorne's concerns about the negative effects of isolation on his characters, he provides some ambivalent and ambiguous characters (such as Owen Warland in "Artist of the Beautiful") who require a kind of isolation—as did Hawthorne himself in his early years—in order to thrive as artists and human beings. By being familiar with a number of works by the same writer you can begin to discern particular kinds of concerns and techniques that characterize and help to shed light on a writer's work.

As you read multiple works by the same author you'll begin to recognize situations, events, characters, issues, perspectives, styles, and strategies—even recurring words or phrases—that provide a kind of signature, making the poem, story, or play in some way identifiable with that particular writer. In the case of the four Dickinson poems included in this chapter, religion emerges as a central topic linked to a number of issues including faith, immortality, skepticism, and the nature of God. The student selected these poems because he noticed Dickinson's intense interest in religious faith owing to the many poems that explore a variety of religious attitudes in her work. He chose these four because they were closely related, but he also might have found equally useful clusters of poems about love, nature, domestic life, or writing, as well as other topics. What especially intrigued him was some of the information he read about Dickinson's sternly religious father and the orthodox nature of the religious values of her hometown of Amherst, Massachusetts. Since this paper was not a research paper, he did not pursue these issues beyond the level of the general remarks provided in an introduction to her poetry (though he might have). He did, however, use this biographical and historical information as a means of framing his search for poems that were related to one another. In doing so he discovered consistent concerns along with contradictory themes that became the basis of his paper.

The questions provided below should help you to listen to how a writer's works can speak to each other and to you. Additional useful questions will be found in other chapters of this book. See Questions for Writing about Fiction (p. 49), Poetry (p. 64), and Drama (p. 86) and Questions for Critical Reading and Writing (p. 130).

1. What topics reappear in the writer's work? What seem to be the major concerns of the author?
2. Does the author have a definable world view that can be discerned from work to work? Is, for example, the writer liberal, conservative, apolitical, or religious?
3. What social values come through in the author's work? Does he or she seem to identify with a particular group or social class?
4. Is there a consistent voice or point of view from work to work? Is it a persona or the author's actual self?
5. How much of the author's own life experiences and historical moment make their way into the works?
6. Does the author experiment with style from work to work, or are the works mostly consistent with one another?

7. Can the author's work be identified with a literary tradition, such as *carpe diem,* poetry, or revenge tragedy, that aligns his or her work with that of other writers?
8. What is distinctive about the author's writing? Is the language innovative? Are the themes challenging? Are the voices conventional? Is the tone characteristic?
9. Could you identify another work by the same author without a name being attached to it? What are the distinctive features that allow you to do so?
10. Do any of the writer's works seem *not* to be by that writer? Why?
11. What other writers are most like this author in style and content? Why?
12. Has the writer's work evolved over time? Are there significant changes or developments? Are these new ideas and styles, or do the works remain largely the same?
13. How would you characterize the writing habits of the writer? Is it possible to anticipate what goes on in different works or are you surprised by their content or style?
14. Can difficult or ambiguous passages in a work be resolved by referring to a similar passage in another work?
15. What does the writer say about his or her own work? Do you trust the teller or the tale? Which do you think is more reliable?

A SAMPLE IN-DEPTH STUDY: RELIGIOUS FAITH IN FOUR POEMS BY EMILY DICKINSON

The following paper was written for an assignment that called for an analysis (about 750 words) on any topic that could be traced in three or four poems by Dickinson.

Michael Weitz

Professor Pearl

English 270

May 5, 19--

      Religious Faith in Four Poems by Emily Dickinson

      Throughout much of her poetry, Emily Dickinson wrestles with complex notions of God, faith, and religious devotion. She adheres to no consistent view of religion; rather, her poetry reveals a vision of God and faith that is constantly evolving. Dickinson's gods range from the strict and powerful Old Testament father to a loving spiritual guide to an irrational and ridiculous imaginary figure. Through these varying images of God, Dickinson portrays contrasting images of the meaning and validity of religious faith. Her work reveals competing attitudes toward religious devotion as conventional religious piety struggles with a more cynical perception of God and religious worship.

      Dickinson's "I never saw a Moor--" reveals a vision of traditional religious sensibilities. Although the speaker readily admits that "I never spoke with God / Nor visited in Heaven," her devout faith in a supreme being does not waver. The poem appears to be a straightforward profession of true faith stemming from the argument that the proof of God's existence is the universe's existence. Dickinson's imagery therefore evolves from the natural to the supernatural, first establishing her convictions that Moors and Seas exist, in spite of her lack of personal contact with either. This leads to the foundation of her religious faith, again based not on physical experience but on intellectual convictions. The speaker professes that she believes in the existence of Heaven even without conclusive evidence: "Yet certain am I of the spot / As if the Checks were given--." But the appearance of such idealistic views of God and faith in "I never saw a Moor--" are transformed in Dickinson's other poems into a much more skeptical vision of the validity of religious piety.

While faith is portrayed as an authentic and deeply important quality in "I never saw a Moor--," Dickinson's "'Faith' is a fine invention" portrays faith as much less essential. Faith is defined in the poem as "a fine invention," suggesting that it is created by man for man and therefore is not a crucial aspect of the natural universe. Thus the strong idealistic faith of "I never saw a Moor--" becomes discredited in the face of scientific rationalism. The speaker compares religious faith with actual microscopes, both of which are meant to enhance one's vision in some way. But "Faith" is only useful "When Gentlemen can see--" already; in an "Emergency," when one ostensibly cannot see, "Microscopes are prudent." Dickinson pits religion against science, suggesting that science, with its tangible evidence and rational attitude, is a more reliable lens through which to view the world. Faith is irreverently reduced to a mere invention, and one that is ultimately less useful than microscopes or other scientific instruments.

Rational, scientific observations are not the only contributing factor to the portrayal of religious skepticism in Dickinson's poems; nature itself is seen to be incompatible in some ways with conventional religious ideology. In "Apparently with no surprise," the speaker recognizes the inexorable

cycle of natural life and death as a morning frost kills a
flower. But the tension in this poem stems not from the
"happy Flower" struck down by the frost's "accidental power,"
but from the apparent indifference of the "Approving God" who
condones this seemingly cruel and unnecessary death. God is
seen as remote and uncompromising, and it is this perceived
distance between the speaker and God that reveals the increasing absurdity of traditional religious faith. The speaker understands that praying to God or believing in religion cannot
change the course of nature, and as a result feels so help-
lessly distanced from God that religious faith becomes virtu-
ally meaningless.

Dickinson's religious skepticism becomes even more explicit in "I know that He exists," in which the speaker attempts to understand the connection between seeing God and
facing death. In this poem Dickinson characterizes God as a
remote and mysterious figure; the speaker mockingly asserts,
"I know that He exists," even though "He has hid his rare
life / From our gross eyes." The skepticism toward religious
faith in this poem stems from the speaker's recognition of the
paradoxical quest that people undertake to know and to see
God. A successful attempt to see God, to win the game of
hide-and-seek that He apparently is orchestrating, results inevitably in death. With this recognition the speaker comes to
view religion as an absurd and reckless game in which the
prize may be "Bliss" but more likely is "Death's--stiff--
stare--." For to see God and to meet one's death as a result
certainly suggests that the game of trying to see God (the so-
called "fun") is much "too expensive" and that religion itself

is a "jest" that, like the serpent in Genesis, has "crawled
too far."

Ultimately, Dickinson's vision of religious faith in her
poems is one of suspicion and cynicism. She cannot reconcile
the physical world to the spiritual existence that Christian
doctrine teaches, and as a result the traditional perception
of God becomes ludicrous. "I never saw a Moor--" does attempt
to sustain a conventional vision of religious devotion, but
Dickinson's poems overall are far more likely to suggest that
God is elusive, indifferent, and often cruel, thus undermining
the traditional vision of God as a loving father worthy of de-
vout worship. Thus, not only religious faith but also those
who are religiously faithful become targets for Dickinson's
irreverent criticism of conventional belief.

8. The Literary Research Paper

A close reading of a primary source such as a short story, poem, or play can give insights into a work's themes and effects, but sometimes you will want to know more. A published commentary by a critic who knows the work well and is familiar with the author's life and times can provide insights that otherwise may not be available. Such comments and interpretations—known as *secondary sources*—are, of course, not a substitute for the work itself, but they often can take you into a work further than if you made the journey by yourself.

After imagination, good sense, and energy, perhaps the next most important quality for writing a research paper is the ability to organize material. A research paper on a literary topic requires a writer to take account of quite a lot at once: the text, ideas, sources, and documentation techniques all make demands on one's efforts to present a topic clearly and convincingly.

The following list should give you a sense of what goes into creating a research paper. Although some steps on the list can be folded into one another, they offer an overview of the work that will involve you.

1. Choosing a topic
2. Finding sources
3. Evaluating sources
4. Taking notes
5. Developing a thesis
6. Organizing an outline
7. Writing drafts
8. Revising
9. Documenting sources
10. Preparing the final draft and proofreading

Even if you have never written a research paper, you most likely have already had experience choosing a topic, developing a thesis, organizing an outline, and writing a draft that you then revised, proofread, and handed in. Those skills represent six of the ten items on the list. This chapter briefly reviews some of these steps and focuses on the remaining tasks, unique to research paper assignments.

CHOOSING A TOPIC

Chapter 1 discussed the importance of reading a work closely and taking careful notes as a means of generating topics for writing about literature. If you know a work well and record your understanding of it in notes, you'll have impressions and ideas to choose from for potential topics. You may find it useful to review the information on pages 5–7 before reading the advice about putting together a research paper in this chapter.

The student author of the sample research paper "Defining Identity in 'Mending Wall' " (p. 162) was asked to write a five-page paper that demonstrated some familiarity with published critical perspectives on a Robert Frost poem of her choice. Before looking into critical discussions of the poem, she read "Mending Wall" several times, taking notes and making comments in the margin of her textbook on each reading.

What prompted her choice of "Mending Wall" was a class discussion that focused on the poem's speaker's questioning the value and necessity of the wall in contrast to his neighbor's insistence upon it. At one point, however, the boundaries of the discussion opened up to the possibility that the wall is important to both characters in the poem rather than only the neighbor. It is, after all, the speaker, not the neighbor, who repairs the damage to the wall caused by hunters and who initiates the rebuilding of the wall. Why would he do that if he wanted the wall down? Only after having thoroughly examined the poem did the student go to the library to see what professional critics had to say about this question.

FINDING SOURCES

Whether your college library is large or small, its reference librarians can usually help you locate secondary sources about a particular work or author. Unless you choose a very recently published story, poem, or play about which little or nothing has been written, you should be able to find commentaries about a literary work efficiently and quickly. Here are some useful reference sources that can help you to establish both an overview of a potential topic and a list of relevant books and articles. They are useful for topics on fiction and drama as well as poetry.

Annotated List of References

Baker, Nancy L. *A Research Guide for Undergraduate Students: English and American Literature.* 2nd ed. New York: MLA, 1985. Especially designed for students; a useful guide to reference sources.

Bryer, Jackson, ed. *Sixteen Modern American Authors: A Survey of Research and Criticism*. New York: Norton, 1973. Extensive bibliographic essays on Sherwood Anderson, Willa Cather, Hart Crane, Theodore Dreiser, T. S. Eliot, William Faulkner, F. Scott Fitzgerald, Robert Frost, Ernest Hemingway, Eugene O'Neill, Ezra Pound, Edwin Arlington Robinson, John Steinbeck, Wallace Stevens, William Carlos Williams, and Thomas Wolfe.

Corse, Larry B., and Sandra B. Corse. *Articles on American and British Literature: An Index to Selected Periodicals, 1950–1977*. Athens, OH: Swallow Press, 1981. Specifically designed for students using small college libraries.

Eddleman, Floyd E., ed. *American Drama Criticism: Interpretations, 1890–1977*. 2nd ed. Hamden, CT: Shoe String Press, 1979. Supplement 1984.

Elliot, Emory, et al. *Columbia Literary History of the United States*. New York: Columbia UP, 1988. This updates the discussions in Spiller (below) and reflects recent changes in the canon.

Harner, James L. *Literary Research Guide: A Guide to Reference Sources for the Study of Literature in English and Related Topics*. 2nd ed. New York: MLA, 1993. A selective but extensive annotated guide to important bibliographies, abstracts, data bases, histories, surveys, dictionaries, encyclopedias, and handbooks; an invaluable research tool with extensive, useful indexes.

Holman, C. Hugh, and William Harmon. *A Handbook to Literature*. 6th ed. New York: Macmillan, 1992. A thorough dictionary of literary terms that also provides brief, clear overviews of literary movements such as Romanticism.

Kuntz, Joseph M., and Nancy C. Martinez. *Poetry Explication: A Checklist of Interpretation since 1925 of British and American Poems Past and Present*. Boston: Hall, 1980.

MLA International Bibliography of Books and Articles on Modern Language and Literature. New York: MLA, 1921–. Compiled annually; a major source for articles and books.

The New Cambridge Bibliography of English Literature. 5 vols. Cambridge, Eng.: Cambridge UP, 1967–77. An important source on the literature from A.D. 600 to 1950.

The Oxford History of English Literature. 13 vols. Oxford, Eng.: Oxford UP, 1945–, in progress. The most comprehensive literary history.

The Penguin Companion to World Literature. 4 vols. New York: McGraw-Hill, 1969–71. Covers classical, Oriental, African, European, English, and American literature.

Preminger, Alex, and T. V. F. Brogan, eds. *The New Princeton Encyclopedia of Poetry and Poetics*. Princeton, NJ: Princeton UP, 1993. Includes entries on technical terms and poetic movements.

Rees, Robert, and Earl N. Harbert. *Fifteen American Authors before*

1900: Bibliographic Essays on Research and Criticism. Madison: U of Wisconsin P, 1971. Among the writers covered are Stephen Crane and Emily Dickinson.

Spiller, Robert E., et al. *Literary History of the United States.* 4th ed. 2 vols. New York: Macmillan, 1974. Coverage of literary movements and individual writers from colonial times to the 1960s.

Walker, Warren S. *Twentieth-Century Short Story Explication.* 3rd ed. Hamden, CT: Shoe String Press, 1977. A bibliography of criticism on short stories written since 1800; supplements appear every few years.

These sources are available in the reference sections of most college libraries; ask a reference librarian to help you locate them.

Computer Searches

Researchers can locate materials in a variety of sources, including card catalogues, specialized encyclopedias, bibliographies, and indexes to periodicals. Many libraries now also provide computer searches that are linked to a data base of the libraries' holdings. This can be an efficient way to establish a bibliography on a specific topic. If your library has such a service, consult a reference librarian about how to use it and to determine if it is feasible for your topic. If a computer service is not accessible at your library, you can still collect the same information from printed sources.

EVALUATING SOURCES AND TAKING NOTES

Evaluate your sources for their reliability and the quality of their evidence. Check to see if an article or book has been superseded by later studies; try to use up-to-date sources. A popular magazine article will probably not be as authoritative as an article in a scholarly journal. Sources that are well documented with primary and secondary materials usually indicate that the author has done his or her homework. Books printed by university presses and established trade presses are preferable to books privately printed. But there are always exceptions. If you are uncertain about how to assess a book, try to find out something about the author. Are there any other books listed in the catalog that indicate the author's expertise? What do book reviews say about the work? Three valuable indexes to book reviews of literary studies are *Book Review Digest, Book Review Index,* and *Index to Book Reviews in the Humanities.* Your reference librarian can show you how to use these important tools for evaluating books. Reviews can be a quick means to get a broad perspective on writers and their works because reviewers often survey previous approaches to the topic under discussion.

As you prepare a list of reliable sources relevant to your topic, record the necessary bibliographic information so that it will be available when you make up the list of works cited for your paper. (See the illustration of a sample bibliography card.) For a book include the author, complete title, place of publication, publisher, and date. For an article include author, complete title, name of periodical, volume number, date of issue, and inclusive page numbers.

Once you have assembled a tentative bibliography, you will need to take notes on your readings. If you are not using a word processor, use 3×5, 4×6, or 5×8-inch cards for note taking. They are easy to manipulate and can be readily sorted later on when you establish subheadings for your paper. Be sure to keep track of where the information comes from by writing the author's name and page number on each notecard. If you use more than one work by the same author, include a brief title as well as the author's name. (See the illustration of the sample notecard.)

> Lynen, John F. *The Pastoral Art of Robert Frost.*
> New Haven: Yale UP, 1960.

Sample Bibliography Card for a Book

> Symbolic value of the wall   Lynen 29
>   Lynen describes the wall as
> "the symbol of all kinds of
> man-made barriers."
>
> [Do these barriers have any
> positive value?]

Sample Notecard

The sample notecard records the source of information (the complete publishing information is on the bibliography card) and provides a heading that will allow easy sorting later on. Notice that the information is summarized rather than quoted in large chunks. The student also includes a short note asking herself if Lynen's reading could be expanded upon.

Notecards can combine quotations, paraphrases, and summaries; you can also use them to cite your own ideas and give them headings so that you don't lose track of them. As you take notes try to record only points relevant to your topic, though, inevitably, you'll end up not using some of your notes.

DEVELOPING A THESIS AND ORGANIZING THE PAPER

As the notes on "Mending Wall" accumulated, the student sorted them into topics including

```
 1. Publication history of the poem
 2. Frost's experiences as a farmer
 3. Critics' readings of the poem
 4. The speaker's attitude toward the wall
 5. The neighbor's attitude toward the wall
 6. Mythic elements in the poem
 7. Does the wall have any positive value?
 8. How do the speaker and neighbor characterize themselves?
 9. Humor in the poem
10. Frost as a regional poet
```

The student quickly saw that items 1, 2, 6, and 10 were not directly related to her topic concerning why the speaker initiates the rebuilding of the wall. The remaining numbers (3–5, 7–9) are the topics taken up in the paper. The student had begun her reading of secondary sources with a tentative thesis that stemmed from her question about why the poem's speaker helps his neighbor to rebuild the wall. That "why" shaped itself into the expectation that she would have a thesis something like this: "The speaker helps to rebuild the wall because. . . ."

She assumed she would find information that indicated some specific reason. But the more she read the more she discovered that there was no single explanation provided by the poem or by critics' readings of the poem. Instead, through the insights provided by her sources, she began to see that the wall had several important functions in the poem. The perspective she developed into her thesis—that the wall "provided a foundation upon which the men build a personal sense of identity"—allowed her to incorporate a number of the critics' insights into her paper in order to shed light on why the speaker helps to rebuild the wall.

Because the assignment was relatively brief, the student did not write up a formal outline but instead organized her stacks of usable notecards and proceeded to write the first draft from them.

REVISING

After writing your first draft, you should review the advice and revision checklist on page 16 so that you can read your paper with an objective eye. Two days after writing her next-to-last draft, the writer of "Defining Identity in 'Mending Wall' " realized that she had allotted too much space for critical discussions of the humor in the poem that were not directly related to her approach. She realized that it was not essential to point out and discuss the puns in the poem; hence she corrected this by simply deleting most references to the poem's humor. The point is that she saw this herself after she took some time to approach the paper from a fresh perspective.

DOCUMENTING SOURCES

You must acknowledge the use of a source when you (1) quote someone's exact words, (2) summarize or borrow someone's opinions or ideas, or (3) use information and facts that are not considered to be common knowledge. The purpose of this documentation is to acknowledge your sources, to demonstrate that you are familiar with what others have thought about the topic, and to provide your reader access to the same sources. If your paper is not adequately documented, it will be vulnerable to a charge of *plagiarism*—the presentation of someone else's work as your own. Conscious plagiarism is easy to avoid; honesty takes care of that for most people. However, there is a more problematic form of plagiarism that is often inadvertent. Whether inadequate documentation is conscious or not, plagiarism is a serious matter and must be avoided. Papers can be evaluated only by what is on the page, not by their writers' intentions.

Let's look more closely at what constitutes plagiarism. Consider the following passage quoted from A. R. Coulthard, "Frost's 'Mending Wall,' " *Explicator* 45 (Winter 1987): 40:

> "Mending Wall" has many of the features of an "easy" poem aimed at high-minded readers. Its central symbol is the accessible stone wall to represent separation, and it appears to oppose isolating barriers and favor love and trust, the stuff of Golden Treasury of Inspirational Verse.

Now read this plagiarized version:

```
"Mending Wall" is an easy poem that appeals to high-minded
readers who take inspiration from its symbolism of the stone
```

```
wall, which seems to oppose isolating barriers and support
trusting love.
```

Though the writer has shortened the passage and made some changes in the wording, this paragraph is basically the same as Coulthard's. Indeed, several of his phrases are lifted almost intact. (Notice, however, that the plagiarized version seems to have missed Coulthard's irony and, therefore, misinterpreted and misrepresented the passage.) Even if a parenthetical reference had been included at the end of the passage and the source included in "Works Cited," the language of this passage would still be plagiarism because it is presented as the writer's own. Both language and ideas must be acknowledged.

Here is an adequately documented version of the passage:

```
A. R. Coulthard points out that "high-minded readers" mistak-
enly assume that "Mending Wall" is a simple inspirational poem
that uses the symbolic wall to reject isolationism and to sup-
port, instead, a sense of human community (40).
```

This passage makes absolutely clear that the observation is Coulthard's, and it is written in the student's own language with the exception of one quoted phrase. Had Coulthard not been named in the passage, the parenthetical reference would have included his name: (Coulthard 40).

Some mention should be made of the notion of common knowledge before we turn to the standard format for documenting sources. Observations and facts that are widely known and routinely included in many of your sources do not require documentation. It is not necessary to cite a source for the fact that Alfred, Lord Tennyson, was born in 1809 or that Frost writes about New England. Sometimes it will be difficult for you to determine what common knowledge is for a topic that you know little about. If you are in doubt, the best strategy is to supply a reference.

There are two basic ways to document sources. Traditionally, sources have been cited in footnotes at the bottom of each page or in endnotes grouped together at the end of the paper. Here is how a portion of the sample paper on "Mending Wall" would look if footnotes were used instead of parenthetical documentation:

```
It remains one of Frost's more popular poems, and, as Douglas
Wilson notes, "one of the most famous in all of American
poetry."[1]
```

Unlike endnotes, which are double spaced throughout under the title of "Notes" on separate pages at the end of the paper, footnotes appear four

---

[1] Douglas L. Wilson, "The Other Side of the Wall," *Iowa Review* 10 (Winter 1979): 65.

spaces below the text. They are single spaced with double spaces between notes.

No doubt you will have encountered these documentation methods in your reading. A different style is recommended, however, in the third edition of the Modern Language Association's *MLA Handbook for Writers of Research Papers* (1988). The new style employs parenthetical references within the text of the paper; these are keyed to an alphabetical list of works cited at the end of the paper. This method is designed to be less distracting for the reader. Unless you are instructed to follow the footnote or endnote style for documentation, use the new parenthetical method explained in the next section.

The List of Works Cited

Items in the list of works cited are arranged alphabetically according to the author's last name and indented five spaces after the first line. This allows the reader to locate quickly the complete bibliographic information for the author's name cited within the parenthetical reference in the text. The following are common entries for literature papers and should be used as models. If some of your sources are of a different nature, consult Joseph Gibaldi and Walter S. Achtert, *MLA Handbook for Writers of Research Papers,* 3rd ed. (New York: MLA, 1988); many of the bibliographic possibilities you are likely to need are included in this source.

A Book by One Author

```
Hendrickson, Robert.  The Literary Life and Other Curiosities.
     New York: Viking, 1981.
```

Notice that the author's name is in reverse order. This information, along with the full title, place of publication, publisher, and date should be taken from the title and copyright pages of the book. The title is underlined to indicate italics and is also followed by a period. If the city of publication is well known, it is unnecessary to include the state. Use the publication date on the title page; if none appears there use the copyright date (after ©) on the back of the title page.

A Book by Two Authors

```
Horton, Rod W., and Herbert W. Edwards.  Backgrounds of Ameri-
     can Literary Thought.  3rd ed.  Englewood Cliffs: Pren-
     tice, 1974.
```

Only the first author's name is given in reverse order. The edition number appears after the title.

A Book with More Than Three Authors

Abrams, M. H., et al., eds. The Norton Anthology of English
    Literature. 5th ed. 2 vols. New York: Norton, 1986.
    Vol. 1.

The abbreviation *et al.* means "and others." It is used to avoid having to list all fourteen editors of this first volume of a two-volume work.

A Work in a Collection by the Same Author

O'Connor, Flannery. "Greenleaf." The Complete Stories. By
    O'Connor. New York: Farrar, 1971. 311-34.

Page numbers are given because the reference is to only a single story in the collection.

A Work in a Collection by Different Writers

Frost, Robert. "Design." Poetry: An Introduction. Ed. Mi-
    chael Meyer. Boston: Bedford-St. Martin's P, 1995. 311.

The hyphenated publisher's name indicates a publisher's imprint: Bedford Books of St. Martin's Press.

A Translated Book

Grass, Günter. The Tin Drum. Trans. Ralph Manheim. New York:
    Vintage-Random, 1962.

An Introduction, Preface, Foreword, or Afterword

Johnson, Thomas H. Introduction. Final Harvest: Emily Dickin-
    son's Poems. By Emily Dickinson. Boston: Little, Brown,
    1961. vii-xiv.

This cites the introduction by Johnson. Notice that a colon is used between the book's main title and subtitle. To cite a poem in this book use this method:

Dickinson, Emily. "A Tooth upon Our Peace." Final Harvest:
    Emily Dickinson's Poems. Ed. Thomas H. Johnson. Boston:
    Little, Brown, 1961. 110.

An Encyclopedia

"Wordsworth, William." The New Encyclopaedia Britannica. 1984
    ed.

Because this encyclopedia is organized alphabetically, no page number or other information is given, only the edition number (if available) and date.

```
Morrow, Lance.   "Scribble, Scribble, Eh, Mr. Toad."   Time
     24 Feb. 1986: 84.
```

The citation for an unsigned article would begin with the title and be alphabetized by the first word of the title other than "a," "an," or "the."

An Article in a Scholarly Journal with
Continuous Pagination beyond a Single Issue

```
Mahar, William J.   "Black English in Early Blackface Min-
     strelsy: A New Interpretation of the Sources of Minstrel
     Show Dialect."   American Quarterly 37 (1985): 260-85.
```

Because this journal uses continuous pagination instead of separate pagination for each issue, it is not necessary to include the month, season, or number of the issue. Only one of the quarterly issues will have pages numbered 260–85. If you are not certain whether a journal's pages are numbered continuously throughout a volume, supply the month, season, or issue number, as in the next entry.

An Article in a Scholarly Journal with
Separate Pagination for Each Issue

```
Updike, John.   "The Cultural Situation of the American Writer."
     American Studies International 15 (Spring 1977): 19-28.
```

By noting the spring issue, the entry saves a reader looking through each issue of the 1977 volume for the correct article on pages 19–28.

An Article in a Newspaper

```
Ziegler, Philip.   "The Lure of Gossip, the Rules of History."
     New York Times 23 Feb. 1986: sec. 7: 1+.
```

This citation indicates that the article appears on page 1 of section 7 and continues onto another page.

A Lecture

```
Stern, Milton.   "Melville's View of Law."   English 270 class
     lecture.   University of Connecticut, Storrs, 12 Mar. 1992.
```

Parenthetical References

A list of works cited is not an adequate indication of how you have used sources in your paper. You must also provide the precise location of quotations and other information by using parenthetical references within the text of the paper. You do this by citing the author's name (or the source's title if the work is anonymous) and the page number.

Collins points out that "Nabokov was misunderstood by early
reviewers of his work" (28).

or

Nabokov's first critics misinterpreted his stories (Collins
28).

Either way a reader will find the complete bibliographic entry in the list of
works cited under Collins's name and know that the information cited in
the paper appears on page 28. Notice that the end punctuation comes after
the parentheses.

If you have listed more than one work by the same author, you would
add a brief title to the parenthetical reference to distinguish between them.
You could also include the full title in your text.

Nabokov's first critics misinterpreted his stories (Collins
"Early Reviews" 28).

or

Collins points out in "Early Reviews of Nabokov's Fiction" that
his early work was misinterpreted by reviewers (28).

There can be many variations on what is included in a parenthetical reference,
depending on the nature of the entry in the list of works cited. But the general
principle is simple enough: provide enough parenthetical information for
a reader to find the work in "Works Cited." Examine the sample research
paper for more examples of works cited and strategies for including parenthetical references. If you are puzzled by a given situation, ask your reference
librarian to show you the *MLA Handbook.*

ROBERT FROST (1874-1963)
Mending Wall   1914

Something there is that doesn't love a wall,
That sends the frozen-ground-swell under it,
And spills the upper boulders in the sun;
And makes gaps even two can pass abreast.
The work of hunters is another thing: 5
I have come after them and made repair
Where they have left not one stone on a stone,
But they would have the rabbit out of hiding,
To please the yelping dogs. The gaps I mean,
No one has seen them made or heard them made,   10
But at spring mending-time we find them there.
I let my neighbor know beyond the hill;
And on a day we meet to walk the line

And set the wall between us once again.
We keep the wall between us as we go.   15
To each the boulders that have fallen to each.
And some are loaves and some so nearly balls
We have to use a spell to make them balance:
"Stay where you are until our backs are turned!"
We wear our fingers rough with handling them.   20
Oh, just another kind of outdoor game,
One on a side. It comes to little more:
There where it is we do not need the wall:
He is all pine and I am apple orchard.
My apple trees will never get across   25
And eat the cones under his pines, I tell him.
He only says, "Good fences make good neighbors."
Spring is the mischief in me, and I wonder
If I could put a notion in his head:
"*Why* do they make good neighbors? Isn't it   30
Where there are cows? But here there are no cows.
Before I built a wall I'd ask to know
What I was walling in or walling out,
And to whom I was like to give offense.
Something there is that doesn't love a wall,   35
That wants it down." I could say "Elves" to him,
But it's not elves exactly, and I'd rather
He said it for himself. I see him there
Bringing a stone grasped firmly by the top
In each hand, like an old-stone savage armed.   40
He moves in darkness as it seems to me,
Not of woods only and the shade of trees.
He will not go behind his father's saying,
And he likes having thought of it so well
He says again, "Good fences make good neighbors."   45

A SAMPLE RESEARCH PAPER:
DEFINING IDENTITY IN "MENDING WALL"

The following research paper by Juliana Daniels follows the format
described in the *MLA Handbook for Writers of Research Papers* (1988). This
format is discussed in the preceding section on documentation and in Chapter
1, in the section "Manuscript Form" (p. 17). Though the sample paper is
short, it illustrates many of the techniques and strategies useful for writing
an essay that includes secondary sources. Notice that when you cite poetry
lines no abbreviation is used in the parenthetical documentation. Simply use
the word *line* or *lines* in that first citation along with the number(s), and
then just use the number(s) in subsequent citations after having established
that the number(s) refers to lines.

Juliana Daniels

Professor Caron

English 109-11

December 6, 19--

Defining Identity in "Mending Wall"

Robert Frost's poem "Mending Wall" has been the object of much critical scrutiny since its publication in 1914. It remains one of Frost's more popular poems, and, as Douglas L. Wilson notes, "one of the most famous in all of American poetry" (65). Perhaps partly as a result of its widespread popularity and frequent inclusion in literature anthologies, critics have tended to treat "Mending Wall" as a fairly straightforward poem that is easily accessible to high school students as well as professional scholars. But over the years there have been decided trends in the critical interpretations of this poem. These trends manifest themselves mostly in debates over which character, the speaker or his neighbor, has a clearer understanding of the real significance of the crumbling stone wall they endeavor to mend. However, scholars have overlooked the important ways that the wall helps each man to define himself in relation to the other. The wall not only offers the men a tangible way to demarcate their property but also affords them a way to clearly define their relationship with each other. Thus the wall does far more than just, as the neighbor asserts, make "good neighbors" (line 27)--it provides a foundation upon which the men may build a personal sense of identity.

This notion of identity as a significant theme in the poem has often been ignored by critics in favor of discussions

of the meaning of the wall itself. Many previous interpretations of "Mending Wall" have focused on the speaker's supposed
insight, crediting him with the wisdom to recognize the unnat-
urally limiting and divisive qualities inherent in the wall.
After all, it is the speaker who twice mentions that "Something there is that doesn't love a wall" (35), thereby challenging his neighbor's firm defense of the wall as the means
of creating "good neighbors" (27). Charles Watson acknowledges the common tendency of readers to interpret the poem as
"the meditation of a right-minded man who, even as he partici-
pates in the annual wall-mending rite, indulges privately in
some gently mocking reflections on his neighbor's mindless adherence to his father's belief in walls" (653). The speaker's
apparent "right-mindedness," as well as the appeal of joining
him in his supposed aversion to artificial boundaries between
people, effectively lulls readers into a mistaken faith in the
speaker's negative perception of both the wall and his "recal-
citrant and plodding neighbor [who] is a slave to the rituals
of the quotidian" (Lentricchia 11).

This original critical trend of favoring the speaker's
vision of the wall as meaningless and the neighbor as mindless
has been countered by numerous readings of the poem in which
the neighbor's point of view is deemed the wiser and more valuable. Fritz Oehlschlaeger, among others, suggests the possibility of interpreting "Mending Wall" in favor of the
neighbor's perspective, maintaining that it is the neighbor
"who understands both the intransigence of natural fact and
the need to limit human ego. This understanding makes the
Yankee farmer, not the speaker, the truly neighborly figure in

the poem" (244). In this case the neighbor is credited with
the understanding that established boundaries provide the necessary foundations for strong and successful relationships between people. His repeated assertion that "Good fences make
good neighbors" (27, 45) suggests that walls are "the essential barriers that must exist between man and man if the individual is to preserve his own soul, and mutual understanding
is to survive and flourish" (Ward 428).

However, the real wisdom in "Mending Wall" lies not in
deciding whose point of view is more admirable but in recog-
nizing that although the wall is perceived differently by the
two men, it is essential in defining both of them. That is,
the sense of identity that each man has in relation to the
other deeply depends upon the existence of the wall that di-
vides them and the way that they conceive of the wall. The
neighbor can more readily acknowledge and articulate his desire for the wall to remain in place, but the speaker also
does his part to ensure that the wall dividing their property
does not crumble. For they each realize, on some level, that
if the wall that defines the limits of their land were to disappear, then their sense of the established social order would
also disappear, along with their identity as a part of that
social order. As James R. Dawes points out, these "men can
only interact when reassured by the constructed alienation of
the wall" (300). So they work together to keep the wall
firmly in place, keeping themselves separated in order to
maintain their individual sense of self.

Part of the speaker's sense of identity lies in his role
as a questioner, a challenger, a rebel thinker. He twice men-

tions his recognition that "Something there is that doesn't love a wall" (35), and seems pleased to ally himself with the forces of nature that conspire to destroy that wall which becomes, as John Lynen notes, "the symbol for all kinds of man-made barriers" (29). Yet the speaker's pleasure at minimizing the importance of the wall results less from any inherent properties of the actual wall than it does from the sense of superiority over his neighbor which this belief affords him. The speaker's created sense of identity as an insightful, clever "free-thinker" is corroborated by his belief that "the neighbor's adherence to his father's saying suggests the narrowness and blind habit of the primitive" (Lynen 28); it is his opposition to the neighbor which defines the speaker in the poem. The speaker declares that he can think of no good reason for maintaining the wall, as there are no cows to contain and his "apple trees will never get across / And eat the cones under his [neighbor's] pines" (25-26). Clearly, his belief in his own wisdom leads to his sense of superiority over his neighbor, the "old-stone savage" (40) who "moves in darkness" (41). Thus, the existence of the wall provides the speaker with the means to identify himself as superior to his neighbor.

It is revealing to note that in spite of the speaker's superfluous objections to the rebuilding of the wall, it is he who initiates its repair each spring. He acknowledges that "I let my neighbor know beyond the hill; / And on a day we meet to walk the line / And set the wall between us once again" (12-14). He also explains how he repeatedly replaces the stones on the wall after hunters dislodge them: "I have come

after them and made repair / Where they have left not one
stone on a stone, / But they would have the rabbit out of hiding" (6-8). Thus, the speaker's behavior indicates that he
does in fact believe in the importance of the wall, diligently
restoring it whenever the stones are knocked out of place.
This apparent contradiction between the speaker's actions and
his purported beliefs suggests a subtle recognition of the importance of maintaining the wall. The speaker fancies himself
a genuine liberal, responding to his neighbor's conservative
refrain "Good fences make good neighbors" (27) with the question "Why do they make good neighbors?" (30). The answer lies
in the reader's understanding that the wall is crucial to
maintaining the speaker's own self image. Perhaps the wall is
not needed to fence in cows or trees, but it is necessary in
order for the speaker to define himself in relation to the way
his neighbor conceives of the wall. The speaker's superfluous
objections to the wall are nothing more than fancy, for without the wall the speaker would be unable to define himself in
opposition to his neighbor.

While the speaker defines his neighbor as a closed-minded
primitive, thereby validating his notion of himself as much
superior to him, the neighbor defines himself as someone who,
unlike the speaker, can acknowledge the importance of the
wall. He finds it necessary to tell the speaker two separate
times that "Good fences make good neighbors" (27, 45), suggesting his recognition that the speaker resists acknowledging
the merit of his father's saying. Thus the neighbor is able
to define himself in relation to the speaker, believing himself to clearly possess more valuable knowledge about fences

and about relationships than his seemingly flighty neighbor
does. The humor of this poem lies in the irony that both men
consider themselves to have sharper perceptions and broader
knowledge than the other, thus contributing to their individual sense of superiority.

Marion Montgomery explains that a "wise person knows that
a wall is a point of reference, a touchstone of sanity, and
that it must be not only maintained but respected as well"
(147). But the wall in "Mending Wall" goes beyond a reference
point that protects merely one's privacy and individuality; it
actually offers two people the foundation they need in order
to be able to relate to each other and to understand themselves. Without the ritual of rebuilding the wall, neither
the speaker nor the neighbor would have a way to compare himself to the other and thus reaffirm his own vision of himself.
The confrontation between the two men in "Mending Wall" is as
much of a ritual as the actual mending of the wall and is
maintained as the poem "concludes with the fence having been
mended and with the reader expecting the same movement to take
place in succeeding years" (Bowen 14). Both the speaker and
his neighbor "walk the line" (13) together, each complicit in
the rebuilding and re-enforcing of the established barrier
that allows them to maintain a sense of personal identity.

Works Cited

Bowen, J. K. "The Persona in Frost's 'Mending Wall': Mended
    or Amended." CEA Critic 31 (November 1968): 14.

Dawes, James R. "Masculinity and Transgression in Robert
    Frost." American Literature 65 (June 1993): 297-312.

Frost, Robert. "Mending Wall." Poetry: An Introduction. Ed.
    Michael Meyer. Boston: Bedford-St. Martin's, 1995. 298.

Lentricchia, Frank. "Experience as Meaning: Robert Frost's
    'Mending Wall.'" CEA Critic 34 (May 1972): 8-12.

Lynen, John F. The Pastoral Art of Robert Frost. New Haven:
    Yale UP, 1960. 27-31.

Montgomery, Marion. "Robert Frost and His Use of Barriers:
    Man vs. Nature toward God." Robert Frost: A Collection
    of Critical Essays. Ed. James M. Cox. Englewood Cliffs:
    Prentice, 1962. 138-50.

Oehlschlaeger, Fritz. "Fences Make Neighbors: Process, Iden-
    tity, and Ego in Robert Frost's 'Mending Wall.'" Arizona
    Quarterly (40 Autumn 1984): 242-54.

Ward, William S. "Lifted Pot Lids and Unmended Walls." Col-
    lege English 27 (February 1966): 428-29.

Watson, Charles N. "Frost's Wall: The View from the Other
    Side." New England Quarterly 44 (December 1971): 653-56.

Wilson, Douglas L. "The Other Side of the Wall." Iowa Review
    10 (Winter 1979): 65-75.

9. Taking Essay Examinations

PREPARING FOR AN ESSAY EXAM

Keep Up with the Reading

The best way to prepare for an examination is to keep up with the reading. If you begin the course with a commitment to completing the reading assignments on time, you will not have to read in a frenzy and cram just days before the test. The readings should be a pleasure, not a frantic ordeal. Moreover, you'll find that your instructor's comments and class discussion will make more sense to you and that you'll be able to participate in class discussion. As you prepare for the exam you should be rereading texts rather than reading for the first time. It may not be possible to reread everything but you'll at least be able to scan a familiar text and reread passages that are particularly important.

Take Notes and Annotate the Text

Don't rely exclusively on your memory. The typical literature class includes a hefty amount of reading, so unless you take notes, annotate the text with your own comments, and underline important passages, you're likely to forget material that could be useful for responding to an examination question (see pp. 3–5 for a discussion of these matters). The more you can retrieve from your reading the more prepared you'll be for reviewing significant material for the exam. These notes can be used to illustrate points that were made in class. By briefly quoting an important phrase or line from the text you can provide supporting evidence that will make your argument convincing. Consider, for example, the difference between writing that "Marvell's speaker in 'To His Coy Mistress' says that they won't be able to love after they die" and writing that "the speaker intones that 'The grave's a fine and private place, / But none, I think, do there embrace.' " No one expects you to memorize the entire poem, but recalling a few lines here and there can transform a sleepy generality into an illustrative, persuasive argument.

Anticipate Questions

As you review the readings keep in mind the class discussions and the focus provided by your instructor. Very often class discussions and the instructor's emphasis become the basis for essay questions. You may not see the exact same topics on the exam, but you might find that the matters you've discussed in class will serve as a means of responding to an essay question. If, for example, class discussion of John Updike's "A & P" (see p. 24) centered on the story's small-town New England setting, you could use that conservative, traditional, puritanical setting to answer a question such as "Discuss how the conflicts that Sammy encounters in 'A & P' are related to the story's theme." A discussion of the intolerant rigidity of this New England town could be connected to A & P "policy" and the crabbed values associated with Lengel that lead to Sammy's quitting his job in protest of such policies. The point is that you'll be well prepared for an essay exam when you can shape the material you've studied so that it is responsive to whatever kind of reasonable questions you encounter on the exam. Reasonable questions? Yes, your instructor is more likely to offer you an opportunity to demonstrate your familiarity with and understanding of the text than to set a trap that, for instance, demands you discuss how Updike's work experience as an adolescent informs the story when no mention was ever made of that in class or in your reading.

You can also anticipate questions by considering the generic questions for writing about fiction (p. 49), poetry (p. 64), and drama (p. 86) and the questions for critical reading and writing (p. 130), along with the questions for writing about an author in depth (p. 143). Not all of these questions will necessarily be relevant to every work that you read, but they cover a wide range of concerns that should allow you to organize your reading, note taking, and reviewing so that you're not taken by surprise during the exam.

Studying with a classmate or a small group from class can be a stimulating and fruitful means of discovering and organizing the major topics and themes of the course. This method of brainstorming can be useful not only for studying for exams, but throughout the semester as a way to understand and review course readings. And, finally, you needn't be shy about asking your instructor what types of questions might appear on the exam and how best to study for them. You may not get a very specific reply but almost any information is more useful than none.

TYPES OF EXAMS

Closed-Book versus Open-Book Exams

Closed-book exams require more memorization and recall than open-book exams, which permit you to use your text and perhaps even your notes to answer questions. Obviously dates, names, definitions, and other details play less of a role in an open-book exam. An open-book exam requires no less preparation, however, because you'll need to be intimately familiar with the texts and the major ideas, themes, and issues that you've studied in order to quickly and efficiently support your points with relevant, specific evidence. Since every student has the same advantage of having access to the text, preparation remains the key to answering the questions. Some students find open-book exams more difficult than closed-book tests, because they risk spending too much time reading, scanning, and searching for material and not enough time writing a response that draws upon the knowledge and understanding that their reading and studying has provided them. It's best to limit the time you allow yourself to review the text and/or notes, so that you devote an adequate amount of time to getting your ideas down on paper.

Essay Questions

Essay questions generally fall within one of the following familiar categories. If you can recognize quickly what is being asked of you, you will be able to respond to them more efficiently.

1. Explication. Explication calls for a line-by-line explanation of a passage of poetry or prose that considers, for example, diction, figures of speech, symbolism, sound, form, and theme in an effort to describe how language creates meaning (for a more detailed discussion of explication, see pp. 18–20).

2. Definition. Defining a term and then applying it to a writer or work is a frequent exam exercise. Consider: "Define *romanticism*. To what extent can Hawthorne's *The Scarlet Letter* be regarded as a romantic story?" This sort of question requires that you first describe what constitutes a romantic literary work and then explain how *The Scarlet Letter* does (and doesn't) fit the bill.

3. Analysis. An analytical question focuses on a particular part of a literary work. You might be asked, for example, to analyze the significance of images in Diane Ackerman's poem "A Fine, A Private Place" (p. 37). This sort of question requires you not only to discuss a specific element of the poem but to explain also how that element contributes to the poem's overall effect (for a more detailed discussion of analysis, see pp. 23–24).

4. Comparison and Contrast. Comparison and contrast calls for a discussion of the similarities and/or differences between writers, works, or elements of works, for example, "Compare and contrast Lengel's sensibilities in John Updike's 'A & P' (p. 24) with John Wright's in Susan Glaspell's *Trifles* (p. 73)." Despite the obvious differences in age and circumstances between these characters, a discussion of their responses to people—particularly to women—reveals some intriguing similarities (for a more detailed discussion of comparison and contrast, see pp. 33–35).

5. Discussion of a Critical Perspective. A brief quotation by a critic about a work is usually designed to stimulate a response that requires you to agree

with, disagree with, or qualify a critic's perspective. Usually it is not so important whether you agree or disagree with the critic; what matters is the quality of your argument. Think about how you might wrestle with this assessment of Robert Frost written by Lionel Trilling: "The manifest America of Mr. Frost's poems may be pastoral; the actual America is tragic." With some qualifications (surely not every one of Frost's poems is "tragic") this could provide a useful way of talking about a poem such as "Mending Wall" (p. 161).

6. Imaginative Questions. To a degree every question requires imagination regardless of whether it's being asked or answered. However, some questions require more imaginative leaps to arrive at the center of an issue than others do. Consider, for example, the intellectual agility needed to respond to this question: "How do you think Dickens's Mr. Gradgrind from *Hard Times* and the narrator of Frost's 'Mending Wall' would respond to Sammy's character in Updike's 'A & P'?" As tricky as this triangulation of topics may seem, there is plenty to discuss concerning Gradgrind's literal-mindedness, the narrator's imagination, and Sammy's rejection of "policy." Or try a simpler but no less interesting version: "How do you think Frost would review Marvell's 'To His Coy Mistress' and Ackerman's 'A Fine, A Private Place'?" Such questions certainly require detailed, reasoned responses, but they also leave room for creativity and even wit.

STRATEGIES FOR WRITING ESSAY EXAMS

Your hands may be sweaty and your heart pounding as you begin the exam, but as long as you're prepared and you keep in mind some basic strategies for writing essay exams, you should be able to respond to questions with confidence and a genuine sense of accomplishment.

1. Before you begin writing, read through the entire exam. If there are choices to be made, make certain you know how many questions must be answered (only one out of four, not two). Note how many points each question is worth; spend more time on the two worth forty points each and perhaps leave the twenty-point question for last.

2. Budget your time. If there are short-answer questions, do not allow them to absorb you so that you cannot do justice to the longer essay questions. Follow the suggested time limits for each question; if none are offered, then create your own schedule in proportion to the points allotted for each question.

3. Depending upon your own sensibilities, you may want to begin with the easiest or hardest questions. It doesn't really matter which you begin with as long as you pace yourself to avoid running out of time.

4. Be sure that you understand the question. Does it ask you to compare and/or contrast, define, analyze, explicate, or use some other approach?

Determine how many elements there are to the question so that you don't inadvertently miss part of the question. Do not spend time copying the question.

5. Make some brief notes about how you plan to answer the question; even a simple list of what you'll need to cover can serve as a useful outline.

6. Address the question; avoid unnecessary summaries or irrelevant asides. Focus on the particular elements enumerated or implied by the question.

7. After beginning the essay, write a clear thesis that describes the major topics you will discuss: "*The Scarlet Letter* is typical of Hawthorne's concerns as a writer owing to its treatment of sin, guilt, isolation, and secrecy."

8. Support and illustrate your answer with specific, relevant references to the text. The more specificity—the more you demonstrate a familiarity with the text (rather than simply providing a plot summary)—the better the answer.

9. Don't overlap and repeat responses to questions; your instructor will recognize such padding. If two different questions are about the same work or writer, demonstrate the breadth and depth of your knowledge of the subject.

10. Allow time to proofread and to qualify and to add more supporting material if necessary. At this final stage, too, it's worth remembering that Mark Twain liked to remind his readers that the difference between the right word and the almost right word is the difference between lightning and the lightning bug.

10. Glossary
of Literary Terms

Accent The emphasis, or STRESS, given a syllable in pronunciation. We say "*syl*lable" not "syl*la*ble," "*em*phasis" not "em*pha*sis." Accents can also be used to emphasize a particular word in a sentence: *Is* she con*tent* with the *con*tents of the *yel*low *pack*age? See also METER.

Act A major division in the action of a play. The ends of acts are typically indicated by lowering the curtain or turning up the houselights. Playwrights frequently employ acts to accommodate changes in time, setting, characters onstage, or mood. In many full-length plays, acts are further divided into scenes, which often mark a point in the action when the location changes or when a new character enters. See also SCENE.

Action What happens in a story or drama. Action may involve both external, physical actions, such as quarrels, journeys, or confronting adversaries, and internal, psychological actions, such as learning something about others or oneself, making decisions, or gaining perspective.

Allegory A narration or description usually restricted to a single meaning because its events, actions, characters, settings, and objects represent specific abstractions or ideas. Although the elements in an allegory may be interesting in themselves, the emphasis tends to be on what they ultimately mean. Characters may be given names such as Hope, Pride, Youth, and Charity; they have few if any personal qualities beyond their abstract meanings. These personifications are not symbols because, for instance, the meaning of a character named Charity is precisely that virtue. See also SYMBOL.

Alliteration The repetition of the same consonant sounds in a sequence of words, usually at the beginning of a word or stressed syllable: "*de*scen*d*ing *d*ew*d*rops"; "*l*uscious *l*emons." Alliteration is based on the sounds of letters, rather than the spelling of words; for example, "*k*een" and "*c*ar" alliterate, but "*c*ar" and "*c*ite" do not. Used sparingly, alliteration can intensify ideas by emphasizing key words, but when used too self-consciously, it can be distracting, even ridiculous, rather than effective. See also ASSONANCE, CONSONANCE.

Allusion A brief reference to a person, place, thing, event, or idea in history or literature. Allusions conjure up biblical authority, scenes from Shakespeare's plays, historic figures, wars, great love stories, and anything else that might enrich an author's work. Allusions imply reading and cultural experiences shared by the writer and reader, functioning as a kind of shorthand whereby the recalling of something outside the work supplies an emotional or intellectual context, such as a poem about current racial struggles calling up the memory of Abraham Lincoln.

Ambiguity Allows for two or more simultaneous interpretations of a word, phrase, action, or situation, all of which can be supported by the context of a work. Deliberate ambiguity can contribute to the effectiveness and richness of a work, for example, in the open-ended conclusion to Hawthorne's "Young Goodman Brown." However, unintentional ambiguity obscures meaning and can confuse readers.

Anagram A word or phrase made from the letters of another word or phrase, as "heart" is an anagram of "earth." Anagrams have often been considered merely an exercise of one's ingenuity, but sometimes writers use anagrams to conceal proper names or veiled messages, or to suggest important connections between words, as in "hated" and death."

Anapestic meter See FOOT.

Antagonist The character, force, or collection of forces in fiction or drama that opposes the PROTAGONIST and gives rise to the conflict of the story; an opponent of the protagonist, such as Iago in Shakespeare's play *Othello*. See also CHARACTER, CONFLICT.

Antihero A protagonist who has the opposite of most of the traditional attributes of a hero. He or she may be bewildered, ineffectual, deluded, or merely pathetic. Often what antiheroes learn, if they learn anything at all, is that the world isolates them in an existence devoid of God and absolute values. Yossarian from Joseph Heller's *Catch-22* is an example of an antihero. See also CHARACTER.

Approximate rhyme See RHYME.

Archetype A term used to describe universal symbols that evoke deep and sometimes unconscious responses in a reader. In literature, characters, images, and themes that symbolically embody universal meanings and basic human experiences, regardless of when or where they live, are considered archetypes. Common literary archetypes include stories of quests, initiations, scapegoats, descents to the underworld, and ascents to heaven. See also MYTHOLOGICAL CRITICISM.

Aside In drama, a speech directed to the audience that supposedly is not audible to the other characters onstage at the time. When Hamlet first appears onstage, for example, his aside "A little more than kin, and less than kind!" gives the audience a strong sense of his alienation from King Claudius. See also SOLILOQUY.

Assonance The repetition of internal vowel sounds in nearby words that do not end the same, for example, "asl*ee*p under a tr*ee*," or "*ea*ch *evening.*" Similar endings result in rhyme, as in as*leep* in the *deep*. Assonance is a strong means of emphasizing important words in a line. See also ALLITERATION, CONSONANCE.

Ballad Traditionally, a ballad is a song, transmitted orally from generation to generation, that tells a story and that eventually is written down. As such, ballads usually cannot be traced to a particular author or group of authors. Typically, ballads are dramatic, condensed, and impersonal narratives, such as "Bonny Barbara Allan." A **literary ballad** is a narrative poem that is written in deliberate imitation of the language, form, and spirit of the traditional ballad, such as Keats's "La Belle Dame Sans Merci." See also BALLAD STANZA, QUATRAIN.

Ballad stanza A four-line stanza, known as a QUATRAIN, consisting of alternating eight- and six-syllable lines. Usually only the second and fourth lines rhyme (an *abcb* pattern). Coleridge adopted the ballad stanza in "The Rime of the Ancient Mariner":

All in a hot and copper sky
The bloody Sun, at noon,
Right up above the mast did stand,
No bigger than the Moon.

See also BALLAD, QUATRAIN.

Biographical criticism An approach to literature which suggests that knowledge of the author's life experiences can aid in the understanding of his or her work. While biographical information can sometimes complicate one's interpretation of a work, and some formalist critics (such as the New Critics) disparage the use of the author's biography as a tool for textual interpretation, learning about the life of the author can often enrich a reader's appreciation for that author's work. See also FORMALIST CRITICISM, NEW CRITICISM.

Blank verse Unrhymed iambic pentameter. Blank verse is the English verse form closest to the natural rhythms of English speech and therefore is the most common pattern found in traditional English narrative and dramatic poetry from Shakespeare to the early twentieth century. Shakespeare's plays use blank verse extensively. See also IAMBIC PENTAMETER.

Cacophony Language that is discordant and difficult to pronounce, such as this line from John Updike's "Player Piano": "never my numb plunker fumbles." Cacophony ("bad sound") may be unintentional in the writer's sense of music, or it may be used consciously for deliberate dramatic effect. See also EUPHONY.

Caesura A pause within a line of poetry that contributes to the rhythm of the line. A caesura can occur anywhere within a line and need not be indicated by punctuation. In scanning a line, caesuras are indicated by a double vertical line (‖). See also METER, RHYTHM, SCANSION.

Canon Those works generally considered by scholars, critics, and teachers to be the most important to read and study, which collectively constitute the "masterpieces" of literature. Since the 1960s, the traditional English and American literary canon, consisting mostly of works by white male writers, has been rapidly expanding to include many female writers and writers of varying ethnic backgrounds.

Carpe diem The Latin phrase meaning "seize the day." This is a very common literary theme, especially in lyric poetry, which emphasizes that life is short, time is fleeting, and that one should make the most of present pleasures. Robert Herrick's poem "To the Virgins, to Make Much of Time" employs the *carpe diem* theme.

Catharsis Meaning "purgation," *catharsis* describes the release of the emotions of pity and fear by the audience at the end of a tragedy. In his *Poetics,* Aristotle discusses the importance of catharsis. The audience faces the misfortunes of the protagonist, which elicit pity and compassion. Simultaneously, the audience also confronts the failure of the protagonist, thus receiving a frightening reminder of human limitations and frailties. Ultimately, however, both these negative emotions are purged, because the tragic protagonist's suffering is an affirmation of human values rather than a despairing denial of them. See also TRAGEDY.

Character, characterization A character is a person presented in a dramatic or narrative work, and characterization is the process by which a writer makes that character seem real to the reader. A **hero** or **heroine,** often called the PROTAGONIST, is the central character who engages the reader's interest and empathy. The ANTAGONIST is the character, force, or collection of forces that stands directly opposed to the protagonist and gives rise to the conflict of the story. A **static character** does not change throughout the work, and the reader's knowledge of that character does not grow, whereas a **dynamic character** undergoes some kind of change because of the action in the plot. A **flat character** embodies one or two qualities, ideas, or traits that can be readily described in a brief summary. They are not psychologically complex characters and therefore are readily accessible to readers. Some flat characters are recognized as **stock characters;** they embody stereotypes such as the "dumb blonde" or the "mean stepfather." They become types rather than individuals. **Round characters** are more complex than flat or stock characters, and often display the inconsistencies and internal conflicts found in most real people. They are more fully developed, and therefore are harder to summarize. Authors have two major methods of presenting characters: **showing** and **telling. Showing** allows the author to present a character talking and acting, and lets the reader infer what kind of person the character is. In **telling,** the author intervenes to describe and sometimes evaluate the character for the reader. Characters can be convincing whether they are presented by showing or by telling, as long as their actions are motivated. **Motivated action** by the characters occurs when the reader or audience is offered reasons for how the characters behave, what they say, and the decisions they make. **Plausi-**

ble action is action by a character in a story that seems reasonable, given the motivations presented. See also PLOT.

Chorus In Greek tragedies (especially those of Aeschylus and Sophocles), a group of people who serve mainly as commentators on the characters and events. They add to the audience's understanding of the play by expressing traditional moral, religious, and social attitudes. The role of the chorus in dramatic works evolved through the sixteenth century, and the chorus occasionally is still used by modern playwrights such as T. S. Eliot in *Murder in the Cathedral*. See also DRAMA.

Classical unities Derived from Renaissance interpretations of Aristotle's *Poetics, classical unities* refers to three principles to which it was said that plays should adhere: unity of time, unity of place, and unity of action. Unity of time demands that the play's storyline confine itself to one twenty-four-hour period. Unity of place requires that the play restrict its setting to one location. Unity of action means that the play must develop only one line of action, without digressions or elaborate sub-plots. Unity of action also means that comedy and tragedy must be kept entirely separate; there can be no mixing of comic scenes with the high seriousness of tragedy and no blending of permanent pain and suffering with laughter. See also COMEDY, DRAMA, TRAGEDY.

Cliché An idea or expression that has become tired and trite from overuse, its freshness and clarity having worn off. Clichés often anesthetize readers, and are usually a sign of weak writing. See also SENTIMENTALITY, STOCK RESPONSES.

Climax See PLOT.

Closet drama A play that is written to be read rather than performed onstage. In this kind of drama, literary art outweighs all other considerations. See also DRAMA.

Colloquial Refers to a type of informal diction that reflects casual, conversational language and often includes slang expressions. See also DICTION.

Comedy A work intended to interest, involve, and amuse the reader or audience, in which no terrible disaster occurs and that ends happily for the main characters. **High comedy** refers to verbal wit, such as puns, whereas **low comedy** is generally associated with physical action and is less intellectual. **Romantic comedy** involves a love affair that meets with various obstacles (like disapproving parents, mistaken identities, deceptions, or other sorts of misunderstandings) but overcomes them to end in a blissful union. Shakespeare's comedies, such as *A Midsummer Night's Dream,* are considered romantic comedies.

Comedy of manners A satiric play that focuses on the fashions, conventions, and morals of middle- and upper-class society. Characters in comedies of manners tend to be more types than individualized personalities. Comedies of manners typically downplay plot complications (usually involving lovers) and emphasize clever, refined dialogue whose humor is pointed and whose purpose is to reform as well as entertain. Molière's seventeenth-century play *Tartuffe* is an example of a comedy of manners. See also SATIRE.

Comic relief A humorous scene or incident that alleviates tension in an otherwise serious work. In many instances these moments enhance the thematic significance of the story in addition to providing laughter. When Hamlet jokes with the gravediggers we laugh, but something hauntingly serious about the humor also intensifies our more serious emotions.

Conflict The struggle within the plot between opposing forces. The PROTAGONIST engages in the conflict with the ANTAGONIST, which may take the form of a character, society, nature, or an aspect of the protagonist's personality. See also CHARACTER, PLOT.

Connotation Associations and implications that go beyond the literal meaning of a word, which derive from how the word has been commonly used and the associations people make with it. For example, the word *eagle* connotes ideas of liberty and freedom that have little to do with the word's literal meaning. See also DENOTATION.

Consonance A common type of near rhyme that consists of identical consonant sounds preceded by different vowel sounds: *home, same; worth, breath*. See also RHYME.

Contextual symbol See SYMBOL.

Controlling metaphor See METAPHOR.

Convention A characteristic of a literary genre (often unrealistic) that is understood and accepted by audiences because it has come, through usage and time, to be recognized as a familiar technique. For example, the division of a play into acts and scenes is a dramatic convention, as are soliloquies and asides. FLASHBACKS and FORESHADOWING are examples of literary conventions.

Conventional symbol See SYMBOL.

Cosmic irony See IRONY.

Couplet Two consecutive lines of poetry that usually rhyme and have the same meter. A **heroic couplet** is a couplet written in rhymed iambic pentameter.

Crisis A turning point in the action of a story that has a powerful effect on the protagonist. Opposing forces come together decisively to lead to the climax of the plot. See also PLOT.

Dactylic meter See FOOT.

Deconstructionism An approach to literature which suggests that literary works do not yield fixed, single meanings, because language can never say exactly what we intend it to mean. Deconstructionism seeks to destabilize meaning by examining the gaps and ambiguities of the language of a text. Deconstructionists pay close attention to language in order to discover and describe how a variety of possible readings are generated by the elements of a text. See also NEW CRITICISM.

Denotation The dictionary meaning of a word. See also CONNOTATION.

Dénouement A French term meaning "unraveling" or "unknotting," used to describe the resolution of the plot following the climax. See also PLOT, RESOLUTION.

Dialect A type of informal diction. Dialects are spoken by definable groups of people from a particular geographic region, economic group, or social class. Writers use dialect to contrast and express differences in educational, class, social, and regional backgrounds of their characters. See also DICTION.

Dialogue The verbal exchanges between characters. Dialogue makes the characters seem real to the reader or audience by revealing firsthand their thoughts, responses, and emotional states. See also DICTION.

Diction A writer's choice of words, phrases, sentence structures, and figurative language, which combine to help create meaning. **Formal diction** consists of a dignified, impersonal, and elevated use of language; it follows the rules of syntax exactly and is often characterized by complex words and lofty tone. **Middle diction** maintains correct language usage, but is less elevated than formal diction; it reflects the way most educated people speak. **Informal diction** represents the plain language of everyday use, and often includes idiomatic expressions, slang, contractions, and many simple, common words. **Poetic diction** refers to the way poets sometimes employ an elevated diction that deviates significantly from the common speech and writing of their time, choosing words for their supposedly inherent poetic qualities. Since the eighteenth century, however, poets have been incorporating all kinds of diction in their work and so there is no longer an automatic distinction between the language of a poet and the language of everyday speech. See also DIALECT.

Didactic poetry Poetry designed to teach an ethical, moral, or religious lesson. Michael Wigglesworth's Puritan poem *Day of Doom* is an example of didactic poetry.

Doggerel A derogatory term used to describe poetry whose subject is trite and whose rhythm and sounds are monotonously heavy-handed.

Drama Derived from the Greek word *dram,* meaning "to do" or "to perform," the term *drama* may refer to a single play, a group of plays ("Jacobean drama") or to all plays ("world drama"). Drama is designed for performance in a theater; actors take on the roles of characters, perform indicated actions, and speak the dialogue written in the script. **Play** is a general term for a work of dramatic literature, and a **playwright** is a writer who makes plays.

Dramatic irony See IRONY.

Dramatic monologue A type of lyric poem in which a character (the speaker) addresses a distinct but silent audience imagined to be present in the poem in such a way as to reveal a dramatic situation and, often, unintentionally, some aspect of his or her temperament or personality. See also LYRIC.

Dynamic character See CHARACTER.

Editorial omniscience See NARRATOR.

Electra complex The female version of the Oedipus complex. *Electra complex* is a term used to describe the psychological conflict of a daughter's unconscious rivalry with her mother for her father's attention. The name comes from the Greek legend of Electra, who avenged the death of her father, Agamemnon, by killing her mother. See also OEDIPUS COMPLEX, PSYCHOLOGICAL CRITICISM.

Elegy A mournful, contemplative lyric poem written to commemorate someone who is dead, often ending in a consolation. Tennyson's *In Memoriam,* written on the death of Arthur Hallam, is an elegy. *Elegy* may also refer to a serious meditative poem produced to express the speaker's melancholy thoughts. See also LYRIC.

End rhyme See RHYME.

End-stopped line A poetic line that has a pause at the end. End-stopped lines reflect normal speech patterns and are often marked by punctuation. The first line of Keats's "Endymion" is an example of an end-stopped line; the natural pause coincides with the end of the line, and is marked by a period:

A thing of beauty is a joy forever.

English sonnet See SONNET.

Enjambment In poetry, when one line ends without a pause and continues into the next line for its meaning. This is also called a **run-on line.** The transition between the first two lines of Wordsworth's poem "My Heart Leaps Up" demonstrates enjambment:

My heart leaps up when I behold
A rainbow in the sky:

Epic A long narrative poem, told in a formal, elevated style, that focuses on a serious subject and chronicles heroic deeds and events important to a culture or nation. Milton's *Paradise Lost,* which attempts to "justify the ways of God to man," is an epic. See also NARRATIVE POEM.

Epigram A brief, pointed, and witty poem that usually makes a satiric or humorous point. Epigrams are most often written in couplets, but take no prescribed form.

Escape literature See FORMULAIC LITERATURE.

Euphony *Euphony* ("good sound") refers to language that is smooth and musically pleasant to the ear. See also CACOPHONY.

Exact rhyme See RHYME.

Exposition A narrative device, often used at the beginning of a work, that provides necessary background information about the characters and their circumstances. Exposition explains what has gone on before, the relationships between characters, the development of a theme, and the introduction of a conflict. See also FLASHBACK.

Extended metaphor See METAPHOR.

Eye rhyme See RHYME.

Falling action See PLOT.

Falling meter See METER.

Farce A form of humor based on exaggerated, improbable incongruities. Farce involves rapid shifts in action and emotion, as well as slapstick comedy and extravagant dialogue. Malvolio, in Shakespeare's *Twelfth Night,* is a farcical character.

Feminine rhyme See RHYME.

Feminist criticism An approach to literature that seeks to correct or supplement what may be regarded as a predominantly male-dominated critical perspective with a feminist consciousness. Feminist criticism places literature in a social context and uses a broad range of disciplines, including history, sociology, psychology, and linguistics, to provide a perspective sensitive to feminist issues. Feminist theories also attempt to understand representation from a woman's point of view and to explain women's writing strategies as specific to their social conditions. See also SOCIOLOGICAL CRITICISM.

Figures of speech Ways of using language that deviate from the literal, denotative meanings of words in order to suggest additional meanings or effects. Figures of speech say one thing in terms of something else, such as when an eager funeral director is described as a vulture. See also METAPHOR, SIMILE.

First-person narrator See NARRATOR.

Fixed form A poem that may be categorized by the pattern of its lines, meter, rhythm, or stanzas. A sonnet is a fixed form of poetry because by definition it must have fourteen lines. Other fixed forms include LIMERICK, SESTINA, and VILLANELLE. However, poems written in a fixed form may not always fit into categories precisely, because writers sometimes vary traditional forms to create innovative effects. See also OPEN FORM.

Flashback A narrated scene that marks a break in the narrative in order to inform the reader or audience member about events that took place before the opening scene of a work. See also EXPOSITION.

Flat character See CHARACTER.

Foil A character in a work whose behavior and values contrast with those of another character in order to highlight the distinctive temperament of that character (usually the protagonist). In Shakespeare's *Hamlet,* Laertes acts as a foil to Hamlet, because his willingness to act underscores Hamlet's inability to do so.

Foot The metrical unit by which a line of poetry is measured. A foot usually consists of one stressed and one or two unstressed syllables. An *iambic foot,* which consists of one unstressed syllable followed by one stressed syllable ("away"), is the most common metrical foot in English poetry. A *trochaic foot* consists of one stressed syllable followed by an unstressed syllable ("lovely"). An *anapestic foot* is two unstressed syllables followed by one stressed one ("understand"). A *dactylic foot* is one stressed syllable followed by two unstressed ones ("desperate"). A *spondee* is a foot consisting of two stressed syllables ("dead set"), but is not a sustained metrical foot and is used mainly for variety or emphasis. See also IAMBIC PENTAMETER, LINE, METER.

Foreshadowing The introduction early in a story of verbal and dramatic hints that suggest what is to come later.

Form The overall structure or shape of a work, which frequently follows an established design. Forms may refer to a literary type (narrative form, short story form) or to patterns of meter, lines, and rhymes (stanza form, verse form). See also FIXED FORM, OPEN FORM.

Formal diction See DICTION.

Formalist criticism An approach to literature that focuses on the formal elements of a work, such as its language, structure, and tone. Formalist critics offer intense examinations of the relationship between form and meaning in a work, emphasizing the subtle complexity in how a work is arranged. Formalists pay special attention to diction, irony, paradox, metaphor, and symbol, as well as larger elements such as plot, characterization, and narrative technique. Formalist critics read literature as an independent work of art rather than as a reflection of the author's state of mind or as a representation of a moment in history. Therefore, anything outside of the work, including historical influences and authorial intent, is generally not examined by formalist critics. See also NEW CRITICISM.

Formula literature Often characterized as "escape literature," formula literature follows a pattern of conventional reader expectations. Romance novels, westerns, science fiction, and detective stories are all examples of formula literature; while the details of individual stories vary, the basic ingredients of each kind of story are the same. Formula literature offers happy endings (the hero "gets the girl," the detective cracks the case), entertains wide audiences, and sells tremendously well.

Found poem An unintentional poem discovered in a nonpoetic context, such as a conversation, news story, or advertisement. Found poems serve as reminders that everyday language often contains what can be considered poetry, or that poetry is definable as any text read as a poem.

Free verse Also called *open form poetry,* free verse refers to poems characterized by their nonconformity to established patterns of meter, rhyme, and stanza. Free verse uses elements such as speech patterns, grammar, emphasis, and breath pauses to decide line breaks, and usually does not rhyme. See OPEN FORM.

Genre A French word meaning kind or type. The major genres in literature are poetry, fiction, drama, and essays. Genre can also refer to more specific types of literature such as comedy, tragedy, epic poetry, or science fiction.

Haiku A style of lyric poetry borrowed from the Japanese that typically presents an intense emotion or vivid image of nature, which, traditionally, is designed to lead to a spiritual insight. Haiku is a fixed poetic form, consisting of seventeen syllables organized into three unrhymed lines of five, seven, and five syllables. Today, however, many poets vary the syllabic count in their haiku. See also FIXED FORM.

Hamartia A term coined by Aristotle to describe "some error or frailty" that brings about misfortune for a tragic hero. The concept of hamartia is closely related to that of the tragic flaw: both lead to the downfall of the protagonist in a tragedy. Hamartia may be interpreted as an internal weakness in a character (like greed or passion or HUBRIS); however, it may also refer to a mistake that a character makes that is based not on a personal failure, but on circumstances outside the protagonist's personality and control. See also TRAGEDY.

Hero, heroine See CHARACTER.

Heroic couplet See COUPLET.

High comedy See COMEDY.

Historical criticism An approach to literature that uses history as a means of understanding a literary work more clearly. Such criticism moves beyond both the facts of an author's personal life and the text itself in order to examine the social and intellectual currents in which the author composed the work. See also NEW HISTORICISM.

Hubris Excessive pride or self-confidence that leads a protagonist to disregard a divine warning or to violate an important moral law. In tragedies, hubris is a very common form of hamartia. See also HAMARTIA, TRAGEDY.

Hyperbole A boldly exaggerated statement that adds emphasis without intending to be literally true, as in the statement "He ate everything in the house." Hyperbole (also called **overstatement**) may be used for serious, comic, or ironic effect. See also FIGURES OF SPEECH.

Iambic meter See FOOT.

Iambic pentameter A metrical pattern in poetry which consists of five iambic feet per line. (An iamb, or iambic foot, consists of one unstressed syllable followed by a stressed syllable.) See also METER, FOOT.

Image A word, phrase, or figure of speech (especially a SIMILE or a METAPHOR) that addresses the senses, suggesting mental pictures of sights, sounds, smells, tastes, feelings, or actions. Images offer sensory impressions to the reader and also convey emotions and moods through their verbal pictures. See also FIGURES OF SPEECH.

Implied metaphor See METAPHOR.

In medias res See PLOT.

Informal diction See DICTION.

Internal rhyme See RHYME.

Irony A literary device that uses contradictory statements or situations to reveal a reality different from what appears to be true. It is ironic for a firehouse to burn down, or for a police station to be burglarized. **Verbal irony** is a figure of speech that occurs when a person says one thing but means the opposite. **Sarcasm** is a strong form of verbal irony that is calculated to hurt someone through, for example, false praise. **Dramatic irony** creates a discrepancy between what a character believes or says and what the reader or audience member knows to be true. **Tragic irony** is a form of dramatic irony found in tragedies such as *Oedipus the King,* in which Oedipus searches for the person responsible for the plague that ravishes his city and ironically ends up hunting himself. **Situational irony** exists when there is an incongruity between what is expected to happen and what actually happens due to forces beyond human comprehension or control. The suicide of the seemingly successful main character in Edwin Arlington Robinson's poem "Richard Cory" is an example of situational irony. **Cosmic irony** occurs when a writer uses God, destiny, or fate to dash the hopes and expectations of a character or of humankind in general. In cosmic irony, a discrepancy exists between what a character aspires to and what universal forces provide. Stephen Crane's poem "A Man Said to the Universe" is a good example of cosmic irony, because the universe acknowledges no obligation to the man's assertion of his own existence.

Italian sonnet See SONNET.

Limerick A light, humorous style of fixed form poetry. Its usual form consists of five lines with the rhyme scheme *aabba;* lines 1, 2, and 5 contain three feet, while lines 3 and 4 usually contain two feet. Limericks range in subject matter from the silly to the obscene, and since Edward Lear popularized them in the nineteenth century, children and adults have enjoyed these comic poems. See also FIXED FORM.

Limited omniscience See POINT OF VIEW.

Line A sequence of words printed as a separate entity on the page. In poetry, lines are usually measured by the number of feet they contain. The names for various line lengths are as follows:

monometer: one foot	pentameter: five feet
dimeter: two feet	hexameter: six feet
trimeter: three feet	heptameter: seven feet
tetrameter: four feet	octameter: eight feet

The number of feet in a line, coupled with the name of the foot, describes the metrical qualities of that line. See also END-STOPPED LINE, ENJAMBMENT, FOOT, METER.

Literary ballad See BALLAD.

Literary symbol See SYMBOL.

Litotes See UNDERSTATEMENT.

Low comedy See COMEDY.

Lyric A type of brief poem that expresses the personal emotions and thoughts of a single speaker. It is important to realize, however, that although the lyric is uttered in the first person, the speaker is not necessarily the poet. There are many varieties of lyric poetry, including the DRAMATIC MONOLOGUE, ELEGY, HAIKU, ODE, and SONNET forms.

Marxist criticism An approach to literature that focuses on the ideological content of a work—its explicit and implicit assumptions and values about matters such as culture, race, class, and power. Marxist criticism, based largely on the writings of Karl Marx, typically aims at not only revealing and clarifying ideological issues but also correcting social injustices. Some Marxist critics use literature to describe the competing socioeconomic interests that too often advance capitalist interests such as money and power rather than socialist interests such as morality and justice. They argue that literature and literary criticism are essentially political because they either challenge or support economic oppression. Because of this strong emphasis on the political aspects of texts, Marxist criticism focuses more on the content and themes of literature than on its form. See also SOCIOLOGICAL CRITICISM.

Masculine rhyme See RHYME.

Melodrama A term applied to any literary work that relies on implausible events and sensational action for its effect. The conflicts in melodramas typically arise out of plot rather than characterization; often a virtuous individual must somehow confront and overcome a wicked oppressor. Usually, a melodramatic story ends happily, with the protagonist defeating the antagonist at the last possible moment. Thus, melodramas entertain the reader or audience with exciting action while still conforming to a traditional sense of justice. See SENTIMENTALITY.

Metaphor A metaphor is a figure of speech that makes a comparison between two unlike things, without using the word *like* or *as*. Metaphors assert the identity of dissimilar things, as when Macbeth asserts that life *is* a "brief candle." Metaphors can be subtle and powerful, and can transform people, places, objects, and ideas into whatever the writer imagines them to be. An **implied metaphor** is a more subtle comparison; the terms being compared are not so specifically explained. For example, to describe a stubborn man unwilling to leave, one could say that he was "a mule standing his ground." This is a fairly explicit metaphor; the man is being compared to a mule. But to say that the man "brayed his refusal to leave" is to create an implied metaphor, because the subject (the man) is never overtly identified as a mule. Braying is associated with the mule, a notoriously stubborn creature, and so the comparison between the stubborn man and the mule is sustained. Implied metaphors can slip by inattentive readers who are not sensitive to such carefully chosen, highly concentrated language. An **extended metaphor** is a sustained comparison in which part or all of a poem consists of a series of related metaphors. Robert Francis's poem "Catch" relies on an extended metaphor that compares poetry to playing catch. A **controlling metaphor** runs through an entire work and determines the form or nature of that work. The controlling metaphor in Anne

Bradstreet's poem "The Author to Her Book" likens her book to a child. **Synecdoche** is a kind of metaphor in which a part of something is used to signify the whole, as when a gossip is called a "wagging tongue," or when ten ships are called "ten sails." Sometimes, synecdoche refers to the whole being used to signify the part, as in the phrase "Boston won the baseball game." Clearly, the entire city of Boston did not participate in the game; the whole of Boston is being used to signify the individuals who played and won the game. **Metonymy** is a type of metaphor in which something closely associated with a subject is substituted for it. In this way, we speak of the "silver screen" to mean motion pictures, "the crown" to stand for the king, "the White House" to stand for the activities of the president. See also FIGURES OF SPEECH, PERSONIFICATION, SIMILE.

Meter When a rhythmic pattern of stresses recurs in a poem, it is called *meter*. Metrical patterns are determined by the type and number of feet in a line of verse; combining the name of a line length with the name of a foot concisely describes the meter of the line. **Rising meter** refers to metrical feet which move from unstressed to stressed sounds, such as the iambic foot and the anapestic foot. **Falling meter** refers to metrical feet which move from stressed to unstressed sounds, such as the trochaic foot and the dactylic foot. See also ACCENT, FOOT, IAMBIC PENTAMETER, LINE.

Metonymy See METAPHOR.

Middle diction See DICTION.

Motivated action See CHARACTER.

Mythological criticism An approach to literature that seeks to identify what in a work creates deep universal responses in readers, by paying close attention to the hopes, fears, and expectations of entire cultures. Mythological critics (sometimes called *archetypal critics*) look for underlying, recurrent patterns in literature that reveal universal meanings and basic human experiences for readers regardless of when and where they live. These critics attempt to explain how archetypes (the characters, images, and themes that symbolically embody universal meanings and experiences) are embodied in literary works in order to make larger connections that explain a particular work's lasting appeal. Mythological critics may specialize in areas such as classical literature, philology, anthropology, psychology, and cultural history, but they all emphasize the assumptions and values of various cultures. See also ARCHETYPE.

Naive narrator See NARRATOR.

Narrative poem A poem that tells a story. A narrative poem may be short or long, and the story it relates may be simple or complex. See also BALLAD, EPIC.

Narrator The voice of the person telling the story, not to be confused with the author's voice. With a **first-person narrator,** the *I* in the story presents the point of view of only one character. The reader is restricted to the perceptions, thoughts, and feelings of that single character. For example, in Melville's "Bartleby, the Scrivener," the lawyer is the first-person narrator of the story. First-person narrators can play either a major or a minor role in the story they are telling. An **unreliable narrator** reveals an interpretation of events that is somehow different from the author's own interpretation of those events. Often, the unreliable narrator's perception of plot, characters, and setting becomes the actual subject of the story, as in Melville's "Bartleby, the Scrivener." Narrators can be unreliable for a number of reasons: they might lack self-knowledge (like Melville's lawyer), they might be inexperienced, they might even be insane. **Naive narrators** are usually characterized by youthful innocence, such as Mark Twain's Huck Finn or J. D. Salinger's Holden Caulfield. An **omniscient narrator** is an all-knowing narrator who is not a character in the story and who can move from place to place and pass back and forth through time, slipping into and out of characters as no human being possibly could in real life. Omniscient narrators can report the thoughts and feelings of the characters, as well as their words and actions. The narrator of *The Scarlet Letter* is an omniscient narrator. **Editorial omniscience** refers to an intrusion by the narrator in order to evaluate a character for a reader, as when the narrator of *The Scarlet Letter* describes Hester's relationship to the Puritan community. Narration that allows the characters' actions and thoughts to speak for themselves is called **neutral omniscience.** Most modern writers use neutral omniscience so that readers can reach their own conclusions. **Limited omniscience** occurs when an author restricts a narrator to the single perspective of either a major or minor character. The way people, places, and events appear to that character is the way they appear to the reader. Sometimes a limited omniscient narrator can see into more than one character, particularly in a work that focuses on two characters alternately from one chapter to the next. Short stories, however, are frequently limited to a single character's point of view. See also PERSONA, POINT OF VIEW, STREAM-OF-CONSCIOUSNESS TECHNIQUE.

Near rhyme See RHYME.

Neutral omniscience See NARRATOR.

New Criticism An approach to literature made popular between the 1940s and the 1960s that evolved out of formalist criticism. New Critics suggest that detailed analysis of the language of a literary text can uncover important layers of meaning in that work. New Criticism consciously downplays the historical influences, authorial intentions, and social contexts that surround texts in order to focus on explication—extremely close textual analysis. Critics such as John Crowe Ransom, I. A. Richards, and Robert Penn Warren are commonly associated with New Criticism. See also FORMALIST CRITICISM.

New Historicism An approach to literature that emphasizes the interaction between the historic context of the work and a modern reader's understanding and interpretation of the work. New Historicists attempt to describe the culture of a period by reading many different kinds of texts and paying close attention to many different dimensions of a culture, including political, economic, social, and aesthetic concerns. They regard texts not simply as a reflection of the culture that produced them but also as productive of that culture playing an active role in the social and political conflicts of an age. New Historicism acknowledges and then explores various versions of "history," sensitizing us to the fact that the history on which we choose to focus is colored by being reconstructed from our own present circumstances. See also HISTORICAL CRITICISM.

Objective point of view See POINT OF VIEW.

Octave A poetic stanza of eight lines, usually forming one part of a sonnet. See also SONNET, STANZA.

Ode A relatively lengthy lyric poem that often expresses lofty emotions in a dignified style. Odes are characterized by a serious topic, such as truth, art, freedom, justice, or the meaning of life; their tone tends to be formal. There is no prescribed pattern that defines an ode; some odes repeat the same pattern in each stanza, while others introduce a new pattern in each stanza. See also LYRIC.

Oedipus complex A Freudian term derived from Sophocles' tragedy *Oedipus the King*. It describes a psychological complex that is predicated on a boy's unconscious rivalry with his father for his mother's love and his desire to eliminate his father in order to take his father's place with his mother. The female equivalent of this complex is called the **Electra complex.** See also ELECTRA COMPLEX, PSYCHOLOGICAL CRITICISM.

Off rhyme See RHYME.

Omniscient narrator See NARRATOR.

One-act play A play that takes place in a single location and unfolds as one continuous action. The characters in a one-act play are presented economically and the action is sharply focused. See also DRAMA.

Onomatopoeia A term referring to the use of a word that resembles the sound it denotes. *Buzz, rattle, bang,* and *sizzle* all reflect onomatopoeia. Onomatopoeia can also consist of more than one word; writers sometimes create lines or whole passages in which the sound of the words helps to convey their meanings.

Open form Sometimes called "free verse," open form poetry does not conform to established patterns of METER, RHYME, and STANZA. Such poetry derives its rhythmic qualities from the repetition of words, phrases, or grammatical structures, the arrangement of words on the printed page, or by some other means. The poet e. e. cummings wrote open form poetry; his poems do not have measurable meters, but they do have RHYTHM. See also FIXED FORM.

Organic form Refers to works whose formal characteristics are not rigidly predetermined but follow the movement of thought or emotion being expressed. Such works are said to grow like living organisms, following their own individual patterns rather than external fixed rules that govern, for example, the form of a SONNET.

Overstatement See HYPERBOLE.

Oxymoron A condensed form of paradox in which two contradictory words are used together, as in "sweet sorrow" or "jumbo shrimp." See also PARADOX.

Paradox A statement that initially appears to be contradictory but then, on closer inspection, turns out to make sense. For example, John Donne ends his sonnet "Death, Be Not Proud" with the paradoxical statement "Death, thou shalt die." To solve the paradox, it is necessary to discover the sense that underlies the statement. Paradox is useful in poetry because it arrests a reader's attention by its seemingly stubborn refusal to make sense.

Parody A humorous imitation of another, usually serious, work. It can take any fixed or open form, because parodists imitate the tone, language, and shape of the original in order to deflate the subject matter, making the original work seem absurd. Anthony Hecht's poem "Dover Bitch" is a famous parody of Matthew Arnold's well-known "Dover Beach." Parody may also be used as a form of literary criticism to expose the defects in a work. But sometimes parody becomes an affectionate acknowledgment that a well-known work has become both institutionalized in our culture and fair game for some fun. For example, Peter DeVries's "To His Importunate Mistress" gently mocks Andrew Marvell's "To His Coy Mistress."

Persona Literally, a *persona* is a mask. In literature, a *persona* is a speaker created by a writer to tell a story or to speak in a poem. A persona is not a character in a story or narrative, nor does a persona necessarily directly reflect the author's personal voice. A persona is a separate self, created by and distinct from the author, through which he or she speaks. See also NARRATOR.

Personification A form of metaphor in which human characteristics are attributed to nonhuman things. Personification offers the writer a way to give the world life and motion by assigning familiar human behaviors and emotions to animals, inanimate objects, and abstract ideas. For example, in Keats's "Ode on a Grecian Urn," the speaker refers to the urn as an "unravished bride of quietness." See also METAPHOR.

Petrarchan sonnet See SONNET.

Picture poem A type of open form poetry in which the poet arranges the lines of the poem so as to create a particular shape on the page. The shape of the poem embodies its subject; the poem becomes a picture of what the poem is describing. George Herbert's "Easter Wings" is an example of a picture poem. See also OPEN FORM.

Plausible action See CHARACTER.

Play See DRAMA.

Playwright See DRAMA.

Plot An author's selection and arrangement of incidents in a story to shape the action and give the story a particular focus. Discussions of plot include not just what happens, but also how and why things happen the way they do. Stories that are written in a **pyramidal pattern** divide the plot into three essential parts. The first part is the **rising action,** in which complication creates some sort of conflict for the protagonist. The second part is the **climax,** the moment of greatest emotional tension in a narrative, usually marking a turning point in the plot at which the rising action reverses to become the falling action. The third part, the **falling action** (or RESOLUTION), is characterized by diminishing tensions and the resolution of the plot's conflicts and complications. ***In medias res*** is a term used to describe the common strategy of beginning a story in the middle of the action. In this type of plot, we enter the story on the verge of some important moment. See also CHARACTER, CRISIS, RESOLUTION, SUBPLOT.

Poetic diction See DICTION.

Point of view Refers to who tells us a story and how it is told. What we know and how we feel about the events in a work are shaped by the author's choice of point of view. The teller of the story, the narrator, inevitably affects our understanding of the characters' actions by filtering what is told through his or her own perspective. The various points of view that writers draw upon can be grouped into two broad categories: (1) the third-person narrator uses *he, she,* or *they* to tell the story and does not participate in the action; and (2) the first-person narrator uses *I* and is a major or minor participant in the action. In addition, a second-person narrator, *you,* is also possible, but is rarely used because of the awkwardness of thrusting the reader into the story, as in "You are minding your own business on a park bench when a drunk steps out and demands your lunch bag." An **objective point of view** employs a third-person narrator who does not see into the mind of any character. From this detached and impersonal perspective, the narrator reports action and dialogue without telling us directly what the characters think and feel. Since no analysis or interpretation is provided by the narrator, this point of view places a premium on dialogue, actions, and details to reveal character to the reader. See also NARRATOR, STREAM-OF-CONSCIOUSNESS TECHNIQUE.

Problem play Popularized by Henrik Ibsen, a problem play is a type of drama that presents a social issue in order to awaken the audience to it. These plays usually reject romantic plots in favor of holding up a mirror that reflects not simply what the audience wants to see but what the playwright sees in them. Often, a problem play will propose a solution to the problem that does not coincide with prevailing opinion. The term is also used to refer to certain Shakespeare plays that do not fit the categories of tragedy, comedy, or romance. See also DRAMA.

Prologue The opening speech or dialogue of a play, especially a classic

Greek play, that usually gives the exposition necessary to follow the subsequent action. Today the term also refers to the introduction to any literary work. See also DRAMA, EXPOSITION.

Proscenium arch The arch over the front of a stage from which the curtain hangs and which, together with the curtain, separates the stage from the audience.

Prose poem A kind of open form poetry that is printed as prose and represents the most clear opposite of fixed form poetry. Prose poems are densely compact and often make use of striking imagery and figures of speech. See also FIXED FORM, OPEN FORM.

Protagonist The main character of a narrative; its central character who engages the reader's interest and empathy. See also CHARACTER.

Psychological criticism An approach to literature that draws upon psycho-analytic theories, especially those of Sigmund Freud or Jacques Lacan to understand more fully the text, the writer, and the reader. The basis of this approach is the idea of the existence of a human unconscious— those impulses, desires, and feelings about which a person is unaware but which influence emotions and behavior. Critics use psychological approaches to explore the motivations of characters and the symbolic meanings of events, while biographers speculate about a writer's own motivations—conscious or unconscious—in a literary work. Psycholog-ical approaches are also used to describe and analyze the reader's per-sonal responses to a text.

Pun A play on words that relies on a word's having more than one meaning or sounding like another word. Shakespeare and other writers use puns extensively, for serious and comic purposes; in *Romeo and Juliet* (III.i.101), the dying Mercutio puns, "Ask for me tomorrow and you shall find me a grave man." Puns have serious literary uses, but since the eighteenth century, puns have been used almost purely for humorous effect. See also COMEDY.

Pyramidal pattern See PLOT.

Quatrain A four-line stanza. Quatrains are the most common stanzaic form in the English language; they can have various meters and rhyme schemes. See also METER, RHYME, STANZA.

Reader-response criticism An approach to literature that focuses on the reader rather than the work itself, by attempting to describe what goes on in the reader's mind during the reading of a text. Hence, the con-sciousness of the reader—produced by reading the work—is the actual subject of reader-response criticism. These critics are not after a "correct" reading of the text or what the author presumably intended; instead, they are interested in the reader's individual experience with the text. Thus, there is no single definitive reading of a work, because readers create rather than discover absolute meanings in texts. However, this approach is not a rationale for mistaken or bizarre readings, but an exploration of the possibilities for a plurality of readings. This kind of strategy calls attention to how we read and what influences our readings, and what that reveals about ourselves.

Recognition The moment in a story when previously unknown or withheld information is revealed to the protagonist, resulting in the discovery of the truth of his or her situation and, usually, a decisive change in course for that character. In *Oedipus the King,* the moment of recognition comes when Oedipus finally realizes that he has killed his father and married his mother.

Resolution The conclusion of a plot's conflicts and complications. The resolution, also known as the **falling action,** follows the climax in the plot. See also DÉNOUEMENT, PLOT.

Revenge tragedy See TRAGEDY.

Reversal The point in a story when the protagonist's fortunes turn in an unexpected direction. See also PLOT.

Rhyme The repetition of identical or similar concluding syllables in different words, most often at the ends of lines. Rhyme is predominantly a function of sound rather than spelling; thus, words that end with the same vowel sounds rhyme, for instance *day, grey, bouquet, weigh,* and words with the same consonant ending rhyme, for instance *vain, feign, rein, lane.* Words do not have to be spelled the same way or look alike to rhyme. In fact, words may look alike but not rhyme at all. This is called **eye rhyme,** as with *bough* and *cough,* or *brow* and *blow.*

> **End rhyme** is the most common form of rhyme in poetry; the rhyme comes at the end of the lines.

It runs through the reeds
  And away it proceeds,
Through meadow and glade,
  In sun and in shade.

The **rhyme scheme** of a poem describes the pattern of end rhymes. Rhyme schemes are mapped out by noting patterns of rhyme with small letters: the first rhyme sound is designated *a,* the second becomes *b,* the third *c,* and so on. Thus, the rhyme scheme of the stanza above is *aabb.* **Internal rhyme** places at least one of the rhymed words within the line, as in "Dividing and gliding and sliding" or "In mist or cloud, on mast or shroud." **Masculine rhyme** describes the rhyming of single-syllable words, such as *grade* and *shade.* Masculine rhyme also occurs when rhyming words of more than one syllable, when the same sound occurs in a final stressed syllable, as in *defend* and *contend, betray* and *away.* **Feminine rhyme** consists of a rhymed stressed syllable followed by one or more identical unstressed syllables, as in *butter, clutter; gratitude, attitude; quivering, shivering.* All the examples so far have illustrated **exact rhymes,** because they share the same stressed vowel sounds as well as sharing sounds that follow the vowel. In **near rhyme** (also called **off rhyme, slant rhyme,** and **approximate rhyme**), the sounds are almost but not exactly alike. A common form of near rhyme is CONSONANCE, which consists of identical consonant sounds preceded by different vowel sounds: *home, same; worth, breath.*

Rhyme scheme See RHYME.

Rhythm A term used to refer to the recurrence of stressed and unstressed sounds in poetry. Depending on how sounds are arranged, the rhythm of a poem may be fast or slow, choppy or smooth. Poets use rhythm to create pleasurable sound patterns and to reinforce meanings. Rhythm in prose arises from patterned repetitions of sounds and pauses that create looser rhythmic effects. See also METER.

Rising action See PLOT.

Rising meter See METER.

Romantic comedy See COMEDY.

Round character See CHARACTER.

Run-on line See ENJAMBMENT.

Sarcasm See IRONY.

Satire The literary art of ridiculing a folly or vice in order to expose or correct it. The object of satire is usually some human frailty; people, institutions, ideas, and things are all fair game for satirists. Satire evokes attitudes of amusement, contempt, scorn, or indignation toward its faulty subject in the hope of somehow improving it. See also IRONY, PARODY.

Scansion The process of measuring the stresses in a line of verse in order to determine the metrical pattern of the line. See also LINE, METER.

Scene In drama, a scene is a subdivision of an ACT. In modern plays, scenes usually consist of units of action in which there are no changes in the setting or breaks in the continuity of time. According to traditional conventions, a scene changes when the location of the action shifts or when a new character enters. See also ACT, CONVENTION, DRAMA.

Script The written text of a play, which includes the dialogue between characters, stage directions, and often other expository information. See also DRAMA, EXPOSITION, PROLOGUE, STAGE DIRECTIONS.

Sentimentality A pejorative term used to describe the effort by an author to induce emotional responses in the reader that exceed what the situation warrants. Sentimentality especially pertains to such emotions as pathos and sympathy; it cons readers into falling for the mass murderer who is devoted to stray cats, and it requires that readers do not examine such illogical responses. Clichés and stock responses are the key ingredients of sentimentality in literature. See also CLICHÉ, STOCK RESPONSES.

Sestet A stanza consisting of exactly six lines. See also STANZA.

Sestina A type of fixed form poetry consisting of thirty-six lines of any length divided into six sestets and a three-line concluding stanza called an *envoy.* The six words at the end of the first sestet's lines must also appear at the ends of the other five sestets, in varying order. These six words must also appear in the envoy, where they often resonate important themes. An example of this highly demanding form of poetry is Elizabeth Bishop's "Sestina." See also SESTET.

Setting The physical and social context in which the action of a story occurs. The major elements of setting are the time, the place, and the social environment that frames the characters. Setting can be used to evoke a mood or atmosphere that will prepare the reader for what is to come, as in Nathaniel Hawthorne's short story "Young Goodman Brown." Sometimes, writers choose a particular setting because of traditional associations with that setting that are closely related to the action of a story. For example, stories filled with adventure or romance often take place in exotic locales.

Shakespearean sonnet See SONNET.

Showing See CHARACTER.

Simile A common figure of speech that makes an explicit comparison between two things by using words such as *like, as, than, appears,* and *seems:* "A sip of Mrs. Cook's coffee is like a punch in the stomach." The effectiveness of this simile is created by the differences between the two things compared. There would be no simile if the comparison were stated this way: "Mrs. Cook's coffee is as strong as the cafeteria's coffee." This is a literal translation because Mrs. Cook's coffee is compared with something like it—another kind of coffee. See also FIGURES OF SPEECH, METAPHOR.

Situational irony See IRONY.

Slant rhyme See RHYME.

Sociological criticism An approach to literature that examines social groups, relationships, and values as they are manifested in literature. Sociological approaches emphasize the nature and effect of the social forces that shape power relationships between groups or classes of people. Such readings treat literature as either a document reflecting social conditions or a product of those conditions. The former view brings into focus the social milieu; the latter emphasizes the work. Two important forms of sociological criticism are Marxist and feminist approaches. See also FEMINIST CRITICISM, MARXIST CRITICISM.

Soliloquy A dramatic convention by means of which a character, alone onstage, utters his or her thoughts aloud. Playwrights use soliloquies as a convenient way to inform the audience about a character's motivations and state of mind. Shakespeare's Hamlet delivers perhaps the best known of all soliloquies, which begins: "To be or not to be." See also ASIDE, CONVENTION.

Sonnet A fixed form of lyric poetry that consists of fourteen lines, usually written in iambic pentameter. There are two basic types of sonnets, the Italian and the English. The **Italian sonnet,** also known as the **Petrarchan sonnet,** is divided into an octave, which typically rhymes *abbaabba,* and a sestet, which may have varying rhyme schemes. Common rhyme patterns in the sestet are *cdecde, cdcdcd,* and *cdccdc.* Very often the octave presents a situation, attitude, or problem that the sestet comments upon or resolves, as in John Keats's "On First Looking into Chapman's Homer." The **English sonnet,** also known as the **Shakespearean sonnet,** is organized into three quatrains and a couplet, which typically rhyme *abab cdcd efef gg.* This rhyme scheme is more suited to English poetry because English has fewer rhyming words than Italian. English sonnets, because of their four-part organization, also have more flexibility with respect to where thematic breaks can occur. Frequently, however, the most pronounced break or turn comes with the concluding couplet, as in Shakespeare's "Shall I compare thee to a summer's day?" See also COUPLET, IAMBIC PENTAMETER, LINE, OCTAVE, QUATRAIN, SESTET.

Speaker The voice used by an author to tell a story or speak a poem. The speaker is often a created identity, and should not automatically be equated with the author's self. See also NARRATOR, PERSONA, POINT OF VIEW.

Spondaic meter See FOOT.

Stage directions A playwright's written instructions about how the actors are to move and behave in a play. They explain in which direction characters should move, what facial expressions they should assume, and so on. See also DRAMA, SCRIPT.

Stanza In poetry, *stanza* refers to a grouping of lines, set off by a space, that usually has a set pattern of meter and rhyme. See also LINE, METER, RHYME.

Static character See CHARACTER.

Stock character See CHARACTER.

Stock responses Predictable, conventional reactions to language, characters, symbols, or situations. The flag, motherhood, puppies, God, and peace are common objects used to elicit stock responses from unsophisticated audiences. See also CLICHÉ, SENTIMENTALITY.

Stream-of-consciousness technique The most intense use of a central consciousness in narration. The stream-of-consciousness technique takes a reader inside a character's mind to reveal perceptions, thoughts, and feelings on a conscious or unconscious level. This technique suggests the flow of thought as well as its content; hence, complete sentences may give way to fragments as the character's mind makes rapid associations free of conventional logic or transitions. James Joyce's novel *Ulysses* makes extensive use of this narrative technique. See also NARRATOR, POINT OF VIEW.

Stress The emphasis, or accent, given a syllable in pronunciation. See also ACCENT.

Style The distinctive and unique manner in which a writer arranges words to achieve particular effects. Style essentially combines the idea to be expressed with the individuality of the author. These arrangements include individual word choices as well as matters such as the length of sentences, their structure, tone, and use of irony. See also DICTION, IRONY, TONE.

Subplot The secondary action of a story, complete and interesting in its own right, that reinforces or contrasts with the main plot. There may be more than one subplot, and sometimes as many as three, four, or even more, running through a piece of fiction. Subplots are generally either analogous to the main plot, thereby enhancing our understanding of it, or extraneous to the main plot, to provide relief from it. See also PLOT.

Suspense The anxious anticipation of a reader or an audience as to the outcome of a story, especially concerning the character or characters with whom sympathetic attachments are formed. Suspense helps to secure and sustain the interest of the reader or audience throughout a work.

Symbol A person, object, image, word, or event that evokes a range of additional meaning beyond and usually more abstract than its literal significance. Symbols are economical devices for evoking complex ideas without having to resort to painstaking explanations that would make a story more like an essay than an experience. **Conventional symbols** have meanings that are widely recognized by a society or culture. Some conventional symbols are the Christian cross, the Star of David, a swastika, or a nation's flag. Writers use conventional symbols to reinforce meanings. Kate Chopin, for example, emphasizes the spring setting in "The Story of an Hour" as a way of suggesting the renewed sense of life that Mrs. Mallard feels when she thinks herself free from her husband. A **literary** or **contextual symbol** can be a setting, character, action, object, name, or anything else in a work that maintains its literal significance while suggesting other meanings. Such symbols go beyond conventional symbols; they gain their symbolic meaning within the context of a specific story. For example, the white whale in Melville's *Moby-Dick* takes on multiple symbolic meanings in the work, but these meanings do not automatically carry over into other stories about whales. The meanings suggested by Melville's whale are specific to that text; therefore, it becomes a contextual symbol. See also ALLEGORY.

Synecdoche See METAPHOR.

Syntax The ordering of words into meaningful verbal patterns such as phrases, clauses, and sentences. Poets often manipulate syntax, changing conventional word order, to place certain emphasis on particular words. Emily Dickinson, for instance, writes about being surprised by a snake in her poem "A narrow Fellow in the Grass," and includes this line: "His notice sudden is." In addition to the alliterative hissing *s*-sounds here, Dickinson also effectively manipulates the line's syntax so that the verb *is* appears unexpectedly at the end, making the snake's hissing presence all the more "sudden."

Telling Scc CHARACTER.

Tercet A three-line stanza. See also STANZA, TRIPLET.

Terza rima An interlocking three-line rhyme scheme: *aba, bcb, cdc, ded,* and so on. Dante's *The Divine Comedy* and Frost's "Acquainted with the Night" are written in terza rima. See also RHYME, TERCET.

Theme The central meaning or dominant idea in a literary work. A theme provides a unifying point around which the plot, characters, setting, point of view, symbols, and other elements of a work are organized. It is important not to mistake the theme for the actual subject of the work; the theme refers to the abstract concept that is made concrete through the images, characterization, and action of the text. In nonfiction, however, the theme generally refers to the main topic of the discourse.

Thesis The central idea of an essay. The thesis is a complete sentence (although sometimes it may require more than one sentence) that establishes the topic of the essay in clear, unambiguous language.

Tone The author's implicit attitude toward the reader or the people, places, and events in a work as revealed by the elements of the author's style. Tone may be characterized as serious or ironic, sad or happy, private or public, angry or affectionate, bitter or nostalgic, or any other attitudes and feelings that human beings experience. See also STYLE.

Tragedy A story that presents courageous individuals who confront powerful forces within or outside themselves with a dignity that reveals the breadth and depth of the human spirit in the face of failure, defeat, and even death. Tragedies recount an individual's downfall; they usually begin high and end low. Shakespeare is known for his tragedies, including *Macbeth, King Lear, Othello,* and *Hamlet.* The **revenge tragedy** is a well-established type of drama that can be traced back to Greek and Roman plays, particularly through the Roman playwright Seneca (c. 3 B.C.–A.D. 63). Revenge tragedies basically consist of a murder that has to be avenged by a relative of the victim. Typically, the victim's ghost appears to demand revenge, and invariably madness of some sort is worked into subsequent events, which ultimately end in the deaths of the murderer, the avenger, and a number of other characters. Shakespeare's *Hamlet* subscribes to the basic ingredients of revenge tragedy, but it also transcends these conventions because Hamlet contemplates not merely revenge but suicide and the meaning of life itself. A **tragic flaw** is an error or defect in the tragic hero that leads to his downfall, such as greed, pride, or ambition. This flaw may be a result of bad character, bad judgment, an inherited weakness, or any other defect of character. **Tragic irony** is a form of dramatic irony found in tragedies such as *Oedipus the King,* in which Oedipus ironically ends up hunting himself. See also COMEDY, DRAMA.

Tragic flaw See TRAGEDY.

Tragic irony See IRONY, TRAGEDY.

Tragicomedy A type of drama that combines certain elements of both tragedy and comedy. The play's plot tends to be serious, leading to a terrible catastrophe, until an unexpected turn in events leads to a reversal of circumstance, and the story ends happily. Tragicomedy often employs a romantic, fast-moving plot dealing with love, jealousy, disguises, treachery, intrigue, and surprises, all moving toward a melodramatic resolution. Shakespeare's *Merchant of Venice* is a tragicomedy. See also COMEDY, DRAMA, MELODRAMA, TRAGEDY.

Triplet A tercet in which all three lines rhyme. See also TERCET.

Trochaic meter See FOOT.

Understatement The opposite of hyperbole, *understatement* (or litotes) refers to a figure of speech that says less than is intended. Understatement usually has an ironic effect, and sometimes may be used for comic purposes, as in Mark Twain's statement, "The reports of my death are greatly exaggerated." See also HYPERBOLE, IRONY.

Unities See CLASSICAL UNITIES.

Unreliable narrator See NARRATOR.

Verbal irony See IRONY.

Verse A generic term used to describe poetic lines composed in a measured rhythmical pattern, that are often, but not necessarily, rhymed. See also LINE, METER, RHYME, RHYTHM.

Villanelle A type of fixed form poetry consisting of nineteen lines of any length divided into six stanzas: five tercets and a concluding quatrain. The first and third lines of the initial tercet rhyme; these rhymes are repeated in each subsequent tercet (*aba*) and in the final two lines of the quatrain (*abaa*). Line 1 appears in its entirety as lines 6, 12, and 18, while line 3 reappears as lines 9, 15, and 19. Dylan Thomas's "Do not go gentle into that good night" is a villanelle. See also FIXED FORM, QUATRAIN, RHYME, TERCET.

Well-made play A realistic style of play that employs conventions including plenty of suspense created by meticulous plotting. Well-made plays are tightly and logically constructed, and lead to a logical resolution that is favorable to the protagonist. This dramatic structure was popularized in France by Eugène Scribe (1791–1861) and Victorien Sardou (1831–1908) and was adopted by Henrik Ibsen. See also CHARACTER, PLOT.

Acknowledgments *(continued from p. iv)*

Susan Glaspell. *Trifles* by Susan Glaspell. Copyright © 1951 by Walter H. Baker Company. Text Revised, Prompt Book Added and New Material. *Trifles* is the sole property of the author and is fully protected under the copyright laws of the United States, the British Empire including the Dominion of Canada, and all other countries of the Copyright Union, and is subject to royalty. The play may not be acted by professionals or amateurs without formal permission in writing and the payment of royalty. All rights, including professional, amateur, stock, radio and television broadcasting, motion picture, recitation, lecturing public reading, and the rights of translation in foreign languages are reserved. All inquiries should be directed to Baker's Plays, 100 Chauncy Street, Boston, MA, 02111.

William Hathaway. "Oh, Oh" from *Light Year '86*. This poem was originally published in the *Cincinnati Poetry Review*. Reprinted by permission of the author.

Harriet Hawkins. "Should We Study *King Kong* or *King Lear?*" from "From *King Lear* to *King Kong* and Back: Shakespeare in Popular Modern Genres" in *"Bad" Shakespeare: Revelations of the Shakespeare Cannon*, ed. Maurice Cherney, Fairleigh Dickinson University Press, 1988. Reprinted by permission of Associated University Presses.

Robert Hayden. "Those Winter Sundays" reprinted from *Angle of Ascent: New and Selected Poems by Robert Hayden*, with the permission of Liveright Publishing Corporation. Copyright © 1966 by Robert Hayden.

Annette Kolodny. "On the Commitments of Feminist Criticism" from *Dancing Through the Minefield: Some Observations on the Theory, Practice and Politics of a Feminist Literary Criticism. Feminist Studies* 6, 1980. Copyright © by Annette Kolodny; all rights reserved. Reprinted by permission of the author.

Chris Leggett. "On 'Catch': Tossing a Poem Together" by Chris Leggett. Reprinted by permission of the author.

Marge Piercy. "The Secretary Chant" from *Circles on the Water* by Marge Piercy. Copyright © 1982 by Marge Piercy. Reprinted by permission of Alfred A. Knopf, Inc.

Pedro Salinas. "Presagios" from *The Complete Poems of Pedro Salinas*. Copyright © Herederos de Pedro Salinas. Reprinted by permission of Mercedes Casanovas, Barcelona.

Susan Sontag. "Against Interpretation" from *Against Interpretation* by Susan Sontag. Copyright © 1964 by Susan Sontag. Reprinted by permission of Farrar, Straus and Giroux, Inc.

John Updike. "A & P" from *Pigeon Feathers and Other Stories* by John Updike. Copyright © 1962 by John Updike. Reprinted by permission of Alfred A. Knopf, Inc. Originally appeared in "The New Yorker." "Dog's Death" from *Midpoint and Other Poems* by John Updike. Copyright © 1969 by John Updike. Reprinted by permission of Alfred A. Knopf, Inc.